Emerging forces in environmental governance

Emerging forces in environmental governance

Edited by Norichika Kanie and Peter M. Haas

United Nations University Press

TOKYO • NEW YORK • PARIS

MDC Publishers Sdn Bhd
MALAYSIA

United Nations University Press
United Nations University
53—70, Jingumae 5-chome,
Shibuya-ku, Tokyo, 150-8925, Japan
Tel: +81-3-3499-2811
Fax: +81-3-3406-7345
E-mail: sales@hq.unu.edu
General enquiries: press@hq.unu.edu
http://www.unu.edu

Published for ASEAN Countries

by

MDC Publishers Sdn. Bhd.
MDC Building, 2717 & 2718,
Jalan Permata Empat, Taman Permata,
Ulu Kelang, 53300 Kuala Lumpur.
Tel: 03-41086600   Fax: 03-41081506.
E-mail: inquiries@mdcp.com.my
http://www.mdcppd.com.my

Printed by: MDC Printers & Book Binders Sdn. Bhd.

ISBN 967-70-0921-4

2006

Contents

List of tables and figures   viii

Foreword.   x
   A. H. Zakri

Acknowledgements.   xiii

Introduction.   1
   Norichika Kanie and Peter M. Haas

Multilateral institutions

1   Multilateral environmental institutions and coordinating
    mechanisms   15
       Toru Iwama

2   Consolidating global environmental governance: New lessons
    from the GEF?   35
       Jake Werksman

3   The effectiveness of the WTO and WIPO: Lessons for
    environmental governance?.   51
       Laura B. Campbell

Multilevel governance

4 The case for regional environmental organizations............ 71
Jonathan R. Strand

5 Global environmental governance in terms of vertical
linkages 86
Norichika Kanie

Science-policy interface for environmental governance

6 Science policy for multilateral environmental governance..... 115
Peter M. Haas

7 The IPCC: Its roles in international negotiation and domestic
decision-making on climate change policies.................... 137
Yasuko Kameyama

NGOs and environmental governance

8 Institutionalization of NGO involvement in policy functions
for global environmental governance 157
Satoko Mori

9 Civil society protest and participation: Civic engagement
within the multilateral governance regime..................... 176
Dana R. Fisher

Business/industry and environmental governance

10 Balancing TNCs, the states, and the international system in
global environmental governance: A critical perspective 203
Harris Gleckman

11 The private business sector in global environmental
diplomacy... 216
Mikoto Usui

Conclusion

12 Conclusion: Institutional design and institutional reform for
sustainable development 263
Peter M. Haas, Norichika Kanie, and Craig N. Murphy

Acronyms 282

List of contributors 288

Index 290

List of tables and figures

Tables

4.1 Select list of international organizations with environmental functions 75

5.1 Conceptualizing interactive diplomacy 90

5.2 Forces and barriers around vertical linkages................. 107

6.1 Provisions for science in selected MEAs..................... 120

9.1 NGO observers versus protesters at international meetings 184

9.2 Disassociation indices for international meetings............ 185

9.3 Participant distribution at the Human Dike protest 189

9.4 Participant distribution at the Another World is Possible protest... 190

9.5 How do protesters hear about a demonstration? The Human Dike 190

9.6 How do protesters hear about a demonstration? The Another World is Possible protest........................... 191

9.7 With whom do protesters come to demonstrations? The Human Dike 191

9.8 With whom do protesters come to demonstrations? The Another World is Possible protest........................... 191

9.9 What percentage of protesters received funding to attend? The Human Dike 192

9.10 What percentage of protesters received funding to attend? The Another World is Possible protest...................... 192

10.1 Selected factors that create differences between national
environmental regimes   204
10.2 Parallel structures between components of state regulatory
systems and voluntary environmental management systems   207
10.3 Features that differentiate between VEM and a state
regulatory system affecting business activities   208
10.4 Special international aspects of voluntary environmental
management   211
10.5 Possible tools to achieve a better balance between corporate
interests and the interests represented by the interstate
system   213
11.1 An integrative perspective on corporate game change
strategies towards sustainability   220
11.2 Rational motivations for mutual engagement of
multinational corporations and environmental NGOs........   236
11.3 Key dimensions of pro-poor business community ....
partnerships for addressing the bottom tier of the world
market...   238
11.4 Type 2 outcomes: Two parallel showcases of multi-party
partnerships/initiatives   249
12.1 Matrix of functions   267

Figures

4.1 Idealized bargaining model of environmental governance ...   81
7.1 Role of the IPCC: Official mandate   141
7.2 Role of the IPCC: Perceptions of different actors   142

Foreword

There is consensus that the current system of international environmental governance is in need of improvement. Greater effectiveness, coordination, and compliance, it is argued, will ultimately improve the quality of the environment. Debates over how to achieve this goal, through both structural and procedural reform, have generated a number of specific proposals. These range from the partial strategic integration of related multilateral environmental agreements and/or their functions to the creation of a full-fledged world environment organization. The dramatic nature of some of these proposals reflects an increasing sense of urgency in regard to both the physical and human aspects of the sustainable development challenge.

Though reform is needed, it can only be undertaken when the benefits of doing so far outweigh the costs. At present, it seems that much of the current debate over international environmental governance reform has been fuelled more by speculation on expected benefits than by careful, detailed analysis and the consideration of possible negative effects.

It is important that in our enthusiasm for fixing the weaknesses in the current system we do not inadvertently destroy its strengths. One of the chief criticisms of international environmental governance today is that it lacks coherency, and is rife with inefficiencies and overlap that greatly reduce the potential effectiveness of the system and place unnecessary burdens on countries.

These weaknesses, however, do not mean that the current system is devoid of positive features that are worthy of recognition and preservation. In particular, there are three positive aspects of international environmental governance in its current form that should be retained. First, fragmentation, though often criticized, is not entirely harmful. Indeed, fragmentation can breed innovation, whereby different institutional arrangements evolve to address emerging environmental problems. Second, the current system is flexible. Since scientific and technological developments are constantly reshaping the types of challenges we face, as well as our capacity to deal with them, institutions must be able to reflect and respond to these continual changes. International environmental governance structures as they exist today also provide a certain level of autonomy to multilateral environmental agreements, and this is crucial for institutions that deal with a wide variety of complex and often unique environmental issues. Any reform of the current system must take care to preserve the benefits derived from the fragmentation, flexibility, and autonomy of the current system for international environmental governance.

At the same time, there are some obvious gaps and weaknesses within the existing system. One of the most critical relates to the question of financing. Effective environmental management and protection requires a larger and more predictable funding base. Here again, while there are economies of scale and function to be gained from carefully thought out reform, we cannot expect institutional change to make up for what essentially amounts to a lack of political will.

Another problem is the separate treatment of the environment in the policy-making process. Environmental concerns must be mainstreamed within decision-making at both the national and the international level. Much focus has concentrated on the prospect of achieving this goal by strengthening the institutions of international environmental governance. In our efforts to ensure that environmental concerns are made a global priority, we cannot overlook the need to elevate the level of consideration given to environmental issues within the other institutions of national and international governance. That is, environmental issues must be incorporate into judicial, educational, social, health, financial, trade, and security-related institutions at both these levels.

Promoting better integration of the environment into other sectors and institutions would help to ensure that the powerful processes of globalization do not overshadow environmental problems. It would also allow the global environment to benefit from the unique strengths offered by each of these institutions, such as the access of non-governmental actors to a future international criminal court, the dispute-settlement process of the World Trade Organization, and the binding decision-making powers of the UN Security Council.

As the debate over international environmental governance reform gains momentum, it is important to maintain an approach that views reform as an ongoing process rather than as an end in itself. In this context, it is unlikely that there is any one overarching solution to the problems of international environmental governance. These are complex problems that will require a variety of innovative solutions. Indeed, the debate about proposed reforms is an important part of the process. The Institute of Advanced Studies at the United Nations University has engaged in these discussions to inform policy-makers and provide impartial analysis for future decisions surrounding reform. It is our hope that this volume can contribute to this debate and inform further deliberations.

The recognition of the inherent weaknesses of the international environmental governance structure has prompted many debates for a more integrated, binding, coordinated, and synergistic system. Yet, to date, there have been few studies that have looked carefully at the shortcomings of the current system or analysed the proposed reforms that have gained currency in policy circles. This volume, *Emerging Forces in Environmental Governance*, and a second volume, entitled *Reforming International Governance: From Institutional Limits to Innovative Solutions*, are both results of a joint project with the Kita Kyushu University and the Center for Global Partnership in Japan. Each work seeks to address these questions and provide substantive analysis as follow-up to the debates about governance that took place at the World Summit on Sustainable Development. As we strive to create the most effective institutional arrangements possible to protect our environment and promote sustainable development, such discussions will undoubtedly continue in the future. This volume represents an important contribution to those goals.

A. H. Zakri, Director, UNU-IAS

Acknowledgements

This book represents only a part of the effort of many people. As co-editors of the book, we would like to express our appreciation to all the people who have invested effort and support in the course of making this book.

First and foremost we would like to thank Bradnee Chambers, who has been an excellent collaborator from the outset of the joint research initiative that led to this publication. Without his help this book would never have been possible. We also thank Shona Dodds, who worked with us from the early stages of project development and invested lots of her time in this project.

We would also like to thank all the contributors to this book and to the other volume edited by Bradnee Chambers as well as those who participated in two workshops held in Hawaii in spring 2001 and in New York in spring 2002. Among those whose names are not listed in the volume, we would particularly like to express our gratitude to Yozo Yokota, Professor of Chuo University and special adviser to the Rector of the United Nations University, who has given effective supervision to the project and participated in the Hawaii workshop despite his extremely busy schedule. We would also like to thank Marc Levy from Columbia University's Center for International Earth Science Information Network (CIESIN), who participated in and gave a presentation at our New York workshop.

Norichika Kanie was fortunate in receiving a great deal of moral and technical support from many people for the workshops and in getting the manuscript together. These include Keizo Takemi, Kiyoshi Yamada, and other staffs of the Hawaii Tokai International Collage, where we had the first workshop, staffs of the UNU centre, UNU/IAS, and UNU New York office, in particular Mary Esther, Scott McQuade and Gareth Johnston of UNU Press, Masumi Matsumoto from the University of Kitakyushu, and Kayoko Kanie, who has given not only moral support to Kanie as his wife but also served as an assistant to the project management, especially during the first year of the project.

Norichika Kanie would like to express his appreciation to Hiroshi Oka-moto, Dean of the Faculty of Law and Policy Studies at the University of Kitakyushu, and the former Dean of the faculty, Hisakazu Nakamichi, who let him proceed with a rather large-scale project on behalf of the faculty.

This project was realized only with a generous support from the Japan Foundation Center for Global Partnership (CGP). It was originally the CGP's idea to create interaction between scholars from Japan and the USA in order to stimulate ideas from both sides. In particular, thanks are due to Shunsuke Sogo and Junichi Chano, who gave the project encouragement and support, and to the President of the CGP, Hideya Taida, and former President, Yoshihiko Wakumoto.

Last but obviously not least, we would like to thank A. H. Zakri, Director of the UNU/IAS, and the former Director of the UNU/IAS, Tarcisio Della Senta, both of whom gave us an opportunity to work closely with the institute and its international network of excellent people.

We hope that this book will be able to contribute to our understanding of environmental governance and our efforts to protect the environment of the earth.

Norichika Kanie and Peter M. Haas
Ookayama, Tokyo and Amherst, Massachusetts

Introduction

Norichika Kanie and Peter M. Haas

Throughout the process leading up to the 2002 World Summit on Sustainable Development (WSSD) the international community endorsed the need to integrate better three dimensions of sustainable development: the environmental, social, and economic dimensions of development. In the words of Dr Elim Salim, former Minister for Environment in Indonesia and the chair of the main committee to the WSSD and its preparatory committees (prepcoms), these three dimensions of sustainable development are similar to the components that make up a lemon tea. When putting sugar and lemon into the tea, those components cannot be seen in the cup. They are melted and integrated into the body of the lemon tea. Similarly, effective sustainable development planning seamlessly integrates the environmental, social, and economic dimensions of development so that all three dimensions are taken into account for public and private decision-making.

Despite years of effort at reform, however, existing multilateral environmental institutions are not yet well designed for such policy integration, as the historical development of environmental institutions shows. In 1972, when the institutionalization of international environmental policy-making really began, the issues were focused mainly on the conservation and management of natural resources, both living and inanimate. No one could have predicted, or even imagined at that time, the severity or variety of problems that would arise by the twenty-first century, including such previously unrecognized threats as stratospheric

1

ozone depletion and trade in hazardous wastes. Today there exist over 500 multilateral environmental agreements (MEAs) and a plethora of international organizations, doing the best they can to respond to environmental challenges that range from climate change to persistent organic pollutants. In addition new planning doctrines of critical loads, integrated assessment, and public participation have emerged and been applied to multilateral management efforts. The manner in which environmental institutions have developed in response to these problems has, however, largely been *ad hoc* and fragmented. Collectively, these institutions serve as a reflection of the muddled hierarchy of real-world issues that compete for global attention.

The apparently disjointed approach to environmental governance can, largely, be attributed to the very nature and complexity of environmental problems. Environmental processes are governed by laws of nature that are not amenable to conventional bargaining within the domestic or international policy-making process. Environmental policy-makers have to struggle, from the outset, with the issue of "scientific uncertainty" as well as incompatibilities between the ethical and political ramifications of the precautionary principle. In many ways, the current international legislative environment is not conducive to the development of coordinated, or synergistic, approaches to collective environmental – and sustainable development – problem-solving. Particular international agreements are often negotiated by way of "specific" regimes that are considered in relative isolation. Each agreement is tackled by, more or less, artificially decomposing the causal complexities involved for the sake of practical "manageability". Agreements are negotiated by specialized ministries or functional organizations within forums that are detached from the negotiating arenas of other international agreements. Furthermore, the process of consensus-building within the context of the non-cooperative games which are characteristic of global multilateral treaty-making involves a plethora of *ad hoc* log rolling. This, all too often, obscures the interconnectedness of the goals to be shared among different issue-specific regimes. The treaty-making process is also extremely time-consuming. It has taken over a decade to advance from the agenda-setting stage, via a framework agreement, to the negotiation of the first operational protocol for collective action. Even after the protocol agreement, ratification of the protocol is a matter of how governments can create a consensus at the domestic level, and if a government turns out to be unwilling to ratify the protocol and brings back the issue of scientific uncertainty again for political reasons, there is still a possibility that the whole negotiation process can unexpectedly be taken back to an earlier stage, which may consume extra time.

To date international environmental policy-making has generally been segregated on the basis of topic, sector, or territory. The result is the negotiation of treaties that often overlap and conflict with one another. This engenders unnecessary complications at the national level as signatories struggle to meet their obligations under multiple agreements. At the international level, some coordination efforts exist between environmental institutions through mechanisms such as the Inter-agency Coordination Committee and the Commission for Sustainable Development, but these institutions are far too weak to integrate the three dimensions of sustainable development effectively. They seem to have served more as a pooling regime rather than an effective coordination regime.

And yet the process moves. Describing the difficulty of the endeavour should still not blind us, as analysts, to the fact that amazing accomplishments have been achieved multilaterally over the last 30 years. Most governments created environmental agencies, and, since 1992, units responsible for sustainable development. Public expenditures on the enviroment in the advanced industrialized countries now routinely run between 2 and 3 per cent of GNP. The market for pollution-control technology is conservatively estimated at $600 billion per year, and this market did not even exist in 1972. It was created as a consequence of governments adopting policies in order to achieve environmental protection and sustainable development. As mentioned above, hundreds of MEAs have been adopted. Many of these MEAs have actually been effective at improving collective environmental quality through inducing states to change policies in a manner conducive to a cleaner environment. Stratospheric ozone pollution has been reduced. European acid rain is greatly reduced. Oil spills in the oceans are down in number and volume. The quality of many regional seas has been stabilized, if not improved. In the face of sustained economic growth throughout the last 30 years these are not inconsiderable accomplishments. But still the challenge remains to do better, and to progress from environmental protection to sustainable development.[1]

We, as social scientists and citizens of the world, have already recognized that certain inherent links exist between human activities and the natural environment on which they depend. We know, for example, that there are a number of different gases that all lead to climate change, acid rain, and ozone loss. Similarly, we recognize that the climate, forests, oceans, wetlands, and diverse biosystems are naturally co-dependent within the global ecosystem.

There is growing interest in identifying the ways and means of creating a more effective synergy between the multitude of environmental institutions that exist at the local, national, regional, and global levels, and between those levels. The need for a common understanding of the interrelationships between different elements and dimensions of the environment, and sustainable development, extends well beyond the limitations of current scientific knowledge.

The multilateral approach to these issues still remains fragmented in terms of methods and mechanisms of scientific assessment and the development of consensual knowledge. This is also the case in regard to human capacity-building and the arts of domestic-regional-international interfacing in policy-making. At present it is unlikely that the tendency simply to piggyback institutions will produce a coherent, holistic approach to the governance of global sustainable development.

This volume addresses the various new channels of multilateral environmental governance that have appeared within an increasingly globalized international system at the end of the twentieth century. While states ultimately continue to make and enforce international law, they are increasingly dependent upon multilateral institutions, organized science, NGOs and social movements, and business and industry for formulating their views and conducting policy. This collective research project started with the premise that it is the emerging forces emanating from these multi-actors which facilitate creating institutional synergism in environmental governance. In other words, the authors believe that the state alone is not enough to propel changes.

As it is science that makes the environmental aspect of sustainable development "speak", the science-politics interface can be one of the most crucial facets of environmental regime-building. Yet there remains a great amount of scope for improved efficiency in the process of forging consensual knowledge, by identifying and utilizing the natural synergies that exist within the environment itself. Recent research reveals that most conflicts within the process of environmental regime-building are located at a cognitive level. What may appear to be political disagreements are often underpinned by disagreements about empirical data, analysis, and the formulation of assumptions regarding the causal relationships that underlie a given problem.

The interaction between science and politics has undergone institutional innovations during the past two decades, in that government-designated expert groups and independent scientists have, to a large degree, been incorporated within the negotiation setting. Yet it is now the case that most treaty negotiations have entered a stage where a greater role is envisaged for the social-scientific disciplines. Social sciences can provide two important contributions to a better understanding of global change and sustainable development. The first is through research on the human dimensions of global change, such as the large-scale demographic and social forces that drive societies to behave in potentially unsustainable manners. The IPCC, for instance, has turned to the use of social scientists to write reports on the human activities that generate greenhouse gases and thus are the root causes of climate change. Secondly, social scientists can study the diplomatic process by which states try to address shared environmental risks meaningfully, and thus contribute to improvements in the process. For instance, whereas states have endorsed scientifically derived "critical loads" for the protection of certain endangered ecosystems (such as in the case of European acid rain), in practice they often resort to more modest emission standards called "target loads". Social scientists can help decision-makers understand the process by which critical loads are adopted, and yet target loads are pursued, within a broader process of trying to move target load commitments closer to the critical loads which will be more beneficial for the sustainable development of the endangered ecosystems.

This volume is but one of many reflexive efforts by social scientists and environmental diplomats to understand and improve the process of multilateral environmental governance. To some extent sustainable development entails developing mechanisms by which groups who study and understand the development process may be better involved in that process.

Background

In 1999 the United Nations University, in collaboration with over 15 different UN organizations and agencies, agreement secretariats, and specialized agencies, examined the issue of synergy and coordination within international efforts to protect the environment. In the report emanating from this conference, many important questions were raised and several key conclusions reached. These included, for example, whether existing environmental institutions will be "adequate in the medium and long term, or whether deeper structural realignments are necessary".[2]

In regard to this question, one particular recommendation has continually resurfaced. This recommendation lies in the realm of structural change and involves the creation of a world environmental organization (WEO). Although the idea of a new global international environmental organization was once sidelined in the 1992 UN Conference on Environment and Development (UNCED) process, the proposal has regained currency over recent years within the academic literature.[3] There has been something of a time lag between renewed interest in the proposal at the academic level and the more recent interest in the idea from a policy perspective. At a policy level the notion of creating an overarching international environmental organization has been lent credence through a number of recent high-profile statements. These include the comments made recently by Renato Ruggioro,[4] and also the joint declaration of

Brazil, Germany, Singapore, and South Africa at the "Rio + 5" UN-GASS meeting in 1997. Most recently French President Jacques Chirac supported the idea of a WEO in his speech at the 2002 World Summit on Sustainable Development.

Proponents suggest that a world environment organization, or a world environment and development organization (WEDO), could, *inter alia*, facilitate greater coherence in the international environmental and sustainable development regime and increase the political standing of environmental and developmental issues *vis-à-vis* other policy areas, such as international trade as an economic dimension of sustainable development.

While many of the proposals that have been put forward may be attractive at first glance, those seeking to probe deeper into the feasibility and utility of each are confronted with a whole host of complexities and challenges that must be assessed. Many of the complexities are a consequence of the myriad of interrelated functional, political, and legal aspects that comprise the challenge of effective environmental and sustainable development governance. To date, attempts at an in-depth examination of these issues, in a systematic manner, have been rare. It is this factor that has led to this project, which aims to provide an interdisciplinary study of the missing linkages in the existing global environmental governance structure. Although the authors recognize the importance of sustainable development *per se*, the primary focus is on the environmental dimension of sustainable development. Sustainable development is seen from an environmental perspective in this volume.

The idea of launching a research project that looks into the possibilities for the reform of environmental governance structures emerged during Norichika Kanie's discussion with Bradnee Chambers when he worked for the United Nations University Institute of Advanced Studies (UNU/IAS) in 2000. After the elaboration of an earlier proposal, the research project began in 2001 with the support of a generous grant from the Japan Foundation Center for Global Partnership. The project consists of two parts. The first part, the result of which is presented in this volume and which was coordinated by Norichika Kanie, evaluates the state of the art and emerging forces in environmental governance. In this part of the project institutional reform is viewed from the present perspective by evaluating the strengths and weaknesses of the current environmental governance structure. The second part views the reform from the perspectives of various proposals already presented. It looks at actual policy implication of various proposals for institutional reform that have not yet been assessed in a concrete manner. This second part includes an assessment of both strengths and weaknesses of establishing a WEO, and the results are presented in another volume. Since members of the two parts of the project interacted with each other at a workshop and on other occasions, many of the chapters in this volume consider possibilities for the proposals investigated in the latter part (such as the possibility of a WEO) in their recommendations for reform.

The Faculty of Law and Policy Studies at the University of Kitakyushu, where Norichika Kanie was based, hosted the first part of the project, and the UNU/IAS was the host of the second part. Bradnee Chambers of the UNU coordinated the second part.[5] The project was basically designed so that two members of the project would deal with one issue, such as multilateral institutions, the science-policy interface, the NGO-GO interface, the industry-government interface, and multilevel governance.

The project members first met at a workshop in May 2001 in Hawaii to discuss substantive issues. The first draft papers were presented at a two-day workshop in March 2002 in New York, which was held as a side event to the PrepCom3 for the WSSD. Preliminary findings of both parts of the project were also presented as a UNU report to the PrepCom3. Based on the discussion and further research efforts after the second workshop in New York, the final draft papers were submitted and are presented in this volume. Out of the revised papers the authors have also presented a report to the WSSD held in Johannesburg.[6]

Overview of the book

The volume is divided into five sub-themes. The first theme deals with multilateral institutions, and consists of three chapters. It begins with a chapter by Toru Iwama that reviews the existing multilateral environmental or environment-related institutions and coordination structures, with particular attention to the UN system and treaty organs, and gives insights into the interlinkages of the international environmental governance system by proposing their restructuring and revitalization and the creation of new institutions. He shows that there are a number of interrelated functions fulfilled by various multilateral institutions. They have "fulfilled their functions successfully in their own given mandates to protect the environment, but existing multilateral institutions and structures are inadequate to meet the global environmental challenges that international society is now facing". Therefore, he argues, some kind of reform is necessary. Proposals for reform are closely investigated by the other volume coming out of this project, edited by Bradnee Chambers, but Iwama also provides an overview of those various proposals. As he argues, when it comes to creating/reforming something, one of the pressing problems is finance. However, one may realize by a close look at the existing institutions that forces for creating synergies are already emerging within the existing institutional framework, and we may well start looking forward from what we already have to hand.

Such a case seems to exist even in one of the pressing issues, the finance issue. In Chapter 2 Jake Werksman assesses the Global Environment Facility's (GEF) role in consolidating the governance of project finance in areas of the global environment, and draws lessons for a better financial mechanism in environmental governance. Nearly eight years' experience of the GEF, designed through a loose set of institutional links rather than through creating a new international institution, has shown that it has struggled with "the need to avoid the duplication or proliferation of institutions, to tap into the comparative advantages of existing institutions, and to promote partnerships, cooperation, and healthy competition amongst development agencies". In terms of environmental governance, Werksman concludes, the GEF's function of consolidating governance of more than one MEA can lead to greater institutional efficiency, but it may also provide a means for capping and containing developing country demands for increased resources. At the project level, there is evidence that the GEF's position at the centre of more than one MEA has helped it to avoid funding projects in one focal area that could have undermined the objectives of another focal area.

If it is the case that forces for creating symbiotic environmental governance institutions are already emerging even within the existing institutional framework, then we should also consider how the existing structure and functions of the institutional framework could improve global and international governance structures. In other words, we need tools to identify which elements of the structure and function of the institution affect success or failure in achieving the goals of the regime. Lessons may be learned from the experience of other international institutions, Laura Campbell argues, because "successful approaches could serve as a model for environmental governance". Campbell has chosen the cases of the WTO and WIPO, and evaluates them in terms of regime effectiveness in Chapter 3. She argues that, in the context of globalization, issue linkage of environmental issues with other issues such as trade and investment, dispute resolution and enforcement mechanisms, and economic incentives to participate and comply with agreements appears to be an important lesson for developing effective environmental governance structures.

The second sub-theme looks at the linkage between global, regional, national, and local arenas. So far attention has been paid to the linkage at the same level of governance structure and between different issues, called "horizontal linkage", when talking about linkage. However, as 10 years' experience of implementing Agenda 21 has made clear, equally important is how to translate the decisions taken at global level to implementation at the local level, and how local, often fragmented, experience or "best practices" for protecting the environment are accommodated into global regime design. Two chapters are devoted to investigating emerging forces and barriers to narrow the vertical gap. Jonathan Strand examines in Chapter 4 the question of how regional integration may serve as a stepping-stone to environmental governance. Recently, some attention has been paid to vertical linkages, especially in academia, but so far attention has been paid mainly to global and domestic governance, rather than the regional level. Strand argues that there is a paramount role for regional-level coordination of environmental governance and that regional environmental organizations could fill an important niche in multilateral environmental governance. In Chapter 5 Kanie explores domestic-international vertical linkage, and points out emerging forces that may narrow the gap between the domestic and international arenas, as well as identifying barriers to narrowing the gap. The narrowing forces exist in NGO activities, science activities, policies, institutions, and emerging partnerships between some of the stakeholders, but barriers also exist, which are found in the way to disseminate information, language, institutional capacity, and complex MEA requirements.

The next sub-theme is on the emerging forces that exist in the interface between science and policy. In Chapter 6 Peter Haas looks at lessons about the scientific functions that need to be performed to achieve effective multilateral environmental governance, and the institutional design by which such functions may best be performed. He concludes that effective international institutions in the environmental and sustainable development domains have been those that operate through networks composed of multiple international institutions and elements of civil society, rather than centralizing science policy functions. Chapter 7 looks into the case of the IPCC. Yasuko Kameyama assesses the eight gradually expanded roles of the IPCC in the climate change regime: the IPCC as a provider of scientific knowledge to the political process; a body to apply legitimacy to what is written in its reports; a forum to reach political agreements that would not be achievable in the political arena; a corridor for an epistemic community to influence politics; a forum to reach an agreement concerning scientific findings; a tool for researchers to obtain constant research funds; a tool for negotiators to justify their governments' positions; and an organization that disseminates information concerning climate change to the public. She argues that, with rejection of individual political preference, the IPCC roles provide a good guidance for a future scientific organization.

The fourth sub-theme is devoted to relations between non-governmental organizations (NGOs), or civil society organizations

(CSOs), and the environmental governance structure. This nexus is another noteworthy area of emerging forces that facilitate changes to the dynamics of environmental governance. In Chapter 8 Satoko Mori gives an overview of institutionalization of NGO involvement in global environmental governance, particularly focusing on the development after UNCED. Among other things she shows the function of the multi-stakeholder dialogue (MSD) process and the institutional practices of the UNFCCC and the World Bank. Dana Fisher examines more deeply in Chapter 9 the relationship between civil society protest and NGOs' and civil society actors' participation in the international meetings of economic institutions and multilateral regimes by looking at their engagement at particular meetings in recent years. She looks most carefully at the World Bank/International Monetary Fund and the UN Framework Convention on Climate Change. She observes that civil society actors work both within international institutional structures by lobbying members of national delegations as NGO participants, as well as by organizing protests outside of the meetings of such international institutions and multilateral regimes; she suggests that transparency, NGO participation throughout the process, and support of demonstrations by institutional representatives are key to improved environmental governance.

The fifth sub-theme is the interface between business/industry and government. As a business exhibition was symbolically presented in the Sandton International Conference Centre at the WSSD, it is impossible to ignore the role of the business/industry sector in environmental governance. However, there are still positive and negative views towards business/industry involvement in environmental governance activities. Because they are generally recognized substantially as the main force that fosters economic globalization, there are still cautious and sceptical views about their engagement in environment and sustainable development activities. In particular, environmental NGOs or CSOs, which appear to be another kind of emerging force in environmental governance, generally view industry involvement with sceptical eyes. Such a view is very well represented in Chapter 10 by Harris Gleckman. He examines the current balance between international corporate voluntary environmental management and public sector environmental management, and finds that it is, at least from the perspective of the environment, tilted too far in one direction. By recognizing the four components of environmental regulatory systems – namely voluntary codes and standards, self-defined implementation standards, self-financed certification systems, and elective public reporting – and the drivers at the national and international levels, it is possible to construct a number of ways to re-centre the political balance, to create a sustainable business climate, and to enhance global environmental protection. Mikoto Usui provides more positive views towards business/industry partnership in environmental governance. They possess huge power, and thus we should make positive use of them to find a win-win situation. In his informative Chapter 11, Usui explores various types of industry-government relationships. He argues that the multi-stakeholder dialogue programme of the UNCSD as well as the Global Compact have offered an innovative breakthrough at least for evading the impasse of institutional parallelism between private business and CSOs. It is hoped that the "Type 2" outcome of the WSSD will stimulate a variety of tri-sectoral partnering projects that involve a mediatory or brokering role of various UN agencies, the World Bank, and the IFC.

Finally, Peter Haas, Norichika Kanie, and Craig Murphy summarize the emerging forces in environmental governance, reflecting on the chapters in this volume. They present a matrix of functions in environmental governance that provides a mapping of the actor-function relationship. By clarifying who undertakes which function, our understanding of the complex environmental governance structure may advance. Also, the matrix could serve as a hint for further institutionalization or non-institutionalization of emerging forces in environmental governance in the world, since emergence of a WEO is unlikely in the foreseeable future.

In the process leading up to the WSSD a new approach was developed for enhancing "partnerships" between and among various stakeholders in society in implementing measures for sustainable development. As defined by the Commission on Global Governance, partnerships should be at the core of global governance.[7] If so, how shall we enhance partnerships? In what kind of governance structure can we enhance partnership functions? Without understanding the emerging forces in governance, states and civil society cannot establish meaningful partnerships. The authors hope that this volume can help in understanding the emerging forces in environmental governance, and serve as a reference for further discussion on the reform of environmental governance structure.

Notes

1. Haas, Peter M. 2001. "Pollution", in P. J. Simmons and Chantal de Jonge Oudraat (eds) *Managing Global Issues*. Washington, DC: Carnegie Endowment for International Peace, pp. 310–353.
2. United Nations University. 1999. *Inter-linkages: Synergies and Coordination between MEAs*, UNU Report. Tokyo: United Nations University, p. 31.
3. See Esty, Daniel C. 1994. *Greening the GATT*. Washington, DC: Institute for International Economics; Biermann, Frank and Udo E. Simonis. 1998. *A World Environment and Development Organization*, SEF Policy Paper 9. Bonn: SEF, p. 12; Ulfstein, Geir.

1999. "The proposed GEO and its relationship to existing MEAs", paper presented at the International Conference on Synergies and Coordination between Multilateral Environmental Agreements, United Nations University, 14–16 July. *Global Environmental Politics*, Vol. 1, No. 1. February 2001, MIT Press. See also the statement that came out of the Strengthening Global Environmental Governance Conference, New York, 4–5 June 1998.

4. Former Director-General of the WTO.

5. Chambers, W. Bradnee and Jessica F. Green (eds). Forthcoming. *Reforming International Environmental Governance: From Institutional Limits to Innovative Solutions*. Tokyo: United Nations University Press.

6. UNU/IAS. 2002. *International Sustainable Development Governance: The Question of Reform: Key Issues and Proposals*. Tokyo: UNU/IAS.

7. The Commission on Global Governance defines governance as follows. "Governance is the sum of the many ways individuals and institutions, public and private, manage their common affairs. It is a continuing process through which conflicting or diverse interests may be accommodated and cooperative action may be taken. It includes formal institutions and regimes empowered to enforce compliance, as well as informal arrangements that people and institutions either have agreed to or perceive to be in their interest." Commission on Global Governance. 1995. *Our Global Neighbourhood: The Report of the Commission on Global Governance*. Oxford: Oxford University Press.

Multilateral institutions

1

Multilateral environmental institutions and coordinating mechanisms

Toru Iwama

Introduction

Since the UN Conference on the Human Environment in 1972, new, diverse, and complicated environmental problems have emerged. Accordingly, to address these problems, existing multilateral institutions, the UN organs in particular, have been provided with new and additional functions on the one hand and multilateral environmental institutions have been newly established on the other hand, such as the United Nations Environment Programme (UNEP), the Global Environment Facility (GEF), the Commission on Sustainable Development (CSD), etc. In addition, sectoral multilateral environmental agreements (MEAs) have been increasingly concluded, with institutional settings such as a conference or a meeting of the parties (COP/MOP), a secretariat, and specialist subsidiary bodies – these are called treaty organs in this chapter.

There are, however, four problems to be pointed out at the present stage with regard to international environmental governance by multilateral institutions. First, there are missing links between different institutions in policy-making and its implementation, although they are addressing common and related issues. Only an *ad hoc*, fragmental, and disjointed approach has been applied by different institutions. Different treaties or regimes were concluded or established for different sectors of the environment, and these do no address issues in the cross-sectoral and multi-sectoral context. Secondly, there are overlapping or conflicting functions and insufficient coordination among different institutions. Thirdly, there are no powerful, competent institution(s) whose mandates are directly related to international environmental governance. UNEP is only a "catalyst" in the UN system, with a small secretariat in terms of staff numbers and budget. Less attention is paid to the environment in the Second Committee of the General Assembly. The UNEP Executive Director's voice is lower in the UN Secretariat. Fourthly, multilateral environmental institutions have not captured the initiatives of numerous actors, including NGOs and corporations, in policy-making and its implementation.

This chapter reviews the existing multilateral environmental or environment-related institutions and coordination structures, with a particular attention to the UN system and treaty organs, and gives insights into the interlinkages of the international environmental governance system by proposing their restructuring and revitalization and the creation of new institutions.

Existing multilateral institutions

UN organs

The UN organs – principal organs such as the General Assembly, the Economic and Social Council (ECOSOC), the Security Council, the International Court of Justice (ICJ), and the Secretariat, specialized agencies, subsidiary organs, and related agencies – are addressing environmental issues in their respective mandates and their roles have become increasingly important,[1] but only UNEP, the CSD, and the GEF are directly related to international environmental governance as far as their mandates are concerned. The establishment of UNEP and the CSD were historically important in the sense that they followed the two landmark global conferences respectively, the 1972 UN Conference on the Human Environment (UNCHE) and the 1992 UN Conference on Environment and Development (UNCED).

Principal organs

General Assembly

The General Assembly is a principal agenda-setting and policy-making body[2] of the UN system which provides overall guidance to governments, the UN system, and relevant treaty organs. The bulk of the General Assembly's work on environmental issues is carried out by its Second (Economic and Financial) Committee. Owing to its universal membership and broad mandate, the General Assembly has been an appropriate forum to address environmental issues of global concern, although its powers are limited to making recommendations which are not legally binding on member states. Among the achievements of the General Assembly, of historical importance are the convening of the 1972 UN-CHE and the 1992 UNCED, culminating in the establishment of UNEP and the CSD respectively, and of international conferences to conclude MEAs, such as the 1992 United Nations Framework Convention on Climate Change (UNFCCC) and the 1995 agreement for the implementation of the provisions of the United Nations Convention on the Law of the Sea of 10 December 1982, relating to the conservation and management of straddling fish stocks and highly migratory fish stocks.

ECOSOC
Of the three principal councils, only ECOSOC is directly concerned with environmental policies. It receives and merely passes to the General Assembly the reports of the UNEP Governing Council, the UN subsidiary bodies, and the UN specialized and related agencies. However, ECOSOC itself had no environment-oriented main or standing committees or functional commissions[3] before the CSD was created as a functional commission of ECOSOC by the UN General Assembly to ensure the follow-up to UNCED.[4]

Security Council
The mandate of the Security Council is to remove causes of conflicts before they become threats to international peace and security. It is probable that non-military sources of instability in the economic, social, humanitarian, and ecological fields could in the future become threats to international security.[5] However, there are legal and political obstacles to be cleared if environmental threats could be interpreted to mean threats to international security and the Council could enforce the violation of environmental rules.

ICJ
The ICJ, as the principal judicial organ of the United Nations, is empowered to decide legal disputes which are submitted to it by the parties to the dispute. Such disputes include those on environmental matters. The jurisdiction of the Court comprises all cases which the parties refer to it and all matters specially provided for in treaties and conventions in force.[6] The major treaties and conventions for environmental protection adopted since the mid-1980s include provision for the submission of disputes arising from their interpretation and application to the ICJ.[7] There are two recent movements which show that the Court is willing to address

environmental matters. The first is its decision in 1993 to establish
a seven-member Chamber for environmental matters in accordance with
Article 26(1) of the Statute of the Court. However, no disputes have
been submitted to the Chamber. The second is that the Court has decided matters which are directly or indirectly related to environmental
protection. There have been five cases submitted to it: three cases on nuclear weapons and nuclear weapons testing[8] and two cases arising from
environmental damage.[9]

Secretariat
The Secretariat provides administrative services to the General Assembly and its subsidiary bodies. Although it has within itself departments on
political and Security Council affairs, trusteeship and decolonization, and
economic and social affairs, no department exists on environmental affairs. The Secretary-General, the executive officer of the Secretariat, has
little formal power in this matter, but may influence the course of events
of environment-related matters.[10]

Specialized agencies
Of the 16 specialized agencies,[11] the FAO, IBRD, ILO, IMO, UNESCO,
UNIDO, WHO, and WMO are directly involved in environmental protection.[12] They were assigned or gradually assumed some environment-
related functions which are incidental to carrying out their principal
tasks.[13]
 They have made a number of achievements in the area of progressive
development of international environmental law, including the conclusion of MEAs and the issue of guidelines and other "soft" law. They have
sponsored or initiated negotiations to conclude MEAs and are playing an
administrative role as their secretariats. For example, the FAO worked
to conclude the 1951 Rome International Plant Protection Convention,
the 1956 Rome Plant Protection Agreement for the Asian and Pacific
Region, and the 1969 Rome Convention on the Conservation of the
Living Resources of the South-East Atlantic. The IMO (formerly the
IMCO) is responsible for the negotiation and administration of treaties
and conventions related to ocean pollution: the 1972 Convention on the
Prevention of Marine Pollution by Dumping of Wastes and Other Matter
(the London Dumping Convention), the MARPOL 1973/78 Convention,
the 1990 International Convention on Oil Pollution Preparedness, Response, and Cooperation, and so on. The General Assembly of UNESCO
adopted in 1972 the Convention Concerning the Protection of the World
Cultural and Natural Heritage. UNESCO functions as its secretariat.
And the Intergovernmental Committee for the Protection of the Cultural
and Natural Heritage of Outstanding Universal Value (the World Heri-

tage Committee), which was established by this convention to implement its administration, is assisted by a secretariat appointed by the UNESCO Director-General.

Subsidiary organs

Subsidiary organs are established by the General Assembly or by other subdivisions of the UN system.

UNEP

Of primary importance in the UN system for environmental protection is UNEP. UNEP was established as a subsidiary organ of the UN General Assembly[14] to work as a "catalyst" for activities and programmes within the UN system. It promotes international environmental cooperation rather than initiating or mandating environmental programmes on its own account.[15] It serves as a focal point for environmental action and coordination within the UN system, and reports to the General Assembly through ECOSOC. It consists of a 58-member Governing Council and the Environment Secretariat, whose head is the Executive Director.[16] Its administrative cost is covered by the regular budget funds of the United Nations. Additional financing is allocated to its operational activities by the Environment Fund, comprising unrestricted voluntary contributions.

A set of programmes which UNEP has implemented include stimulation of research, collection and coordination of data, publications, education, sponsoring negotiations leading to conclusion of international treaties, and the establishment of specialized environmental organs, as well as the adoption of guidelines and other types of soft law.[17]

In view of the progressive development of international environmental law, UNEP's achievements in sponsoring international negotiations to conclude MEAs are to be noted. It sponsored the negotiations leading to the 1985 Vienna Convention for the Protection of the Ozone Layer (the Vienna Convention), the 1987 Montreal Protocol on Substances that Deplete the Ozone Layer (the Montreal Protocol), and the 1989 Basel Convention on the Control of Transboundary Movements of Hazardous Wastes and Their Disposal (the Basel Convention). The 1998 Convention on Prior Informed Consent Procedure for Certain Hazardous Chemicals and Pesticides in International Trade (the Rotterdam Convention) was negotiated under the auspices of UNEP jointly with the FAO.

UNEP initiated the preparation of the 1992 Convention on Biological Diversity (CBD). UNEP and the WMO co-sponsored the Intergovernmental Panel on Climate Change (IPCC) for the negotiation of a climate regime, culminating in the adoption of the UNFCCC in 1992. UNEP also provided substantive support and expertise for the conclusion of the 1994 Convention to Combat Desertification in Those Countries Experiencing

Serious Drought and/or Desertification, Particularly in Africa (the Desertification Convention). It initiated the regional seas programme for 14 regions with nine conventions and three action plans, as well as their 27 protocols.

UNEP plays a significant role for administering five MEAs as the secretariat of the 1973 Convention on International Trade in Endangered Species of Wild Fauna and Flora (CITES), the 1979 Bonn Convention on the Conservation of Migratory Species of Wild Animals (CMS), the Vienna Convention, the Montreal Protocol, the Basel Convention, and the CBD.

It is noteworthy that there is a remarkable recent trend of "greening" of the existing UN organs, the creation of new environmental organs within the UN system such as the CSD, and development of environmental treaty organs (to be discussed later) on the one hand,[18] but on the other hand they have contributed to dilution of UNEP's mandate and authority.[19]

CSD

The CSD was created by the UN General Assembly as a functional subsidiary organ of ECOSOC,[20] and is composed of 53 members elected for terms of three years' office from the member states of the UN and its specialized agencies. It receives substantive and technical services from the UN Secretariat's Department for Policy Coordination and Sustainable Development.

Its mandate is to receive and consider reports (national, regional, and international) or periodic communications on the progress of implementation of UNCED final documents, including Agenda 21, the Rio Declaration on Environment and Development, and the Non-Legally Binding Authoritative Statement of Principles for a Global Consensus on the Management, Conservation, and Sustainable Development of All Types of Forests, and to elaborate policy guidance and options for future activities to follow up UNCED and to recommend them to the UN General Assembly through ECOSOC.

There is a criticism that no clear distinction has been made with regard to the allocation of responsibilities and mandates between the CSD and UNEP as the main institutions within the UN system.[21] It can be pointed out that the creation of the CSD has indirectly contributed to diluting the authority of UNEP in the area of international environmental cooperation in the UN system.[22]

Others

Other subsidiary organs such as the United Nations Development Programme (UNDP), the United Nations University (UNU), the United

Nations Institute for Training and Research (UNITAR), and the five regional Economic Commissions[23] also perform environment-related functions.

Related agencies and others

The International Atomic Energy Agency (IAEA) is not a specialized agency but is associated with the United Nations as an independent intergovernmental organization. After the 1986 Chernobyl incident, the IAEA sponsored two international conventions of environmental significance and has been extending environmental considerations regarding the use of nuclear energy.

In 1991 the Global Environment Facility (GEF) became operational on a three-year trial basis, and was restructured in 1994 on a permanent basis. It is implemented by the World Bank (IBRD), UNEP, and the UNDP. The World Bank functions to administer GEF, a trust fund, and responsibility for investment projects. Its purpose is to give additional funding to projects in developing countries in four designated areas: reduction of global warming gas emissions, protection of the biosphere, protection of international waters, and protection of the ozone layer.

WTO

In 1994 the World Trade Organization (WTO) was established in the final act of the Uruguay Round of trade negotiations under the General Agreement on Tariffs and Trade (GATT). GATT used to be a development-oriented organization, with the exceptional clause of Article 25. However, the Marrakesh Agreement establishing the WTO recognizes, in its preamble, sustainable development as the overarching objective of the WTO, and it has responded to criticisms of being insufficiently responsive to environmental consequences of world trade by setting up in 1995 the Committee on Trade and Environment (CTE).[24]

Treaty organs

Since the early 1970s a large number of MEAs in the area of oceans, atmosphere, nature, waste, and fisheries have been concluded, with institutional arrangements setting up a conference or a meeting of the parties (COP/MOP) with decision-making powers, a secretariat, and specialist subsidiary bodies.[25] These institutions are called "autonomous institutions" in the sense that they do not constitute traditional intergovernmental organizations (IGOs) but are distinct both from the state parties to a particular agreement and from the existing IGOs on the one hand, and they have their own law-making powers and compliance mechanisms on the other hand.[26] These treaty organs, comprising the COP/MOP, a secretariat, and specialist subsidiary bodies, are included here as multilateral environmental institutions.

MEAs establishing such institutional arrangements include the 1971 Convention on Wetlands of International Importance Especially as Waterfowl Habitat (the Ramsar Convention), the London Dumping Convention, CITES, the CMS, the Basel Convention and its 1999 Protocol on Liability and Compensation, the UNFCCC and its 1997 Kyoto Protocol, the CBD and its 2000 Cartagena Protocol on Biosafety, the Desertification Convention, the 1994 International Tropical Timber Agreement (ITTA), and the Rotterdam Convention.

The secretariat of each agreement is either newly established or affiliated with existing UN organs such as the IMO, UNESCO, the FAO, and UNEP, or an international NGO such as the International Union for Conservation of Nature and Natural Resources (IUCN, now often called the World Conservation Union).

Coordinating institutions/bodies and mechanisms

Since the 1972 UNCHE there has arisen a need for coordination of policies within respective international institutions and among different ones in order to implement environmental goals. This chapter reviews the existing coordinating institutions, bodies, and mechanisms.

Intra-institutional coordination

A newly emerging need for coordination of policies between environment and development has been satisfied within respective international institutions, particularly development-oriented ones, by setting up a new subdivision. For example, the World Bank has recognized the adverse effect of development loans and increasingly structured and conditioned loans in such a way that the development it funds is ecologically sound.[27] It has made major reforms by establishing in 1973 an Office of Environmental Affairs to provide studies of the environmental impacts of the development projects it funds. In 1989 it adopted its Operational Directive on Environmental Assessment, which was revised in 1991. In 1973 the former IMCO Assembly established the Marine Environment Protection Committee. The WTO established the CTE to discuss the environmental aspects of trade and trade-related aspects of environmental measures.

Inter-institutional coordination

Inter-UN organs

In the UN system, the Administrative Committee on Coordination (ACC) consists of the executive heads of the specialized agencies, related agencies, and subsidiary organs, including UNEP. It meets several times a year, chaired by the UN Secretary-General, and coordinates UN policies at the secretariat level. It considers and makes recommendations on coordination of environment-related programmes and projects falling within the purview of more than one of the participating entities. With regard to UNEP-related programmes and projects, it makes a report, drafted by the UNEP Executive Director, to the UNEP Governing Council. Designated Officials for Environmental Matters (DOEM), one of UNEP's organs, help the UNEP Executive Director to draft these reports.

The Inter-Agency Committee on Sustainable Development (IACSD) was established in 1993 as a standing committee of the ACC to advise the ACC on ways and means of addressing issues relating to the follow-up to UNCED by the UN system in order to ensure effective system-wide cooperation and coordination in the implementation of Agenda 21 and other outcomes of UNCED.

There are other organs whose mandates are to coordinate between/among different UN organs: CIDIE (the Committee on International Development Institutions on the Environment) which is a joint organ of multilateral development and financial institutions; GESAMP (the Group of Experts on the Scientific Aspects of Marine Pollution), which is a joint organ of the United Nations, UNEP, the FAO, UNESCO, the WHO, WMO, IMO, and IAEA; the UNEP/WMO joint-sponsored IPCC; and the GEF which is jointly administered by UNEP, the UNDP, and the World Bank, etc.

Inter-treaty organs

Recently COP/MOPs of MEAs have realized the importance of and need for coordination between/among treaty organs since they are dealing with closely related matters, and adopted resolutions to exchange information between/among secretariats and accept observers from each other to participate in COP/MOP meetings. Examples are agreements between the CBD and the Ramsar Convention on the question of biological diversity, and between the UNFCCC and the CBD on the question of climate change.[28]

The 1997 exchange of a memorandum of cooperation between the

CBD's secretariat and that of the Protocol Concerning Specially Protected Areas and Wildlife for the Wider Caribbean Sea Region is a good example, in which both agreed to send their staffs to the other's meetings, exchange information and experience, coordinate their work plans, cooperate in their preparation process, work out joint conservation plans, integrate and unite programmes for domestic implementation of each other's legal instruments, and review other necessary guidelines.

Between UN organs and treaty organs

The same trend can be witnessed in the coordination between UN organs and treaty organs, for example among the UNFCCC, CBD, UNEP, and GEF on climate change issues, between the WTO and MEAs on issues of trade and environment, and among the CBD, FAO, and UNESCO on natural heritage issues.

Proposals for restructuring and revitalizing multilateral institutions and establishing new institutions

The multilateral institutions discussed above are fulfilling a range of interrelated functions, including awareness-raising and agenda-setting; collecting, processing, and disseminating information; setting international standards and regulations; capacity-building and providing financial and technical assistance; and avoiding and settling disputes.[29]

It is fair to say that they have fulfilled their functions successfully within their own given mandates to protect the environment, but existing multilateral institutions and structures are inadequate to meet the global environmental challenges which international society is now facing. Chapter 38 of Agenda 21 calls for a need for the restructuring and revitalization of the UN system to implement Agenda 21 and other conclusions of UNCED. There have been many suggestions and proposals made for that purpose, including those for establishing new institutions and structures and those addressing the four problems cited in the introduction.[30]

Such suggestions and proposals are categorized into two approaches: a vertical approach and a horizontal approach. The former emphasizes the need to centralize functions of different institutions to one institution, either through the creation of a new institution or the strengthening of an existing one. It seeks to generate vertical, "top-down" integration and an overarching authority which either assumes the responsibilities of existing institutions or directs their coordination from above.[31] The latter approach emphasizes the strengthening of an existing institution on the one hand and horizontal system-wide coordination between/among related institutions on the other hand. It is based on the revitalization of institutions, a clear division of their responsibilities, and the avoidance of duplication of their functions.

Vertical approach

Establishing a new UN principal organ

In order for international environmental governance to have a high-profile presence in the UN system, it would seem suitable to establish a principal organ with either environmental legislation or enforcement powers,[32] since no present principal organs can address such a need. The present General Assembly is not suitable as far as its mandate and powers are concerned.[33] The Security Council is not suitable, either, because there are legal and political difficulties to be solved if environmental threats are to be interpreted to mean threats to international security and the Council could enforce the violation of environmental rules, and neither the composition nor the voting system appears suitable for assigning environmental tasks to the Council.[34]

There remain many questions to be answered regarding a new organ's powers, particularly its legislative or norm-making power and its enforcement power, and its composition and voting system. In answering these questions, the following comment should be taken into account:

... any legislative organ must be large enough to be considered reasonably representative of the world community – even if it is provided ... that any proposed legislation must also be approved by the General Assembly. On the other hand, an organ charged with enforcement should, by analogy with the Security Council, be small enough to be able to act effectively.[35]

It has been suggested that the Trusteeship Council which has completed its original task should be restructured into a new one with environmental tasks. A proposed new Trusteeship Council can be categorized into two types: an environmental watchdog for the UN system;[36] and the council entrusted with the task of overall supervision of global environmental protection as well as global common areas.[37] With regard to the latter type of a new council, the Secretary-General's remark should be taken into account – that it could exercise a collective trusteeship for the integrity of the global environment and common areas, such as the oceans, atmosphere, and outer space.[38]

Establishing a new UN specialized agency

In 1991 Sir Geoffrey Palmer proposed the creation of "a proper international environmental agency within the United Nations system that has real power and authority", a new specialized UN agency called the

International Environment Organization (IEO).[39] The structural basis of his proposal is modelled on that of the ILO, where tripartite representatives from government, industry, and employers and employees can participate in decision-making, including standard-setting and rule-making.[40]

According to Palmer, the IEO shall be composed of a general conference comprising all members and a governing council comprising 40 people – 20 representing governments, 10 representing business organizations, and 10 representing environmental organizations and the secretariat.[41] Each member state sends to the conference two government delegates and two others from business and environmental organizations, respectively. The IEO can perform both a legislative and an implementation function. It can take decisions by a two-thirds majority, demand reports from member states, and take measures to secure compliance with its provisions.[42] UNEP may be strengthened and transformed into this type of international intergovernmental organization, a specialized agency which is required to conclude a relationship agreement with the United Nations when being established.

Horizontal approach

Revitalized UN organs

General Assembly
Regarding the General Assembly, it could be recommended that the Fourth Committee in charge of decolonization be restructured into a Committee for Sustainable Development, or that the current load of the Second Committee be redistributed between it and the Fourth Committee, with one of them handling all environment-development-related issues and the other undertaking all other economic and financial ones.[43]

ECOSOC
As Chapter 38.10 of Agenda 21 suggests, the functions of ECOSOC could be revitalized in such a way that it would assist the General Assembly through overseeing system-wide coordination, overviewing the implementation of Agenda 21 and making recommendations in this regard, and undertaking the task of directing system-wide coordination and integration of environmental and developmental aspects in the UN's policies and programmes. ECOSOC could also make appropriate recommendations to the General Assembly, relevant specialized agencies, and member states.

However, at the extreme side of the debate, there is a suggestion that ECOSOC be entirely abolished and its tasks be taken over by the present Second and Third Committees of the General Assembly.[44]

Security Council
A suggestion that the Security Council could be assigned functions of environmental protection is based on the recognition that major or critical environmental destruction may present threats to international security and that the Council has powers to enforce states to comply with its decisions. However, because of its present composition and voting system, and the need for a UN Charter amendment if responsibilities in respect of the enforcement of environmental rules or the prevention of environmental violation are given to the Council, it is more suitable and feasible to create a new principal organ as discussed above.[45]

Secretariat
As Chapter 38.15 of Agenda 21 suggests, strong and effective leadership on the part of the Secretary-General is crucial for global environmental governance, since he/she would be the focal point of the institutional arrangements within the UN system. The Secretary-General plays a key role in the interagency mechanism for coordination and supervision of environmental programme planning and review among the UN organs. In this sense, a supportive system should be established within the Secretariat, including an environmental secretariat to be created under the Secretariat as a unit of the central secretariat of the United Nations.[46]

Specialized agencies
It is recommended that relevant specialized agencies should strengthen their functions of environmental protection in the future, and there needs to be an adjustment and coordination among different agencies initiated by a newly created specialized agency, such as the IEO or a strengthened UNEP.

Strengthened UNEP
UNEP has been criticized for its insufficient clout because it has been unable to fulfil fully its original mandate as a "catalyst" to promote international cooperation in the UN system in the face of growing complexities of environmental problems, owing to the size of its secretariat, its insufficient budget, the impractical location of its headquarters, the lack of weight for the voice of its Executive Director in the UN Secretary-General's Cabinet, the low status of environmental matters in the overcrowded schedule of the Second Committee of the UN General Assembly, and duplication of its functions with other UN organs.[47] UNEP can function as a coordinator of environmental policies in the UN system if some conditions are met.

There are three recommendations addressed to UNEP. The first is to provide "stable, adequate, and predictable financial resources"[48] to UNEP in order to keep its existing mandate as a "catalyst" working. The need should be identified for direct financial support from the UN regular budget to pay for the administration of the UNEP Secretariat. With regard to DOEM (Designated Officials for Environmental Matters), an interagency subsidiary of the ACC created by UNEP, this should be revitalized to ensure it can carry out its coordinating mandate in the ACC.

The second recommendation is to strengthen the existing mandate of UNEP as a "catalyst" with adequate funding. UNEP in particular is called upon to:

- coordinate and promote relevant scientific research
- facilitate information dissemination and exchange
- promote the use of environmental means such as environmental impact assessments
- promote regional and subregional cooperation and coordination
- help governments to meet legal and institutional requirements
- promote closer working relations with development organs such as the UNDP and the World Bank to integrate environmental considerations into development projects
- support negotiations leading to adoption of either treaty laws or soft laws.[49]

Regarding UNEP's role of coordinating functions among convention secretariats, it is to be strengthened in such a way that UNEP functions as a secretariat for each treaty organ, which includes co-location of secretariats established in UNEP.[50]

The third recommendation is to transform UNEP with the present narrow mandate of a "catalyst" into a new full-fledged institution: a UN principal organ, a UN specialized agency, or an operational UN Environment Agency.[51]

Revitalized UNDP

The UNDP round tables and World Bank consultative groups may be used as vehicles for regular national planning and review. The UNDP is the lead agency in the UN system for capacity-building for sustainable development at local, national, and regional levels. It is therefore imperative that the UNDP should keep close working relations with UNEP and that the UNDP resident representatives should be strengthened to coordinate field-level UN technical cooperation activities.[52]

Renewed CSD

The creation of the CSD contributed to diluting the mandate and authority of UNEP. The function of the CSD is questionable. It seems that there was no need to set up a new organ, the CSD, in the UN system when its mandates and functions were covered by the existing organ, UNEP. It also seems that the Commission is unlikely to fulfil any more visionary ambitions for an overarching international environmental organization.[53] Therefore, it is recommended that the CSD be merged into UNEP. If it is not practicable, the mandate and activities of the CSD should be better defined to build on potential strengths which are to be identified in concrete terms.

Revitalized ACC

The role of the ACC should be revitalized as the interagency mechanism for coordination and supervision of environmental programme planning and review among the UN organs and for provision of a vital interface with the multilateral financial institutions. A special board or taskforce may be set up for that purpose by the ACC.[54] In this regard, the direct and strong leadership of the Secretary-General is expected, and all heads of organs and agencies of the UN system are expected to cooperate with the Secretary-General fully in order to make the ACC work effectively.

Due consideration should be given to the creation of a high-level deputy on sustainable development to assist the Secretary-General so that the ACC can exercise its function to the full extent. Relevant UN programmes on environment and development should be reported from all relevant UN organs and agencies to the deputy, which will ensure that those programmes are coordinated and reinforce each other under the chairmanship of the Secretary-General at the ACC.

The recently proposed EMG (Environmental Management Group) headed by the UNEP Executive Director, replacing the Inter-Agency Environmental Coordination Group (IAECG) to achieve better coordination and joint action, should be further elaborated. It is to comprise at its core all the leading UN organs in the field of the environment and human settlements, as well as other UN organs, financial institutions, and organizations outside the UN system, including MEAs' secretariats whenever required.[55]

Coordinated treaty organs

In order to exploit synergies, capture linkages, and avoid duplicating or conflicting decisions among MEAs and to achieve coherence and effectiveness in international environmental governance, a clustering approach to MEAs should be adopted.[56] Clustering could group MEAs either into issue clusters such as atmosphere, oceans, fresh water, biological diversity, and waste, or into functional issue clusters such as capacity-building, environmental assessment, scientific assessment, monitoring, administrative management, reporting, and so on. Clustering should be administered by UNEP based on clear criteria, and the result should be disseminated to secretariats of institutions responsible for initiating or sponsoring negotiations of MEAs. And to enhance interlinkages, coordination, and administrative streamlining, it is recommended that a number of treaty organs operating in related fields be combined into a single one, by co-locating the secretariats of MEAs to UNEP, for example.

Links between policies and funding

International policies to promote sustainable development, particularly in developing countries, are implemented successfully with adequate international financial and technological support. UN development agencies, such as the UNDP, should ensure, in full cooperation with recipient countries and in full coordination with UNEP, that the projects they support be consistent with the recipient country's international environmental requirements, whether they are legally binding or not.

A current international treaty practice of linking the implementation of treaty obligations of developed countries with their funding commitments, which is witnessed in the areas of the ozone layer, climate change, and biological diversity, is highly recommended. In this regard, the role of the GEF, which operates such a funding mechanism, should be further developed.

Conclusions: Options to take

It is often suggested that international environmental governance could be achieved by establishing the interlinkages of multilateral institutions; this requires structural change of existing institutions and/or the creation of new institutions. Proponents suggest that a world environmental organization (WEO) or a world environment and development organization (WEDO) should be established.

This chapter has discussed proposals for restructuring and revitalizing multilateral institutions and establishing new institutions. Among them, a new UN principal organ (the ESC, the Trusteeship Council), a new UN specialized agency (the IEO, UNEPO), or a strengthened UNEP might be equivalent to a WEO or WEDO.

It seems unlikely for a new UN principal organ to be created, because of the limited UN budget, an unwillingness of member states to bear the expense of creating new institutions, their resistance to the expansion of the UN organs, and a foreseeable difficulty of amending the UN Charter. On the other hand, the creation of a new specialized agency seems feasible if the political climate is ripe enough. Technically it does not require the amendment of the Charter, but only needs a relationship agreement with the United Nations. It is expected that a WEO or WEDO as a specialized agency could function to fulfil the interlinkages of multilateral institutions. However, what is crucial is that a WEO or WEDO should take an initiative to coordinate different specialized agencies and other UN organs as far as sustainable development is concerned as a policy issue. A strengthened-UNEP type of WEO or WEDO could also function in full for the interlinkages.

The international community of today is composed of sovereign states – there is no central government and a unitary form of global governance is not feasible. Therefore, coordination and integration can only take place horizontally between/among existing institutions.[57] The WEO or WEDO discussed above is expected to fulfil such a function.

The World Summit on Sustainable Development (WSSD) held in Johannesburg in 2002 was supposed to discuss and agree upon an effective international institutional framework for sustainable development, but could not succeed in producing visible results. It only agreed as one of its objectives to increase effectiveness and efficiency through limiting overlap and duplication of activities of international organizations, within and outside the UN system, based on their mandates and comparative advantages.[58] It also agreed to enhance the roles of the existing UN system – the General Assembly, ECOSOC, the CSD, the UNDP, UNEP, and others – but did not agree to create a WEO or WEDO type of institution.[59] The WSSD reminded academics of the need to elaborate further the effective international institutional framework for environmental governance so that the policy-makers can be persuaded to adopt and implement such governance in order to achieve the common objective of sustainable development in our global society.

Notes

1. See detailed discussion in Caldwell, Lynton K. 1996. *International Environmental Policy*. Durham and London: Duke University Press, pp. 127–139; Morrison, Fred L. and Rüdiger Wolfrum (eds). 2000. *International, Regional and National Environmental Law*. The Hague, London, and Boston: Kluwer Law International, pp. 71–110; Szasz, Paul C. 1992. "Restructuring the international organizational framework", in Edith B. Weiss (ed.) *Environmental Change and International Law: New Challenges and Dimensions*. Tokyo: United Nations University Press, pp. 340–351.
2. Agenda 21, adopted at UNCED in 1992, recognizes the General Assembly as "the supreme policy-making forum" in Chapter 38.1. See UN Doc.A/Conf.151/26/Rev.1 (1993).
3. Szasz, note 1 above, p. 345.
4. GA Res. 47/191 (1992).
5. The diversion case of the Jordan River waters was a good example, where Syria appealed to the Security Council in 1953 to stop Israel from diverting the water. See Caldwell, note 1 above, p. 128.
6. Article 36(1) of the Statute of the International Court of Justice.
7. See examples in Kiss, Alexandre-Charles. 1998. "The International Court of Justice and the protection of the environment", in *Hague Yearbook of International Law*, Vol. 11, pp. 1–2.

8. The Nuclear Tests Case, Order of 22 June 1973; Legality of the Use by a State of Nuclear Weapons in Armed Conflict, Advisory Opinion of 8 July 1996; Legality of the Threat or Use of Nuclear Weapons, Advisory Opinion of 8 July 1996.
9. The Case of Certain Phosphate Lands in Nauru (Nauru v. Australia), Judgment of 26 June 1992; The Gabcíkovo-Nagymaros Case (Hungary v. Slovakia), Judgment of 25 September 1997.
10. Caldwell, note 1 above, p. 128.
11. Food and Agriculture Organization of the United Nations (FAO), International Bank for Reconstruction and Development (IBRD), International Civil Aviation Organization (ICAO), International Development Association (IDA), International Finance Corporation (IFC), International Fund for Agricultural Development (IFAD), International Labour Organization (ILO), International Monetary Fund (IMF), International Telecommunication Union (ITU), International Maritime Organization (IMO), United Nations Educational, Scientific, and Cultural Organization (UNESCO), United Nations Industrial Development Organization (UNIDO), Universal Postal Union (UPU), World Health Organization (WHO), World Intellectual Property Organization (WIPO), and World Meteorological Organization (WMO).
12. Caldwell, note 1 above, p. 134.
13. See details of their respective functions and activities in Szasz, note 1 above, pp. 347–350; Caldwell, ibid., pp. 133–139.
14. General Assembly Resolution 2997 (XXVII) of 15 December 1972.
15. Birnie, Patricia W. and Alan E. Boyle. 1992. International Law and the Environment. Oxford: Oxford University Press, p. 42.
16. The Executive Director is elected by the General Assembly on the nomination of the Secretary-General.
17. Szasz, note 1 above, p. 342.
18. See detailed discussions in Werksman, Jacob (ed.). 1996. Greening International Institutions. London: Earthscan.
19. See Desai, Bharat H. 2000. "Revitalizing international environmental institutions: The UN Task Force Report and beyond", Indian Journal of International Law, Vol. 40, pp. 468–471.
20. Council (ECOSOC) Decision 1993/207.
21. Morrison and Wolfrum, note 1 above, p. 78.
22. Desai, note 19 above, p. 473.
23. ESCAP, ECWA, ECA, ECE, and ECLA.
24. See Tarasofsky, Richard G. 1996. "Ensuring compatibility between multilateral environmental agreements and the GATT/WTO", in Yearbook of International Environmental Law, Vol. 7, p. 52.
25. See detailed discussions about these institutional arrangements in Churchill, Robin R. and Geir Ulfstein. 2000. "Autonomous institutional arrangements in multilateral environmental agreements: A little-noticed phenomenon in international law", American Journal of International Law, Vol. 94, No. 4, pp. 623–659; Röben, Volker. 2000. "Institutional developments under modern international environmental agreements", Max Plank Yearbook of the United Nations, Vol. 4, pp. 363–443.
26. Churchill and Ulfstein, ibid., p. 623.
27. Birnie and Boyle, note 15 above, p. 62.
28. See Kimball, Lee A. 1997. "Institutional linkages between the Convention on Biological Diversity and other international conventions", Review of European Community and International Environmental Law, Vol. 6, No. 3, pp. 239–248.
29. Werksman, note 18 above, pp. xiii–xvii.
30. See in particular Desai, note 19 above, pp. 471–504; Kimball, Lee A. and William C.

Boyd. 1992. "International institutional arrangements for environment and development: A post-Rio assessment", *Review of European Community and International Environmental Law*, Vol. 1, No. 3, pp. 300–304; Palmer, Geoffrey. 1992. "New ways to make international environmental law", *American Journal of International Law*, Vol. 86, No. 2, pp. 278–282; Szasz, note 1 above, pp. 353–384. Palmer (p. 279) analyses the present situation as follows: "There are basically four policy options in the institutional arena. First, things could be left as they are. Second, UNEP could be strengthened and given formal responsibilities. Third, the secretariat approach of the Vienna Convention could be embroidered upon and developed so that a series of secretariats operate for separate environmental issues. At present, that is the way things are heading. The fourth broad option is to create a new international institution."

31. Werksman, note 18 above, p. xxi.
32. The Commission on Global Governance recommended the establishment of an Economic Security Council (ESC) which provides leadership in economic, social, and environmental fields. See Commission on Global Governance. 1995. *Our Global Neighbourhood: The Report of the Commission on Global Governance*. Oxford: Oxford University Press, pp. 153–162.
33. Szasz, note 1 above, pp. 358–359, suggests a "bicameral world parliament" whereby the General Assembly acts in tandem with the new principal organ, so that effective law-making decisions would require adoption by both organs: by the General Assembly representing classic sovereign equality and by a specially balanced organ whose decisions reflect in some realistic way genuine power and interest relationships.
34. *Ibid.*, p. 361.
35. *Ibid.*, p. 365.
36. *Ibid.*, pp. 361–362. Szasz criticizes this idea and instead proposes the establishment of an entirely new principal organ, as stated above.
37. Commission on Global Governance, note 32 above, p. 252; Desai, note 19 above, pp. 498–503.
38. See Note by the Secretary-General, "A New Concept of Trusteeship", UN Doc. A/52/849, 31 March 1998.
39. Palmer, note 30 above, pp. 262, 280–282. Desai, note 19 above, pp. 495–498, proposes the creation of a specialized agency called the United Nations Environment Protection Organization (UNEPO) wherein the existing UNEP could merge.
40. Farr proposes the creation of a global environmental organization (GEO) modelled on the WHO. See Farr, Karen T. 2000. "A new global environmental organization", *Georgia Journal of International and Comparative Law*, Vol. 28, No. 3, pp. 510–525.
41. Palmer, note 28 above, p. 281.
42. *Ibid.*
43. See Szasz, note 1 above, pp. 357–358.
44. *Ibid.*, p. 363.
45. See *ibid.*, p. 361.
46. *Ibid.*, p. 366.
47. See *ibid.*, pp. 351–353; Farr, note 40 above, pp. 501–507.
48. See the Secretary-General's Report of the UN Task Force on Environment and Human Settlements (A/53/463).
49. Chapter 38.22–23 of Agenda 21.
50. Chapter 38.22 (h) of Agenda 21.
51. French, Hilary F. 1995. *Partnership for the Planet: An Environmental Agenda for the United Nations*, Worldwatch Paper No. 126. Washington, DC: Worldwatch Institure, p. 39.
52. See Chapter 38.23–25 of Agenda 21.

53. Werksman, note 18 above, p. xxiii.
54. Kimball and Boyd, note 30 above, p. 301.
55. Desai, note 19 above, p. 481.
56. See Chairman's Summary: Expert Consultations on International Environmental Governance, Cambridge, 28–29 May 2001 (on file with the author).
57. Werksman, note 18 above, p. xxiii.
58. UN Doc.A/CONF.199/L.1, p. 61.
59. *Ibid.*, pp. 64–68.

2

Consolidating global environmental governance: New lessons from the GEF?

Jake Werksman

Introduction and overview

This chapter seeks to draw preliminary lessons from nearly eight years of operation of the Global Environment Facility (GEF). It assesses the GEF's role in consolidating the governance of project finance in areas of global environmental concern. The GEF, in its present "restructured" form, was established in 1994.[1] It was viewed then as a novel experiment in institutional design. It sought to draw upon the capacities of more than one international development agency – the United Nations Development Programme (UNDP), the United Nations Environment Programme (UNEP), and the World Bank – and to serve the needs of more than one multilateral environmental agreement (MEA). Faced with the complexity of these arrangements, the GEF's designers opted to construct the GEF through a loose set of institutional links, rather than to create a new international institution underpinned by a treaty instrument.

The arguments made in favour of this institutional experiment pointed to the need to avoid the duplication or proliferation of institutions, to tap into the comparative advantages of existing institutions, and to promote partnerships, cooperation, and healthy competition amongst development agencies. On the basis of a common set of institutional functions that cut across a number of global environmental challenges, the GEF was asked to consolidate aspects of international environmental governance. The GEF thus represented a significant effort by the international community to engage in what is now fashionably referred to within the context of discussions on international environmental governance as "functional clustering".[2]

The GEF's role and structure were, however, controversial. The history of its negotiation and the concerns raised by its design were reviewed by this author shortly after the GEF Instrument was adopted.[3] That history shows that the concept of a single financial mechanism to serve more than one MEA was promoted by industrialized "donor" countries. Developing countries favoured an approach that would have established separate MEA-specific financial mechanisms operating under the direct authority and control of each MEA conference of parties (COP). The GEF's consolidation of financial functions was seen by some as an effort to limit the amount of overall funding that might otherwise have been available to MEAs. Some were also concerned that functional consolidation would lead to a consolidation of power in the hands of the donors. This concern was heightened by the role that the World Bank would play as the largest of the GEF's three implementing agencies. The implementing agencies were also involved in the negotiations on GEF restructuring and tended to back the positions of their natural constituencies, with UN agencies lining up behind developing countries and the World Bank supporting positions taken by donors. At the time, bodies within the UN system, and those within the so-called "Bretton Woods" system, did not have a track record of close cooperation. Competition for scarce financial resources also raised doubts as to whether this approach to functional clustering could work. Finally, legal ambiguities surrounding the GEF's loose institutional arrangements raised questions as to whether it could be held directly accountable by the COPs for funding MEA implementation and, in turn, whether the GEF could hold the implementing agencies directly accountable for performing their assigned functions.

In an effort to test whether these doubts were justified, this analysis looks for clues in GEF operations at both the level of international governance and the level of project design and implementation. At the level of international governance, the analysis has a dual focus. It assesses whether differences between the governance structures in the MEAs' COPs and the GEF Council have produced divergent or conflicting decisions. It also assesses whether the GEF's lack of a formal institutional status, and its consequent dependence on the World Bank, have adversely affected its ability to act as a strong and objective hub between the competing interests of the MEAs, the GEF's implementing agencies, and the governments and constituencies the GEF was established to serve.

At the project design level, analysis is directed at whether the GEF's consolidation of the financial mechanisms of multiple MEAs with different environmental objectives has led to projects that reap more than one global environmental benefit. It assesses whether, in performing this function, the GEF has helped ensure that projects funded under one MEA do not undermine the objectives of another MEA.

This modest chapter does not draw upon original research, but instead bases its conclusions primarily on two recent documents. The first is the "Second Overall Performance Study of the GEF: Final Draft"[4] (OPS-2), carried out by the GEF's monitoring and evaluation unit at the request of the GEF Council. This study was "designed to assess the extent to which GEF has achieved, or is on its way towards achieving, its main objectives" and produced a wide range of conclusions and recommendations aimed at all aspects of GEF operations.

The second document that provides the basis for this analysis is the "Overall Structure, Process and Procedures of the GEF"[5] (OSPP). This document was prepared by the GEF Secretariat in response to requests of the GEF Council and in consultation with the GEF's implementing agencies, and contains recommendations on how the GEF structure might be reformed to take into account the lessons from OPS-2.

This chapter is therefore by no means comprehensive. It is intended, instead, to highlight that the GEF continues to be an instructive case study for efforts at improving global environmental governance.

The GEF's nuts and bolts

The GEF's primary responsibility is to operate the financial mechanisms of the UN Framework Convention on Climate Change (UNFCCC) and the Convention on Biological Diversity (CBD). It is tasked with providing grants and concessional funding to assist developing countries in meeting the "incremental costs" of implementing their commitments under the UNFCCC and the CBD. The GEF receives most of its funds from those donor (industrialized) countries that are required under these conventions to provide financial assistance to developing countries. The GEF then serves to channel these funds towards eligible projects in developing countries that support the conventions' objectives. The GEF also funds projects in developing countries and countries with economies in transition to protect international waters, and to prevent ozone layer depletion. The UNDP, UNEP, and the World Bank act as the GEF's "implementing agencies", helping developing countries to design and implement eligible projects.

The GEF's legal underpinning is a trust fund, established by a resolution of the World Bank's board of executive directors, with the World Bank serving as the trustee. Responsibility for dispersing the assets of the fund are delegated through the "Instrument for the Establishment of the Global Environment Facility" (the GEF Instrument) to the GEF Council. The council is composed of representatives of those countries that have agreed to participate in the GEF (GEF "participants"). Countries join the GEF by submitting a notification of participation, and, if they wish to contribute to the trust fund, an instrument of commitment. The GEF's legal framework is further bolstered by the adoption, by the governing bodies of each of the implementing agencies, of a resolution approving its participation in accordance with the GEF Instrument. Finally, the MEA COPs are brought into the legal framework through references to the GEF in their treaty instruments, through COP decisions that assign functions and provide guidance to the GEF, and by memoranda of understanding running between the COPs and the GEF Council that set out the COPs' and the GEF's mutual expectations.

In accordance with the GEF Instrument, the participants operate through an assembly and a council. The assembly consists of all the GEF participants, and meets once every three years to review GEF performance and negotiate the replenishment of the GEF trust fund. The GEF's operations are overseen by the GEF Council, which consists of 32 members representing constituency groups formed by the participants. The GEF Council meets at least twice a year to review and approve the GEF's operational policies and programmes and to approve tranches of projects proposed for funding. The day-to-day operations of the GEF are carried out by a secretariat under the direction of a chief executive officer (CEO). The secretariat is based at but is functionally independent from the World Bank.

The GEF Council is made up of 16 constituencies representing developing countries, 14 constituencies from industrialized countries, and two constituencies from economies in transition. It takes decisions by consensus, but if consensus fails, decisions can be taken by a form of democracy through a double-weighted majority system that combines the one-country-one-vote approach of many UN bodies with the one-dollar-one-vote approach of the Bretton Woods institutions: an affirmative vote must gain a 60 per cent majority of the total number of participating countries *as well as* a 60 per cent majority of total contributions.

Managing conflicts and promoting synergies in international governance

In order to perform effectively its role in consolidating functional aspects of the MEAs and of the implementing agencies, the GEF needs sufficient autonomy and authority both to promote synergies and to avoid conflicts amongst competing interests and objectives. The GEF Council, supported by the GEF Secretariat, is required to hold the ring between potentially conflicting demands of the different MEAs that it serves, and between the different international institutions that serve as its implementing agencies. This would appear to require that the GEF have the ability to establish a transparent and accountable relationship with each of these entities, and to manage the relationships between these entities.

With regard to its relationship with MEA COPs the GEF Instrument provides that the GEF Council shall "function under the guidance of, and be accountable to, the [COPs] which shall decide on policies, programme priorities and eligibility criteria for the purposes of the conventions".[6] With regard to the GEF Council's relationship to the implementing agencies, the GEF Instrument indicates that these agencies "shall be accountable to the Council for their GEF-financed activities, including the preparation and cost-effectiveness of GEF projects, and for the implementation of the operational policies, strategies and decisions of the Council within their respective areas of competence".[7]

However, when the GEF Instrument was adopted, aspects of the GEF's institutional design appeared to place at risk its ability to perform these functions effectively. Particular problems are highlighted below.

- *The GEF's governance and decision-making structures are different to the structures that govern the MEAs that the GEF is tasked to serve.* The GEF Council's constituency and voting system is in sharp contrast to the universal membership and consensus-based decision-making procedures employed by the MEA COPs, and is also different from the governance structures of each of the three implementing agencies. Although each of these institutions strives for "universal membership" and enjoys a substantial overlap in parties, it is possible that international institutions with similar memberships but different governance structures can generate inconsistent policies. Donor industrialized-country council members in the GEF enjoy a disproportionately higher number of seats and more heavily weighted votes than developing country council members. Because the GEF Council operates on a constituency basis, while the MEAs do not, there is a potential for gaps to open up between the two governance systems.

- *The GEF is not an autonomous institution, and does not have the capacity to enter into formal legal relationships with other autonomous institutions.* One way of avoiding or managing potential conflicts between the COPs, the implementing agencies, and the GEF would be formalize through an international agreement the respective roles and expectations of each body. The mode of GEF establishment and the text of the GEF Instrument do not appear to give the GEF and its council legal autonomy. For example, while the GEF Council may consider and approve arrangements with other international institutions, it will be the World Bank as trustee that retains the power to "formalize" them.[8] The GEF Instrument therefore left unresolved the issue of what legal form, if any, the links between the GEF and the COPs might take.

- *There is no clearly identified procedure for resolving "disputes" that might arise between the GEF and the COPs, or between GEF and the implementing agencies.* Although the convention texts, the GEF Instrument, and the MOUs set out the respective roles and functions of the COPs, the GEF, and the implementing agencies, no clear and determinative procedure is established to resolve conflicts that might arise between them.

Many in the donor community suggested that informal arrangements, such as observer status for convention representatives at meetings of the GEF Council, could answer concerns about accountability and transparency. Others, more sceptical about the GEF's ability to fulfil the conventions' requirements, sought the advice of the UN Legal Counsel for suggestions on how best to structure this institutional experiment. After reviewing the GEF Instrument and the requirements of the UNFCCC, the Legal Counsel issued an opinion which suggested that the complexity of the relationship anticipated between the GEF and the conventions demanded that this relationship be set out in a "legally binding treaty instrument".[9]

In the end, each COP and the GEF opted to establish links through a memorandum of understanding (MOU) approved by each body.[10] These MOUs have since been interpreted to be non-binding in character.[11] The MOU between the GEF and the UNFCCC COP does anticipate the possibility that

[i]n the event that the COP considers that this specific project decision does not comply with the policies, programme priorities and eligibility criteria established by the COP, it may ask the Council of the GEF for further clarification on the specific project decision and in due time may ask for a reconsideration of that decision.[12]

But this provision does not clarify what procedure should apply if a disagreement between the COP and the GEF Council persists.

With regard to the GEF Council's relationship to the implementing agencies, the respective roles of each agency and its relationship to the GEF Council are sketched out in the GEF Instrument and in the parallel resolutions each implementing agency adopted when endorsing the GEF Instrument. These roles are provided a bit more detail in the "Principles of Cooperation Among the Implementing Agencies" contained in Annex D of the GEF Instrument, and were supposed to be elaborated further in an "interagency agreement" to be concluded on the basis of these principles. That interagency agreement was never negotiated. However, since the GEF's establishment, the GEF Council requested and received from each agency further confirmation that it would assume full accountability to the GEF Council for all GEF projects executed under its sponsorship.[13]

Thus the institutional arrangements that link the GEF Council to the MEA COPs and to the implementing agencies remain legally ill-defined. After eight years of operation, has the looseness of these arrangements undermined the GEF's effectiveness?

The GEF Council and the COPs

Is there any evidence of the GEF Council either failing to abide by the guidance provided to it by the COPs, or of it failing to manage any potential competition for resources between the COPs?

It has often been observed that tensions which arise between international institutions with overlapping memberships may have their roots in policy incoherence within the governments participating in these institutions. Divergence in policies between an environmental institution and an economic institution could be attributable to differences in policies between the environment and treasury ministries that represent that government at each institution. A quick review of the representation at the GEF Council and at MEA COPs suggests that, for many countries, the same ministry does not take the lead at both institutions. Temporary difficulties could also arise from the operation of the GEF's constituency system. Not all parties to the UNFCCC and the CBD have found a place on a GEF constituency. At present 14 are effectively without representation on the GEF Council until they can find a group which allows them to join.[14] This raises the risk that GEF Council would produce decisions that were incompatible with the COP decisions, or that were incompatible with the policies of any of the implementing agencies.

Nonetheless, no specific dispute has, as of yet, arisen between a COP and the GEF Council with regard to the GEF's conformity with COP guidance. This may in part be attributable to political developments since the conventions and the GEF came into force. The north–south tensions that characterized the negotiations on the GEF Instrument have become less apparent as the conventions and the GEF have fallen into routine operation. Thus far, all GEF Council decisions have been taken by consensus, avoiding any potential political fall-out from the application of the GEF's controversial double-weighted majority voting system.

It may also be possible to attribute the absence of conflict between the GEF Council and the COPs to the overlap in individuals who play a prominent role in decision-making in both bodies. A comparison of the individuals currently members and alternates sitting on the GEF Council with attendees at the most recent UNFCCC COP reveals that only 10 of a possible 74 members and alternates also attended the COP.[15] Nonetheless, the overlapping participation in the COPs and the GEF Council of a number of key delegates, particularly those from developing countries, has undoubtedly helped to bring the two sets of institutions together. Council members have helped to explain and build acceptance for the operations of the GEF with colleagues in the COPs, and vice versa.

There is, however, evidence of developing countries, acting through the COPs, registering their continued disapproval of the GEF. This dissatisfaction is reflected, for example, in the continued reluctance of the majority of developing country delegations formally to acknowledge, by COP decision, the GEF's role as *the* operating entity of the conventions' financial mechanisms. At present the UNFCCC COP continues to refer the GEF as "*an* operating entity" of its financial mechanism,[16] while the CBD COP refers to the GEF as "the institutional structure operating the financial mechanism".[17] This language implies that the GEF's relationship with the COPs will remain under review. Specific criticism of the GEF, when it is expressed, is aimed at the inadequacy of available financial resources and the slow pace at which those resources are converted into projects, and not at the GEF's governance structure.

Potential controversies have arisen in the course of the GEF's early operation that could have led to serious conflicts between the COPs and the GEF Council. One arose from differences in the interpretation of the concept of "incremental costs". The UNFCCC, CBD, and the GEF Instrument all indicate that funding for the bulk of the implementation activities to be provided to developing countries under the conventions is to be limited to the "incremental costs" associated with that activity. Early analytical work carried out for the GEF Council began to construct a methodology for determining incremental costs that some developing countries felt was unduly restrictive. The GEF approach was to limit funding only to the costs of those activities that could be shown to implement the convention *and* to achieve "global environmental benefits". This raised concerns that funding for activities under the UNFCCC aimed at helping countries to adapt to the impacts of global warming, or activities under CBD aimed at conserving domestic biodiversity, could be excluded from the GEF portfolio.

The response of the UNFCCC COP was to express its concern over "difficulties encountered by developing country Parties in receiving the necessary financial assistance from the [GEF] due to, *inter alia*, the application of the [GEF] operational policies on ... the application of its concept of incremental costs". The COP called on the GEF to "take steps to facilitate [the] provision of financial resources, including the enhancement of transparency and the flexible and pragmatic application of its concept of incremental costs on a case-by-case basis".[18]

It would appear from the review undertaken by OPS-2 that the GEF Council and the implementing agencies have responded to this guidance. Serious conflicts appear to have been avoided through a flexible and case-by-case application of the concept of incremental costs in the context of negotiations on cost-sharing between host countries and implementing agencies. Its flexible application has been particularly apparent in the context of biodiversity. It should be noted, however, that OPS-2 has described it as "imperative" that the GEF develop clearer and more consistent guidance on the application of the incremental cost concept, including methodology for measuring "global environmental benefits".[19] If future conflicts are to be avoided, any effort to tighten the definition or application of the incremental cost methodology may need to be tracked carefully to avoid excluding projects that are supported by COP guidance.

OPS-2 also noted criticism from certain parties to the CBD that the GEF project portfolio was "relatively weak in supporting activities leading to sustainable use and benefit sharing" of biodiversity.[20] This has been one of the more controversial aspects of the biodiversity debate, as it implies the need for the intervention of international law and institutions into what might otherwise be a largely commercial relationship in order to ensure the "fair and equitable" sharing of benefits. OPS-2 concluded that the lack of GEF funding in this area "may be a reflection of the fact that the [CBD-COP] has not yet been able to provide clear and precise guidance on these matters to the GEF".[21]

Thus it can be suggested that potential conflicts were resolved or at least avoided through the iterative exchanges between a COP's guidance and the GEF Council, without, as of yet, creating the need for more formal arrangements or procedures. OPS-2 found that while the GEF has been responsive to convention guidance, this guidance has tended to be extremely general in nature. The level of generality found in COP guidance to the GEF does diminish the likelihood of a conflict. But it also makes it more difficult for the GEF to demonstrate its responsiveness to convention priorities.

In the next stage of its development the GEF will face an increasing number of MEA bodies with which it will need to build cooperative relationships. The Stockholm Convention on Persistent Organic Pollutants (Stockholm Convention) will use the GEF as its financial mechanism, as will the Cartagena Protocol on Biosafety and the Kyoto Protocol to the UNFCCC. Each of these bodies will be an autonomous institutional arrangement capable of producing guidance to the GEF as to how to direct its resources. OPS-2 has noted that increased competition for resources, in the context of a growing diversity of GEF focal areas, may increase the strain on the GEF's institutional arrangements.

The GEF Council and the implementing agencies

Perhaps the GEF's greatest potential for promoting synergies through its system of governance is by bringing together the implementing agencies, which are often institutional rivals, through a common institutional framework. During a period when the roles and budgets of each of these three institutions have been under heightened scrutiny, the GEF has had the potential to become a forum for fierce competition for credibility and resources.

Each of the agencies was intended to fulfil its role in accordance with its respective "comparative advantage", set out in Annex D of the GEF Instrument. The UNDP is to play the primary role in capacity-building and technical assistance, UNEP in scientific and technical analysis, and the World Bank in managing investment projects. While these roles would appear to be reasonably well defined, developments since the adoption of the GEF Instrument have helped to blur distinctions and increase the potential for competition. In their early years, both convention COPs have instructed the GEF to focus its funding on so-called "enabling activities" – those projects designed to help developing countries prepare for the implementation of their commitments under the treaties. Under both climate change and biodiversity conventions, enabling activities include the preparation of national inventories, planning exercises, and reports, and thus entail a mixture of technical assistance and capacity-building. Each of the implementing agencies has been able to justify its involvement in a share of this kind of project.

While far smaller than the World Bank, the GEF's available resources approach the combined budgets of the UNDP and UNEP. For the UNDP and UNEP, this has meant that participation in the GEF experiment has proved extremely influential on their internal operations. The influence can be positive, by mainstreaming global environmental concerns into general developmental and environmental objectives. GEF participation has also proved beneficial by providing collateral financial and technical benefits to aspects of UNDP and UNEP operations that may not have survived in the absence of GEF funding. There is, for example, anecdotal evidence that some UNDP country offices have benefited from support staff and equipment that could not have been maintained without funding from GEF projects.

It is possible, however, that access to the GEF's resources may have distorted priorities within these agencies. The GEF's focus on global environmental issues is necessarily narrow and top-down, and may have diverted attention away from higher environment and development priorities of developing countries, such as access to potable water and urban air quality. What OPS-2 refers to as the GEF's strength in leveraging co-financing from implementing agencies and other sources of development assistance can also be characterized as a distortion of resource flows that might have otherwise gone to domestic environmental or developmental priorities without the requisite "global environmental benefits".

OPS-2 noted both the benefits of mainstreaming of global environmental concerns into the work of the three implementing agencies and the risks posed by competition amongst them. It suggests that, after an initial difficult period, the competition has proved increasingly positive. OPS-2 also notes, however, that the challenge of managing these relationships is likely to increase over the next stage in the GEF's development. The GEF has begun to expand the range of agencies that are authorized to implement GEF-funded projects. Seven new "executing agencies", including regional development banks and UN specialized agencies, are now eligible to carry out projects in cooperation with the three original implementing agencies.

Conflicts and synergies at the project level

By funding projects that support the implementation of more than one MEA the GEF could be expected to face challenges, in the context of the design of specific projects, where the MEAs' objectives conflict, and to be presented with opportunities for synergies where MEAs' objectives coincide.

With regard to avoiding projects with conflicting objectives, the GEF Instrument prevents the funding of projects that "do not fully conform to the guidance from the relevant Conference of the Parties" of the UNFCCC and the CBD. Projects in the GEF's ozone portfolio "will be consistent with those of the Montreal Protocol on Substances that Deplete the Ozone Layer and its amendments".[22] While these directives do not expressly prohibit the GEF from funding a project in one focal area that might be inconsistent with the objectives of another focal area, the obligation to avoid such conflicts is implicit.

Specific conflicts could have arisen between climate and biodiversity, as well as between climate and ozone. Fast-growing monoculture trees can help manage greenhouse gas emissions by fixing carbon, but they can also contribute to the loss of biodiversity. The GEF's climate change portfolio has, however, avoided investments in such carbon "sinks" projects, focusing instead on technologies and practices aimed at limiting emissions at source. Some chemicals promoted as replacements for ozone-depleting substances in the course of the implementation of the Montreal Protocol are powerful greenhouse gases, and their widespread use could undermine efforts to combat global warming. To avoid such conflicts, the GEF operational policy on ozone provides "the GEF will fund the conversion to the technology with the least impact on global warming that is technically feasible, environmentally sound, and economically acceptable".[23]

With regard to promoting synergies across focal areas, the GEF has developed an operational programme specifically directed at "bringing synergy between three of the GEF focal areas (i.e. Biological Diversity, Climate Change, and International Waters) and land degradation to optimize multiple benefits".[24] The GEF Secretariat has also been involved in efforts amongst convention experts and delegations to try to identify and exploit potential synergies between biodiversity and climate change, including with regard to project implementation.[25]

Having reviewed the GEF's initial efforts to exploit synergies through a multi-convention operational programme, OPS-2 concluded that the GEF should "exercise some caution".

While having some appeal in the sense of being provided opportunities for a more holistic approach, it should be kept in mind that specific convention-related objectives should be kept firmly in mind when setting project objectives. The long history of implementation experience from various types of integrated and multi-purpose projects clearly show very high "mortality rates". GEF would be well advised to avoid falling into the trap of many current international organizations which seem to unable to focus on operational priorities and appear to succumb to the ill-advised temptations to support project designs which serve many objectives indiscriminately and ineffectually.[26]

This word of caution may be increasingly relevant as the GEF is asked to expand the number of MEAs it will serve and the number of focal areas towards which to direct its resources. The addition of the Stockholm Convention to the list of GEF-serviced MEAs, and the eventual entry into force of the Cartagena Protocol on Biosafety and the Kyoto Protocol, will increase the challenge of this balancing act. While Kyoto is unlikely to result in a shift in the GEF's climate change funding, supporting developing countries in the regulation of POPs and in biosafety will be a new venture for the GEF.

Reforming the GEF's overall structure

In light of the many complexities raised in this chapter, the GEF Secretariat has proposed that the loose institutional arrangements that have characterized the past eight years of the GEF's operations be strengthened and clarified. It has identified a number of areas in which the GEF's reliance on other agencies to carry out its functions has constrained its ability to operate effectively. Because the GEF Council sits at the end of a project cycle that originates in each of its eligible countries and passes through three or more separate agencies, it cannot ensure the country-driven nature of the projects it funds, nor the balance of projects across geographical regions. Short of developing its own institutional presence within recipient countries, to address this challenge, the GEF would need to increase its leverage with the implementing agencies.[27]

Supported in part by the recommendations of OPS-2, the GEF Secretariat has flagged the need to "specify the autonomous institutional authority of the GEF". The main reason given for the change is to provide the GEF Secretariat with the authority necessary to enter into arrangements and agreements with a growing number of partners. The GEF Secretariat has proposed two means by which this greater clarity could be achieved: through "instruments of delegation of authority" from the World Bank, as trustee, to the GEF Secretariat, or through an amendment of the GEF Instrument.

The response thus far of the implementing agencies to this call for a greater formal independence of the GEF Secretariat has been sceptical. The UNDP, UNEP, and the World Bank seem to have set aside any institutional rivalries to arrive at a common agreement that transforming the GEF into a formally autonomous institution is not necessary. This consensus may in part derive from a concern that the GEF should not overwhelm the institutions that created it. Furthermore, amending the GEF Instrument for this narrow purpose might invite an unravelling of the delicate package that has functioned reasonably well over the past decade.

Conclusions

Ambivalence in the MEA/GEF relationship

MEA COPs, primarily through developing country delegations, continue to express some dissatisfaction with the GEF. This dissatisfaction is reflected, for example, in the continued reluctance of the majority of developing country delegations formally to acknowledge, by COP decision, the GEF's role as *the* operating entity of the conventions' financial mechanisms. However, specific criticism, when it is expressed, is aimed at the inadequacy of available financial resources and the slow pace at which those resources are converted into projects, and not at the GEF's governance structure. It is not clear whether this dissatisfaction is in any way grounded in continuing concerns about the GEF's governance structure (perceived dominance by donors, dependence on the World Bank, and a lack of direct accountability to the COPs) that formed the basis of earlier criticisms of the GEF.

No specific disputes have arisen involving a divergence of policy at the COPs and at the GEF Council levels. OPS-2 found that while the GEF has been responsive to convention guidance, this guidance has tended to be extremely general in nature, diminishing the likelihood of a conflict but also making it more difficult for the GEF to demonstrate its responsiveness to convention priorities. Any apparent coherence can be attributed only in part to a small degree of overlap in the individuals who represent their governments at both the COPs and the GEF Council.

Since Rio the GEF has been invited by MEA negotiators to operate the financial mechanisms of the Kyoto Protocol, the Cartagena Biosafety Protocol, and the Stockholm Convention on Persistent Organic Pollutants. The GEF also provides support, through its land degradation portfolio, to the UN Convention to Combat Desertification. At one level, this could be taken to reflect a growing confidence in the GEF's effectiveness as a financial mechanism generally, and as a financial mechanism with the specific function of consolidating governance of more than one MEA.

Consolidation and the overall availability of financial resources

Continued calls for the GEF's involvement in the financial mechanisms of new MEAs may also reflect, in the context of an overall decline in ODA, the GEF's position as the only regularly replenished source of funding for the global environment. Some concern has been expressed that the GEF's growing popularity, and the consequent expansion of its focal areas, could "overburden" the GEF's already limited resources.

Consolidation can lead to greater institutional efficiency, but it may also provide a means for capping and containing developing country demands for increased resources.

Synergies at the project level

There is evidence that the GEF's position at the centre of more than one MEA has helped it to avoid funding projects in one focal area that could have undermined the objectives of another focal area. For example, its climate change portfolio has not included sequestration projects, which have been criticized as carrying the risk of promoting forestation projects with an emphasis on monoculture rather than species diversity. Projects that hold the potential to interact with more than one focal area are grouped in a multifocal programme area of their own, which promotes investments consciously designed to be complementary across MEA objectives. OPS-2 has cautioned that the "GEF would be well advised to avoid falling into the trap of many current international organizations which seem to unable to focus on operational priorities and appear to succumb to the ill-advised temptations to support project designs which serve many objectives indiscriminately and ineffectually".[28]

Consolidation and competition amongst implementing agencies

The consolidation of more than one implementing agency into the GEF's operations has led to a degree of competition amongst these agencies, and competition can be healthy. All three agencies are required to report regularly to the GEF Council on their GEF-related portfolios, and have also been called upon to demonstrate, for example, the extent to which they have "mainstreamed" global environmental concerns into their operations. Participation by the UNDP, UNEP, and the World Bank as GEF implementing agencies has led each of these institutions to direct higher levels of resources towards global environmental objectives than they might otherwise have done.

Efforts are under way to promote greater "healthy" competition amongst the IAs and other agencies with the capacity to design and implement GEF projects. These include expanding the number of "executing agencies", including regional development banks and NGOs, as well as the introduction of a "fee system" that would allow agencies to recoup the administrative costs of designing and implementing GEF projects.

There appears to be a shift from the United Nations versus Bretton Woods dynamic that characterized the relationship between the implementing agencies during the GEF restructuring. Recent proposals from the GEF Secretariat to confer upon the GEF an "autonomous institutional authority" have drawn criticism from all three implementing agencies. This suggests that these agencies share a common concern that the GEF's consolidating role should not expand to the extent that it becomes an institutional rival.

Notes

1. "Instrument for the Establishment of the Restructured Global Environment Facility" (hereinafter GEF Instrument). This and all other GEF documents referred to in this chapter are available on www.gefweb.org.
2. See, for example, UNEP. 2001. "Implementing the clustering strategy for multilateral environmental agreements: A framework", background paper by the Secretariat,

UNEP/IGM/4/4, 16 November; Hyvarinen, Joy and Duncan Brack. 2000. *Global Environmental Institutions: Analysis and Options for Change*. London: RIIA.

3. Werksman, Jacob. 1995. "Consolidating governance of the global commons: Insights from the Global Environment Facility", in G. Handl (ed.) *Yearbook of International Environmental Law*, Vol. 6. Oxford: Oxford University Press, p. 27.

4. "Second Overall Performance Study of the GEF: Final Draft", GEF/C.18/7, 11 November 2001 (hereinafter OPS-2).

5. "Overall Structure, Processes and Procedures of the GEF", GEF/C.18/8, 15 November 152001 (hereinafter Overall Structure).

6. GEF Instrument, note 1 above, para 6.

7. *Ibid.*, para 22.

8. *Ibid.*, Annex B, Role and Fiduciary Responsibilities of the Trustee of the GEF Trust Fund, para 7.

9. Memorandum of 22 June 1994 to the Executive Secretary from Hans Corell, Under-Secretary-General for Legal Affairs, Legal Counsel, A/AC.237/74, Annex.

10. See, for example, the Memorandum of Understanding Between the Conference of the Parties to the United Nations Framework Convention on Climate Change and the Council of the Global Environment Facility, Decision 12/Cp.2, Annex. UN Doc. FCCC/CP/1996/15/Add.1 (1996) (hereinafter UNFCCC-GEF MOU).

11. Churchill, Robin R. and Geir Ulfstein. 2000. "Autonomous institutional arrangements in multilateral environmental agreements: A little-noticed phenomenon in international law", *American Journal of International Law*, Vol. 94, No. 4, pp. 623–659.

12. UNFCCC-GEF MOU, note 10 above, para 5.

13. Joint Summary of the Chairs, GEF Council Meeting 22–24 February 1995, Decision on Agenda Item 12: Accountability of implementing agencies for activities of executing agencies; Joint Summary of the Chairs, GEF Council Meeting 18–20 July 1995, Decision on Agenda Item 8: World Bank accountability for executing agency activities.

14. According the GEF website, "the Constituencies for the following new member countries are yet to be determined: Bosnia Herzigovina, Cambodia, Gabon, Grenada, Israel, Kazakhstan, Liberia, Libya, Malta, Namibia, Palau, Seychelles, Syria, Yugoslavia".

15. Report of the Conference of the Parties to the UN Framework Convention on Climate Change at its Seventh Session, FCCC/CP/2001/13 (hereinafter Report of COP-7); GEF website.

16. Report of COP-7, Decision 6/CP.7, "Additional guidance to an operating entity of the financial mechanism", FCCC/CP/2001/13/Add.1.

17. Report of the Conference of the Parties to the Convention on Biological Diversity at its Fifth Meeting, UNEP/CBD/COP/5/23.

18. Report of the Conference of the Parties to the UN Framework Convention on Climate Change at its Second Session, Decision 11/CP.2, Guidance to the Global Environment Facility, FCCC/CP/1996/15/Add.1.

19. OPS-2, note 4 above, para 186 and paras 460 *et seq.*

20. *Ibid.*, para 186.

21. *Ibid.*

22. *Operational Strategy of the Global Environment Facility*, Ch. 1.

23. See *ibid.* for descriptions of principles governing each of the GEF's focal areas.

24. GEF Operational Program No. 12: Integrated Ecosystem Management, April 2000.

25. Report of the first meeting of the *ad hoc* Technical Expert Group on Biological Diversity and Climate Change, Helsinki, 21–25 January 2002, UNEP/CBD/COP/6/INF/6.

26. OPS-2, note 4 above.

27. Overall Structure, note 5 above, paras 13(b) and 30.

28. OPS-2, note 4 above.

3

The effectiveness of the WTO and WIPO: Lessons for environmental governance?

Laura B. Campbell

Introduction

Globalization – the integration of economies through cross-border trade, investment, capital flows, transport, technology transfer, and information exchange – has dramatically changed the context in which environmental governance takes place. Globalization has also changed the roles played by non-state actors such as non-governmental organizations (NGOs), civil society, and the private sector in the development and implementation of international environmental policy. The purposes of this chapter, to identify gaps and weaknesses in the current environmental governance regime and evaluate alternative approaches, entail a fundamental reassessment of how environmental institutions should be structured in the context of globalization.

One institutional change which has been proposed is the creation of a world environment organization (WEO) which could serve as a counterweight to the World Trade Organization's (WTO) global governance over trade. Other reforms being discussed address issues such as institutional transparency and the changing role of non-state actors in environmental governance.

In evaluating proposals for environmental reform, understanding how the structure and functions of other international organizations have influenced their effectiveness in achieving their mandates can serve as a useful tool. The purpose of this chapter is to contribute to the assessment of environmental reform proposals by identifying which elements of the structure and function of other international organizations have affected their success or failure in achieving the goals of their treaty regimes. In some cases, successful approaches could serve as models for environmental governance reform.

This chapter focuses on two international organizations, the World Trade Organization and the World Intellectual Property Organization (WIPO), and provides a qualitative assessment of their effectiveness in selected areas. The most difficult part of this assessment was the selection of indicators of success. Differences between organizational mandates, multiple policy objectives of regimes, and limitations on data collection and analysis made it extremely difficult to measure the extent to which the problems a regime was enacted to address have been resolved. Therefore, indicators related to levels of participation, implementation, and compliance were used where available as the primary basis for conducting a qualitative evaluation.

Both the WTO and WIPO were found to be successful in some areas and failures in others. While world trade has increased significantly since the creation of the WTO, it has not been successful in raising the standard of living in many WTO member countries. WIPO has provided a forum and support which have resulted in the development and adoption of numerous treaties on intellectual property rights, but these treaties have not been effective in protecting these rights, particularly as they are defined in industrialized countries. While industrialized countries tend to be satisfied with the outcomes of the WTO but not those of WIPO, most developing countries hold the opposite view and are largely satisfied with WIPO's work but highly critical of the WTO.

This chapter takes the position that the long-term success of both the WTO and WIPO will depend heavily on their ability to manage issues which are not part of their core mandate. Some of these non-core issues constitute substantive social concerns such as public health, environmental protection, labour standards, and human rights, while others involve procedural matters including institutional transparency and participation of non-governmental actors in activities.

This chapter examines selected functions of the WTO and WIPO and discusses whether they have been generally successful in carrying out these functions. It also presents some conclusions on how the experiences of the WTO and WIPO would be useful to consider in the future development of global environmental governance.

Measuring "effectiveness" and "success"

Evaluating the success of an international organization is an inherently complex task. In addition to analysing implementation and compliance levels, an accurate evaluation requires assessment of other factors which influenced the process, such as political change, civil society, and non-governmental actors as well as economic, security, public health, or environmental crises. Quantifying the interactive effects of these factors on compliance or achievement of the goals of a regime requires extensive data collection and sophisticated computer analysis not undertaken during this project.

While there has been a great deal of research on regime effectiveness since 1984, when Robert Keohane first introduced the international regime as the conceptual framework for the study of international relations,[1] relatively little attention has been paid to the study of international organizations. Ernst Haas, a leader in the research on intergovernmental organizations before and after 1984, has supported the inclusion of the study of intergovernmental organizations within the international regimes' framework,[2] but others have criticized this approach as having resulted in a vague and unclear understanding of the functions of intergovernmental organizations as distinct from regimes. In particular, the need for research on the role of intergovernmental organizations in promoting multilateral cooperation and contributing to the development of regimes has been noted in analysing the role of the secretariat for the General Agreement on Tariffs and Trade (GATT), the WTO's predecessor organization, during the Uruguay Round.[3]

Defining the criteria to measure the success of an intergovernmental organization is an inherently complex task which is further complicated by the need for different approaches for organizations with varying mandates to achieve disparate goals.[4] Obviously, the best indicator that an organization has met its mandate is that the problem which its treaty regime was designed to address has been resolved. Since this is a very difficult factor to measure, the most commonly used indicators of success are related to levels of treaty implementation and compliance. Of course, using implementation and compliance as indicators assumes that the treaty is the best and primary means of addressing the problem. This approach also fails to account for factors other than the international organization which affected the outcome.[5]

The term "regime" is used in this chapter to refer to the body of treaties and agreements for which the intergovernmental organization is responsible. Because the WTO and WIPO have different mandates and regimes, somewhat different criteria were selected to evaluate each organization's performance.

The World Trade Organization

The WTO is responsible for administering the trade agreements adopted in 1994 at the close of the Uruguay Round of multilateral trade negotiations (the WTO Agreements). The WTO Agreements represent an evolution in the multilateral trade regime from a system of tariff reductions in 1948 to a much more comprehensive set of agreements which include the General Agreement on Tariffs and Trade (GATT) on trade in goods, trade in services (the General Agreement on Trade in Services or GATS), non-tariff trade barriers (the Technical Barriers to Trade Agreement or TBT), agriculture, food safety (the Sanitary and Phytosanitary Agreement or SPS), and intellectual property rights (TRIPs).

While the multilateral trade regime does not include a comprehensive agreement on investment, two existing agreements cover certain areas of investment. The Agreement on Trade-Related Investment Measures (TRIMs Agreement) prohibits trade-related investment measures such as local content requirements that are inconsistent with the provisions of the 1994 GATT. The GATS Agreement addresses foreign investment in service areas as one of four modes of supply of services. While negotiations to liberalize investment have been stalled, some countries continue to press for inclusion of investment issues in the Millennium Round negotiations.

The WTO's mandate

The WTO's mandate, as stated in the preamble of the Marrakesh Agreement Establishing the World Trade Organization, is to contribute to the objectives of "raising standards of living, ensuring full employment and a large and steadily growing volume of real income and effective demand, and expanding the production of and trade in goods and services, while allowing for the optimal use of the world's resources in accordance with the objective of sustainable development."

In carrying out its mandate, the WTO provides policy advice to governments, including the development of a framework for implementation of trade agreements; organizes and provides a forum for negotiation of further liberalization in areas already covered by the trade regime and expansion of coverage to new areas; engages in capacity-building activities with developing countries; monitors world trade; oversees review of national trade policies; facilitates consultations among its member countries on trade disputes; resolves complaints about violations and enforces the WTO Agreements, including through the application of penalties; coordinates with other intergovernmental organizations, including the International Monetary Fund, the World Bank, WIPO, and the United Nations Environment Programme; and engages in outreach activities with NGOs.

Evaluation of the WTO's effectiveness

Level of governmental participation in the WTO

As of 1 January 2002, 144 countries are members of the WTO,[6] indicating a very high level of governmental participation in the multilateral trade regime.

Have problems regime designed to address been resolved or improved?

The WTO's success in increasing the production of and trade in goods and services, one of the goals of its mandate, can be assessed by analysing statistics showing changes in levels of production and trade over time. In 2002 the value of world merchandise exports totalled US$6,272 billion, reflecting an increase of US$2,601 billion from 1993.

However, the increase in the value of world exports has not been evenly distributed across countries and regions. For example, between 1995 and 2002 North America's share of world merchandise exports increased from 15.5 per cent to 16.9 per cent, with a total value in 2002 of US$946 billion. By comparison, Africa's share of world merchandise exports increased slightly from 1995 to 2002, from 2.2 to 2.3 per cent, and equalled US$140 billion in 2002. East Asian countries' (excluding Japan and China) share of world merchandise exports rose from 10.3 to 10.4 per cent from 1995 to 2002, and were valued at US$603 billion in 2002.[7]

With respect to the WTO's mandate to raise living standards, world leaders at the Conference on Finance and Development held in 2002 in Monterrey recognized the failure of the global trading system to improve socio-economic conditions in many developing countries, particularly the least developed ones. Data compiled by the United Nations Development Programme (UNDP) illustrate the continuing, and in some cases worsening, differences in economic and human development among countries. The UNDP's *Human Development Report 2003* ranks countries based on life expectancies, literacy rates, levels of education and income per unit of gross domestic product (GDP). In the table showing human and income poverty in developing countries, 35 countries were classified as having a "low human development" level based on factors such as life expectancy, literacy rates, access to clean water, and the percentage of the population living below the national poverty line, defined as earning less than $1 per day.[8]

The report also lists countries on a Human Development Index, according to a ranking system based on life expectancy, literacy rates, educational enrolment, GDP per capita, and other factors. The ranking results show that almost 10 years after the creation of the WTO and adoption of a liberalized trading regime, there is still wide disparity in standards of living among countries and regions, with many countries from the African region near the bottom of the index.[9]

Even though the data show that a huge percentage of the world population still have a very low standard of living a number of years after trade liberalization under the WTO, there is tremendous controversy over how to interpret the economic data. It is not clear, for example, when an income of a few dollars a day may actually represent significant economic progress and a relatively high purchasing power in local markets.

Disputes among WTO member states

By mid-2001, 234 complaints had been filed with the WTO Dispute Settlement Body (DSB) since the entry into force of the Uruguay Round Final Act on 1 January 1995. Of these complaints, developed countries filed two-thirds and developing countries initiated the rest.[10] The highest number of these complaints concern trade defence measures such as antidumping, countervailing, and safeguard measures. Other cases involve issues such as intellectual property, product regulations, and subsidies.

About 75 per cent of the complaints are resolved during the consultation stage and the remainder are decided by WTO panel and appellate body decisions. With some notable exceptions, compliance with the rulings of the DSB has been prompt.

While the WTO has been efficient in resolving disputes and compliance with its rulings has been good, the number of complaints filed is an indication of the high use of trade defence measures by WTO members.

Management of social issues

The WTO's management of social issues – such as the impacts of intellectual property rights protection under TRIPs on public health in developing countries, the relationship between trade and environment, and food safety – has been rocky and subject to intense controversy. Beginning with demonstrations at the 1999 Seattle ministerial meeting, anti-globalization protestors have brought international attention to the threats to social issues posed by liberalization. Demands by developing countries for changes in the TRIPs Agreement to relax IPR rules on pharmaceutical manufacture also highlight the importance of social concerns in the international trade arena.

Impact in shaping future legal and policy regime

The WTO has been very effective in shaping the future trade policy regime before and during the Uruguay Round and in advancing the need for and agenda of the newly launched Millennium Round. However, the WTO's ability to deal effectively with social issues such as environment and public health in the future will have a critical impact on acceptance and advancement of the global trade regime.

*General acceptance of the WTO's work by governments and
non-state actors*

The level of acceptance of the WTO's work and the multilateral trade
regime is mixed. In general, most OECD countries are satisfied with the
WTO's performance and the regime, but many developing countries have
indicated their inability to meet implementation commitments. Many developing countries are very dissatisfied with the TRIPs Agreement as
well as the failure to improve market access for agricultural products and
textiles.

There is a lack of acceptance of the WTO's work by a significant number of NGOs and members of civil society due to their view that trade
liberalization has compromised social and cultural values, such as those
concerning the environment, labour, and human rights.

The World Intellectual Property Organization

International cooperation to protect intellectual property began in 1873
around the time of the International Exhibition of Inventions in Vienna,
when foreign exhibitors declined to participate due to fears about theft of
their ideas. By 1883, the Paris Convention for the Protection of Industrial
Property,[11] the first major treaty to provide international protection for
industrial intellectual property – patents on inventions, trademarks, and
industrial designs – had been adopted by 14 countries. Under the Paris
Convention, an international bureau was created to carry out the administration of the treaty, including organizing meetings of the parties.[12]

By 1886, the Berne Convention for the Protection of Literary and Artistic Works[13] had been adopted, with the purpose of protecting copyrighted materials including written materials such as novels, poems, short
stories, and plays; musical compositions such as songs, operas, and musi-
cals; and works of art such as paintings, drawings, sculpture, and archi-
tectural works. As had been done with the Paris Convention, a bureau
was created to administer the Berne Convention.

In 1893, the bureaus of the Paris and Berne Conventions were combined to create an international organization known as the UN International Bureau for the Protection of Intellectual Property (BIRPI). BIRPI,
first located in Berne and moved to Geneva in 1960 to be closer to other
UN organizations, was the predecessor of the present-day WIPO.

Along with the expansion of trade after the Second World War, intellectual property rights protection became an increasingly important issue on the international agenda. In 1967 the Convention Establishing the
World Intellectual Property Organization[14] was adopted, authorizing the
creation of WIPO. WIPO was established in 1970 and became a special-

ized agency of the United Nations in 1974. As of 15 March 2004, 180 countries are members of WIPO.[15]

WIPO currently administers 23 treaties concerning intellectual property rights, two of which are administered jointly with other organizations. While the Paris and Berne Conventions still constitute the "cornerstone" of the treaty regime managed by WIPO, a number of other agreements have expanded its scope of coverage. In addition to the core treaties which set international standards for intellectual property rights protection, WIPO is also responsible for implementing treaties governing the registration of trademarks and patents and the classification of protected properties.

The treaties making up the international intellectual property rights regime[16] can be divided into three categories: agreements which set standards for intellectual property rights protection, agreements governing the registration of properties, and agreements concerning the classification of patents and trademarks.

Treaties setting standards for intellectual property rights protection

During the early negotiation of the Berne Convention for the Protection of Literary and Artistic Works, some countries favoured the development of a unified international law of copyright protection while others preferred more national independence and cooperation based on reciprocity of rights. The Berne Convention of 1886 reflects a compromise of these two positions, creating some international rights to protection of copyrighted works but reserving for national governments the authority to set most of the terms of these rights, such as the terms of protection. The basic concept was to set some minimum standards and to expand these protections over time, progressively creating a more comprehensive international scheme.[17]

The 1886 Berne Convention was based primarily on the principle of national treatment – the requirement that each party afford the same copyright protection to foreigners as it does to its own citizens. The convention also included minimum international standards of protection for authors which countries were required to recognize. While the Berne Convention has been revised five times and amended twice, its basic structure remains the same as the 1886 version. In each of the subsequent versions, however, authors' rights have been expanded.

The main drawback to utilizing national treatment as the core principle for international intellectual property rights is that an author from a country with very low or no copyright protection would be accorded greater rights in a foreign country with high standards. Likewise, an author from a country with high standards would receive the same low level of protection in a foreign country as that nation's own citizens.

Until the time of the Stockholm Revision Conference in 1967, international copyright protection in the Berne Convention basically reflected the perspective of authors' countries, especially those of Europe. By the time of the Stockholm Conference, many of the convention's 59 members were developing countries whose views on the appropriate extent of copyright protection differed greatly from those of the industrialized countries. Developing countries asserted that access to literary and artistic works created in industrialized countries was essential to their socio-economic development, and that they could not afford to pay for this access under existing copyright treaty law.[18]

In response to demands by the developing countries for concessions, the parties drafted a protocol to the Stockholm Convention. The protocol shortened the terms of protection for copyrighted works and granted compulsory licensing authority to developing countries. Under a compulsory licensing scheme, a developing country could require an author to grant a licence to use his/her work but had to pay "reasonable" compensation for this right. Opposition to the protocol was very high in industrialized countries; the conflicts highlighted at the Stockholm Conference continue to underlie north-south relations on intellectual property rights protection today.[19]

Prior to adoption of the 1883 Paris Convention for the Protection of Industrial Property, differences in both substantive and procedural national patent rules created obstacles to the international assertion of patent rights. For example, in countries where national laws conditioned patentability of an invention on its worldwide novelty, an invention already patented in another country was no longer being considered "novel" and was therefore ineligible for registration. The Paris Convention established an international patent system which gave a patentee IPR protection in all member countries by filing an application in one country. This right was limited by so-called "national working requirements" which allowed importing countries to impose conditions on the sale of patented articles and did not prohibit compulsory licensing. The Paris Convention is also based on the principle of national treatment.[20]

In addition to the Berne and Paris Conventions, WIPO administers eight other treaties which set standards for protection of IPRs, including treaties governing protection of performers, producers, and broadcasters of phonograms, trademarks, and satellite programmes.

Registration treaties

A third set of treaties administered by WIPO are related to the registration of intellectual property rights. Many types of IPR, including patents, trademarks, and industrial designs, must be established through formal registration. The multiplicity of registration procedures in different countries can be a serious barrier for foreign holders to assert their IPR rights. Early efforts to reduce these procedural impediments in the case of trademarks resulted in the Madrid Agreement Concerning the International Registration of Marks[21] in 1891, which provided for international registration effective in all member countries designated by the filer. In 1989 the system established in the Madrid Agreement was amended by the adoption of the Madrid Protocol, which gave greater protection to the holders of internationally registered marks by limiting the impact of challenges to the mark.

Other agreements dealing with registration of intellectual property rights are the Patent Cooperation Treaty, the Budapest Treaty (covering micro-organisms), the Lisbon Agreement (covering appellations of origin), and the Hague Agreement (governing deposit of industrial designs).

Classification treaties

Before registering a trademark or patent, property owners must determine if their creation has already been claimed by someone else. To make searching more feasible, several treaties have been adopted which organize information about registrations into categories. Four treaties cover classification of registered intellectual property rights: the Strasbourg Agreement, the Nice Agreement, the Vienna Agreement, and the Locarno Agreement. The importance of classification of registration information is well illustrated by patents for biotechnology and medicine. From 1980 to 2000 the number of categories for biotechnology rose from 297 to 718, while those for medicine increased from 839 to 1,966. Overall, about 70,000 classifications now exist in the field of technology.[22]

Societal values and intellectual property rights

There is a wide divergence of views over what constitutes intellectual "property", as well as whether and to what extent these private rights should be protected. It is clear that giving an inventor a monopoly over his/her creation provides a strong incentive for innovation. This private benefit, however, also has costs, including underutilization of ideas because they are only available at a price. In poorer countries, the social costs of strong IPR protection are seen as unacceptably high, especially in areas such as public health where IPRs can result in pharmaceutical prices that render medication unattainable by most of the population.

Debates over ... issues regarding the protection of intellectual property rights are no longer merely debates over the ownership of private property rights. Instead IPR has become an integral part of the debates over some of the most critical issues facing the international community today, including environmental protection, wealth transfer, sustainable economic development and the protection of indigenous culture against the ravages of consumerism.[23]

While in industrialized countries the idea of property rights is so ingrained that IPR infringement is automatically equated with stealing, the legal concept of property is a human construct to serve social and economic goals.[24] Even in developed countries, the legal definition of property is constantly changing in response to technological and societal changes.[25] In fact, IPR protection laws are "large-scale intrusions into the free market economy" that involve "manipulating social costs and benefits".[26] The rationale for IPR protection is that the higher prices imposed on consumers are more than offset by the benefits of greater innovation.

Within industrialized countries there is growing disagreement over the benefits of IPR laws for consumers, with a number of experts arguing in favour of reducing levels of protection. On the purely domestic level, however, the social costs and benefits are generally linked – that is, the costs of granting IPR rights are balanced against national social benefits.

International patenting, on the other hand, provides the domestic inventor and by extension the inventor's country with economic benefits while transferring the costs associated with higher prices to the foreign country consumers.[27] It is this "decoupling" and resulting transfer of wealth to the richer countries which own intellectual property rights from the poorer countries which are net importers of protected materials and goods that are at the heart of the international controversy over IPRs.[28]

WIPO's mandate and functions

The WIPO Convention states the objectives of the organization in Article 3:

(i) to promote the protection of intellectual property[29] throughout the world through cooperation among States and, where appropriate, in collaboration with any other international organization,

(ii) to ensure administrative cooperation among the [Paris and Berne] Unions.

Article 4 of the WIPO Convention sets out the activities which WIPO should carry out in order to meet its objectives, stating that WIPO:

(i) shall promote the development of measures designed to facilitate the efficient protection of intellectual property rights throughout the world and to harmonize national legislation in this field . . . ;

(iv) shall encourage the conclusion of international agreements designed to promote the protection of intellectual property;

(v) shall offer its cooperation to States requesting legal-technical assistance in the field of intellectual property;

(vi) shall assemble and disseminate information concerning the protection of intellectual property, carry out and promote studies in the field, and publish the results of such studies;

(vii) shall maintain services facilitating the international protection of intellectual property and, where appropriate, provide for registration in the field and the publication of the data concerning the registrations.

WIPO's effectiveness

Evaluating the effectiveness of WIPO is a complex task not only because of difficulties inherent in setting benchmarks and obtaining data, but because of controversy over the nature of intellectual property and appropriate levels of protection, as discussed above. Different political, economic, cultural, scientific, and technological values are reflected in each nation's views on intellectual property rights. Determining what constitutes success, therefore, is not value neutral.

The basic mandate of WIPO is to promote protection of intellectual property rights by fostering international cooperation. In the past few years the relationship between this goal and social issues such as human health, the environment, and equity has grown increasingly contentious, especially between industrialized and developing countries. In evaluating WIPO's effectiveness in meeting its mandate as set forth in the WIPO Convention, one must take into account the divergence of views on how this mandate is best achieved.

In accord with its mandate, WIPO has provided a forum for the development of rules governing the international treatment of intellectual property rights, and a number of agreements have been completed successfully. WIPO has largely met its mandate to provide for international cooperation and technical assistance to developing countries. However, adoption of IPR treaties developed within WIPO has not been effective in protecting copyrighted and trademarked materials due to weaknesses in both the agreements and enforcement measures. The clearest indicator of WIPO's failure to protect IPRs to the satisfaction of developed countries is the inclusion of these issues within the WTO during the Uruguay Round and the adoption of the Agreement on Trade-Related Intellectual Property Rights (TRIPs).

Discussed below are some possible indicators for measuring WIPO's success in achieving its mandate and influencing further development of the international intellectual property regime. Further research and analysis which would provide a clearer picture of WIPO's success from different perspectives are also proposed.

Level of governmental participation in intellectual property rights treaties

As noted above, 177 countries are members of WIPO. In contrast to the WTO, however, participation in the treaties administered by WIPO is not required as a condition of membership in the organization. Membership of WIPO is open to any country which is a party to any treaty administered by WIPO, a member of the United Nations, or invited by the General Assembly of WIPO to join.

Participation in WIPO's "core" treaties is high: the Paris Convention has 162 parties, the Berne Convention 148 parties, and the Patent Cooperation Treaty 115 parties. In addition, with the major exception of US participation in the Patent Cooperation Treaty, treaty membership includes most developing and developed countries. Since the core treaties have been revised a number of times, more detailed research is needed to determine which versions have been adopted by each country, whether there is a pattern of acceptance that differs among countries with different socio-economic and other conditions, and how these factors reflect on WIPO's effectiveness.

Level of compliance with intellectual property rights treaties

While the WIPO-administered treaties contain some international standards for IPR protection, for the most part national treatment is the underlying principle on which protection is based. In other words, compliance with WIPO treaties does not generally require a country to accord a high level of protection to foreign IPRs, only the same level of protection as is available to domestic IPRs. One of the key goals of WIPO, as set out in the WIPO Convention, is to promote harmonization of national legislation on IPR protection. Therefore, in order to analyse WIPO's effectiveness in promoting IPR protection, national legislation of the parties to each treaty should be examined to determine the terms of protection, procedures for filing and prosecution of rights, available remedies for infringement, including compensation, and level of enforcement.

Dispute resolution

Over the past 20 years, piracy of copyrighted and trademarked goods has increased dramatically due to technological advancements and globalization of trade. Industrialized countries, the owners of most IPRs for these goods, became increasingly frustrated over the failure of WIPO to enforce effectively IPR treaty protections and to develop stronger minimum standards at the international level. At the same time, developing countries' dominance in political negotiations made strengthening standards and enforcement virtually impossible within the WIPO forum.

Although parties to WIPO treaties have recourse to the International Court of Justice to resolve disputes over compliance with treaty provisions, no case has ever been brought to the ICJ. Three possible explanations for the lack of utilization of the ICJ to resolve disputes are the nature of remedies available, the time-consuming and inefficient nature of the process, and the fact that IPRs are basically private property rights and the ICJ is designed to handle state-to-state disputes.

Lack of enforcement of existing standards has been widely perceived as a major failure of WIPO. The objective of strengthening enforcement was one of the key reasons that industrialized countries, led by the USA, moved the issue of IPR protection to a different forum, the General Agreement on Tariffs and Trade.

WIPO recently set up an Advisory Committee on Enforcement of Industrial Property Rights to respond to the need for more effective enforcement of IPR treaties in connection with trade across borders. The approach to enforcement adopted by the advisory committee is to coordinate collective action by all WIPO members to focus on the administrative and procedural problems faced by developing countries and those in transition and to develop best practices for enforcement activities which minimize their cost burdens.[30]

WIPO has also developed rules of procedure for private settlement of disputes, and maintains an extensive list of arbitrators and mediators with expertise in IPR issues and knowledge of the rules of procedure which it makes available to all parties.

In the exploding area of disputes over internet domain names, WIPO has created an online service for dispute resolution. In 2000, 1,850 disputes were settled through this system. Trademark owners can also file complaints online using model documents available for downloading. The online dispute resolution process generates an enforceable decision within two months and appears to be a good example of WIPO's utilization of new technology to improve enforcement. At the same time, the process reduces the time and cost involved in more traditional dispute settlement. Fees paid for this service are expected to increase and become an important income stream for WIPO, which is largely self-financing.

Knowledge management

From looking at its mandate, it is clear that many of WIPO's functions are in the area of knowledge management. Coordinating the development of measures to facilitate the "efficient" protection of intellectual property, performing administrative tasks related to implementation of IPR treaties, assembling and disseminating information, providing legal and technical assistance, and maintaining other services such as registration of IPRs are all related to knowledge management.

In many areas of knowledge management WIPO appears to be quite effective, though it is difficult to assess this accurately without further research into WIPO's activities and their impact on governments and other participants in the IPR regime. Of critical importance to effective knowledge management in the future is WIPO's use of information and communications technology. Several recent initiatives have been undertaken to enhance WIPO's capacity to organize, process, and disseminate information to various actors in the field of international IPR protection.

One recently created programme is WIPOnet, designed to promote international information sharing and the progressive development and application of global standards. If successful, WIPOnet will both facilitate digital exchange between countries of IPR-related information and also promote integration of developing countries into the global digital environment.[31]

Under the auspices of the WIPO Worldwide Academy, WIPO provides an internet-based distance learning centre and develops training materials on a client-specific basis.

A four-year effort aimed at automating the activities related to administration of the Patent Cooperation Treaty – the so-called IMPACT project (Information Management for the Patent Cooperation Treaty) – was recently undertaken by WIPO and is expected to be completed by 2006. When completed, this system would allow for electronic filing for patent and trademark registration as well as improved services for registrants. This computerization will be critical to WIPO's ability to manage an international patent system in the future, as the number of applications increased by 25 times between 1979 and 2000. In 2000 there were already 23,000 registrations of trademarks and 7,300 filings related to patent registration, and a great deal of growth is expected in the future.[32]

The goals of WIPOnet, the WIPO Worldwide Academy, and the IMPACT Project are ambitious and still in early stages of development. To evaluate their effectiveness would require much more detailed data on the success of the programmes in meeting their stated goals.

General acceptance of WIPO's work by governmental stakeholders

For industrialized countries, WIPO is viewed as having failed to promote IPR protection successfully by not brokering treaties which guarantee high levels of protection as well as not obtaining compliance with existing IPR treaties. Industrialized countries also criticize WIPO for not dealing effectively with emerging issues related to technological developments such as biotechnology, digitalization of information and communications, and internet commerce.

For developing countries, obtaining relief from high IPR protection would be an indication of WIPO's success. In certain respects these countries have been satisfied with WIPO's approach, but they are unhappy about its record in addressing issues such as indigenous knowledge, biotechnology, and access to pharmaceuticals.

In evaluating the effectiveness of WIPO in promoting the protection of IPRs, an important indicator of its success is the general acceptance of the purpose and substance of its work by various international stakeholders. As noted above, acceptance of WIPO's work is high among developing countries, but industrialized countries have been far less satisfied. Industrialized countries' dissatisfaction was manifest in their insistence on the inclusion of intellectual property issues in the multilateral trade regime during the Uruguay Round.

Lessons for global environmental governance

From this analysis of the WTO and WIPO, several factors appear to be important in developing effective environmental governance structures: the capacity to link the environment with other issue areas, particularly trade and investment; binding dispute resolution and enforcement mechanisms; and economic incentives to participate in and comply with environmental agreements.

In an increasingly globalized economy, an international organization's ability to adapt to change and address social and economic issues not included in its core mandate will be a key determinant of its success in implementing and advancing its policy agenda.

Notes

1. Keohane, Robert O. 1984. *After Hegemony: Cooperation and Discord in the World Political Economy*.
2. Haas, Ernest. 1983. "Words can hurt you; or who said what to whom about regimes", in Stephen D. Krasner (ed.) *International Regimes*. Cornell University Press.
3. Ryan, Michael P. 1998. "The function-specific and linkage-bargain diplomacy of international intellectual property lawmaking", *University of Pennsylvania Journal of International Economic Law*, Vol. 19, p. 535.
4. See Young, Oran. 1998. "The effectiveness of international environmental regimes", *International Environmental Affairs Journal*, Vol. 10, No. 4, pp. 99–121.
5. *Ibid.*
6. www.wto.org
7. WTO. 2003. *International Trade Statistics 2003*. Geneva: WTO, p. 39.
8. UNDP. 2003. *Human Development Report 2003*. New York: Oxford University Press, pp. 157–159.

9. *Ibid.*, pp. 149–152.

10. WTO. 2001. *Annual Report 2001*. Geneva: WTO, p. 24.

11. Paris Convention for the Protection of Industrial Property, signed in Paris on 20 March 1883. The Paris Convention has been revised or amended seven times since its adoption, in 1900, 1911, 1925, 1934, 1958, 1967, and 1979. There are 162 parties to the convention as of 15 January 2002, but most countries have not ratified the 1979 amendments and 12 had agreed to an earlier version going back to 1925.

12. Unless otherwise noted, the background information and data on WIPO's structure and origin are from the WIPO website, www.wipo.org.

13. Berne Paris Convention for the Protection of Literary and Artistic Works, completed in Paris on 9 September 1896. The Berne Convention has been revised or amended seven times since its adoption, in 1908, 1914, 1928, 1948, 1967, 1971, and 1979. There are 148 parties to the convention as of 15 January 2002, with most countries having agreed to the 1971 version.

14. Signed at Stockholm on 14 July 1967. The convention was amended on 28 September 1979.

15. A list of WIPO member countries can be found on the WIPO website, www.wipo.org/members/members/index.html.

16. In this chapter, the term "international intellectual property rights treaties (or regime)" is used to refer to multilateral treaties. While there are also regional and bilateral agreements on intellectual property rights, they are not covered in this chapter.

17. This discussion of the development and structure of the Berne Convention is taken from Burger, Peter. 2000. "The Bern Convention: Its history and its key role in the future", in Doris E. Long and Anthony D'Amato (eds) *International Intellectual Property*. St Paul, MN: West Group Publishing.

18. *Ibid.*

19. *Ibid.*

20. See Moy, R. Carl. 2000. "The history of the Patent Harmonization Treaty: Economic self-interest as an influence", in Doris E. Long and Anthony D'Amato (eds) *International Intellectual Property*. St Paul, MN: West Group Publishing.

21. Madrid Agreement Concerning the International Registration of Marks, adopted in 1891 and revised in 1900, 1911, 1925, 1934, 1957, 1967, and 1979. As of 18 January 2002 there are 48 parties to the protocol.

22. WIPO website, as of 1 March 2002.

23. Long, Doris E. and Anthony D'Amato (eds). 2000. International Intellectual Property. St Paul, MN: West Group Publishing.

24. *The Economist*. 2001. "Markets for ideas", *The Economist*, 14 April, p. 72.

25. *Ibid.*

26. Moy, note 20 above.

27. This discussion is largely based on Moy, *ibid.*

28. See *ibid.*

29. Article 2 (viii) of the WIPO Convention defines "intellectual property" to include rights related to literary, artistic, and scientific works; performances of performing artists, phonograms, and broadcasts; inventions in all fields of endeavour; scientific discoveries; industrial designs; trademarks, service marks, and commercial names and designations; and protection against unfair competition.

30. See WIPO website.

31. See WIPO website.

32. WIPO website, 1 March 2002.

Multilevel governance

4

The case for regional environmental organizations

Jonathan R. Strand

Introduction[1]

The Bush administration's 2001 decision to withdraw support for legally binding provisions in the Kyoto Protocol is viewed by many observers as a failure of American leadership in the issue area of climate change. Critics in the USA and elsewhere claimed that President Bush, like President Clinton before him, succumbed to domestic political pressures, namely pressure from both labour and business groups.[2] It is perhaps somewhat surprising that the Clinton administration even agreed to the Kyoto Protocol given the known domestic opposition ratification of any such agreement faced in the Senate and even amongst Clinton's own set of advisers and supporters.[3]

The case of the Kyoto Protocol raises a myriad of concerns about global collective action in the absence of strong leadership by the world's only superpower. Moreover, this failure by the USA to contribute to a global collective good and political letdowns in other issue areas such as biodiversity, whaling, and forests have in part led many scholars to call for a global international organization to provide global environmental governance.[4] While the specifics of such an organization are contested, there has been a growing interest in the creation of a world environmental organization (WEO).[5] Proponents of a WEO assert that extant international law, organizations, institutions, and regimes do not have adequate mandates and lack sufficient means to address global environmental problems.[6] Others argue that a WEO could initiate the internalization of transnational environmental externalities.[7] The obvious solution, these and other observers argue, is to create an effective, broad-based, *global* organization.

Exactly how this new institution would be structured and how it would mesh with existing international organizations is unclear. Will the WEO be akin to the International Monetary Fund (IMF) and World Bank in being formally under the United Nations but in reality autonomous from UN control? Could a WEO effectively govern environmental problems without having its decisions being legally binding on members? Furthermore, what internal decision rules will a WEO employ? Will it operate on the principle of one country, one vote, or will votes be weighted based on criteria such as population, GDP, or a measure of economic openness? How will a global institution like the WEO interlink with domestic governmental environmental agencies, non-governmental organizations, and the private sector? Furthermore, what will be the relationship between WEO decisions (public law) and privately established regulations, rules, and standards between corporations (private law)? Additionally, will this new institution address only global environmental problems[8] or will it also tackle regional, national, and local problems?[9] These and countless other questions regarding function, scale, scope, and institutional design loom large, and have been the subject of an ongoing debate in the literature.[10]

Most of the arguments for a multilateral organization to manage transnational environmental problems focus primarily on the formation of a global institution.[11] Despite the compelling case that can be made for a WEO, this chapter argues that an even stronger argument can be made for the regional management of many supranational environmental challenges. The chapter examines the possibility that regional institutions can serve as stepping-stones to regional *and* global environmental governance. The next section of the chapter reviews the arguments for and against the formation of a WEO. The third section presents a general discussion of international cooperation on transnational environmental issues. It is shown that regional-level environmental management has several advantages over a global environmental organization. Next, the chapter discusses the role regional organizations can play and assesses the prospects for them to take up environmental governance tasks, highlighting the interlinkage of regional institutions to both domestic and global environmental governance. It argues that regional environmental governance, nested between domestic and global governance, is one of the "missing links" at the international level. Regional identification and management of environmental problems can be part of a larger, decentralized system of global environmental governance.

Is a world environmental organization the answer?

Compared to other issue areas such as trade, institutional density in the environmental area is low. Global and regional organizations and regimes have been established across a variety of issue areas. Since the end of the Cold War a rising tide of trade integration has swept across most of the world political economy. The evolution of the General Agreement on Tariffs and Trade (GATT) system into the institutionalized World Trade Organization (WTO) in 1995, deepening economic, political, and social integration in Western Europe, the advent of NAFTA (North American Free Trade Area), regional trade integration in East Asia (such as Asia-Pacific Economic Cooperation (APEC) and the East Asian Economic Caucus (EAEC) proposal), and other institutional developments suggest that both global and regional international organizations are now central features of the post-Cold War international system. It has also been noted that there is no global equivalent to a global trade organization such as the WTO in the issue area of the environment. To be sure, almost every international organization has some environmental function and many have environmental agencies, departments, or offices. However, a single mechanism to coordinate and/or manage governance activities is absent.

There is no shortage of tenable answers to explain why there has been little global organization building in the environmental issue area. The environment is a diverse issue area that interfaces with other concerns, such as trade, migration, security, poverty, and health. Hence, a myriad of international organizations and regimes play a role in the management of environmental problems. Another answer rests on the lack of political leadership by the world's largest economy. The fact that the USA has not been actively pursuing institutional alternatives for environmental governance means that it is not providing international leadership, which is important in the creation and maintenance of collective goods. Regardless of the explanation for why there is low institutional density, the multiple shortcomings and outright failings of the current system (perhaps better thought of as a non-system) in the age of globalization are prime factors motivating the arguments of WEO advocates.[12]

Biermann[13] states that supporters of a WEO identify three limits to the current management of environmental problems. First, there is insufficient coordination of efforts to deal with environmental problems. Environmental governance is scattered across many organizations and regimes, and there is a severe lack of synchronization in policy-making and implementation. Furthermore, UN agencies charged with environmental responsibilities often compete with one another over finite resources.[14] Many institutions that deal with environmental problems actually have mandates in other issue areas their leaders see as distinct from the environment. This is perhaps one impetus for the call by the former executive director of the WTO, Renato Ruggiero, for the creation of a WEO. In the view of Ruggiero and others, organizations such as the WTO are not equipped to provide governance outside of their primary mandates, and the apparent solution is to create an issue-specific institution to take over management and thereby provide coordination of environmental problems.[15]

The list of international organizations that have some environmental role is long.[16] Table 4.1[17] displays a non-exhaustive list of international organizations that serve some function in environmental governance. Note that there is much overlap and little coordination even among and across the UN-related organizations listed. The view by many proponents of a WEO is that it would subsume many of the activities of these organizations, or at least act to orchestrate problem identification and policy implementation. In short, "global environmental policies could be made stronger through an independent [WEO] that helps to contain the special interests of individual programs and organizations and to limit double work, overlap, and inconsistencies".[18]

Second, there is a recognized need for capacity building. Developing countries lack the requisite material resources for independent resolution of environmental problems. The dearth of environmental funding is often cited as a primary reason for a new institution; one that can serve as an advocate for an environmental component to the UN's goal that 0.7 per cent of GDP is dedicated to official development assistance (ODA). Exactly what percentage of ODA should be specifically earmarked for environmental funding will be a matter for debate, but clearly there is a need for increased spending by developed countries to enhance the capabilities of developing countries to implement green technologies and undertake environmental education endeavours. Just as the World Bank provides capacity in creating needed infrastructure within developing countries, a WEO could offer developing countries significant resources such as financial assistance, technical advice, and information dissemination.

Often lost in this argument is a clear vision of exactly what capacity-building functions a WEO could provide. Capacity building has a variety of meanings and can be applied to almost any institution and organization (intergovernmental organizations, non-governmental organizations, unions, public schools, private actors, etc.).[19] One of the more problematic aspects of capacity building is identifying when there is *incapacity*.[20] Furthermore, there is a divergence between what developed countries are prepared to provide and the needs of developing countries, contributing to a sense of limited legitimacy for contemporary environmental governance.[21] As Esty and Ivanova[22] put it:

Table 4.1 Select list of international organizations with environmental functions

Organization	Environmental role
African Development Bank	capacity building, environmental impact, water resource management
Asian Development Bank	capacity building, environmental impact, sustainable development
European Bank for Reconstruction and Development	capacity building, sustainable development
Food and Agricultural Organization	forestry and sustainable agriculture
Global Environment Facility	capacity building
Inter-American Development Bank	capacity building, sustainable development
International Atomic Energy Agency	nuclear safety
Inter-Government Authority on Development (formerly IGADD)	food security and environmental protection
International Labor Organization	sustainable agriculture
International Maritime Organization	marine pollution (ICPPS)
International Whaling Commission	conduct of whaling
Helsinki Commission	maintain and improve Baltic marine environment
North American Commission for Environmental Cooperation	surveillance of environmental law in NAFTA members
UN Center for Science and Technology development	capacity building (technology transfer)
UNICEF	poverty and the environment
UN Commission for Human Settlements	environmental refugees
UNDP	sustainable development
UNEP	policy coordination
UN Commission for Sustainable Development	implementation of Agenda 21
UN Population Fund	population management
UN Sudano-Sahelian Office (UNDP)	desertification
UN University	capacity building
World Bank	capacity building, sustainable development
World Health Organization	water quality
World Meteorological Organization	climate change (remote sensing)
World Tourism Organization	ecotourism
World Trade Organization	trade and environmental issues (CTE)

The inadequacy and dispersion of the existing financial mechanisms – scattered across the Global Environmental Facility, UN Development Programme, World Bank, and separate funds such as the Montreal Protocol Finance Mechanism – reinforces the perception of a lack of seriousness in the North about the plight of the South. Furthermore, fundamental principles of good governance such as representativeness, transparency, and accountability are still at issue in many of the institutions with environmental responsibilities. These procedural shortcomings undermine the legitimacy of the system as a whole.

There are several proposals to strengthen the Global Environment Facility (GEF) as a capacity-building framework.[23] One concern of many developing countries, however, is that capacity-building efforts by developed countries will come at a political cost. For instance, one fear is that just as the IMF ties assistance to specific conditions, a stronger GEF might provide only "tied" capacity building. Given the highly controversial nature of IMF conditionality, a WEO that tied capacity-building efforts to domestic policy change by developing countries would probably meet substantial political resistance. This concern could be (partially) surmounted if developing countries had a significant voice in the decision-making mechanisms of a WEO. Nevertheless, there is a real need for capacity building of some sort, and its advocates claim an independent WEO would be able to perform this function.

Third, it is suggested that a WEO could serve to centralize global environmental policy-making. A WEO could be a source of legitimacy and coordinator of organizations and regimes in environmental issue areas. In other words, advocates of a WEO assert that it could serve as an overarching means of synchronizing structural integration. Biermann[24] points to several extant organizations (such as the World Health Organization) that can serve as models for a WEO. In short, a WEO would serve as the overseer and coordinator of information dissemination, environmental standards and rules, and norms regarding environmental policy. The WEO can fill the role that UNEP, NGOs, and other actors have been attempting to fulfil. UNEP was intended to serve as a coordinating body at the international level. But insufficient funding and "deficient authority" result in it "limping from one fiscal crisis to the next".[25] Currently there are at least 20 UN programmes that have core environmental duties, mostly in the area of surveillance and information dissemination. Other international organizations also have environment organs or offices (see Table 4.1). This fragmentation is a serious shortcoming in the environmental governance regime.

Arguably the case in favour of the creation of a WEO is strong. The argument, however, rests on several assumptions.[26] First, it assumes that existing mechanisms for environmental governance cannot be adequately improved. An alternative to a WEO would be to strengthen UNEP or some other existing organization rather than add another organization to the global environmental governance landscape.[27] A second assumption is that a new institution would surmount current shortcomings of global environmental governance. Lack of coordination is perhaps the most serious problem facing the present environmental governance system. But creating a new organization does not necessarily or automatically overcome this and other governance problems. If states resist giving it adequate authority, plentiful resources, and a clear mandate, a WEO may well become another UNEP. Alternatively, Von Moltke[28] suggests that instead of a single mega-organization, it may be the case that a handful of smaller environmental organizations could fill the environmental governance breach. Finally, there is no a priori reason to assume a global institution is the paramount institutional form for environmental management, especially for environmental problems that are not global in scale.[29] In other words, the level of organizational aggregation may not need to be global. As this chapter argues, there is a case to be made that regional organizations can serve as reasonable alternatives to a global organization. The next section provides several reasons why regional organizations may in many cases be advantageous *vis-à-vis* a global environmental organization. There still may be a need for a global organization to address truly global problems, but a single mega-organization may not be the most effective means of dealing with local, national, or regional environmental problems.

Regional stepping-stones to global environmental governance

Substantial empirical and theoretical attention has been paid to the processes of regionalism and globalization. Some authors question whether regionalism and globalism are compatible, part of the same general process of integration, or – at the extreme – diametrically opposed.[30] This issue is often discussed with regard to the proliferation of regional trade areas. Trade integration on a regional scale, along with the metamorphosis of the GATT system into the WTO, has raised a myriad of questions about how issues related to trade are to be grappled with. Quickly any discussion of trade turns into a conversation about the environment. The literature on the intersection of trade issues and environmental issues is extensive.[31] It is not the intention here to discuss the debates in this literature fully, but rather to construct an argument that environmental governance can mirror regional trade integration. Indeed, for many issues (but not all) a regional environmental organization (REO) may have several advantages over a WEO. For several global environmental problems, such as climate change, a global solution may well be the only long-term alternative. Nevertheless, the prospects for a regional alternative to a WEO for local, national, and regional problems need to be explored.

A regional organization would be able to specialize in problems facing member states. As noted by Sandler,[32] environmental problems have differential impacts on states. It seems reasonable that states with shared interests in other issue areas, such as a free trade area or monetary zone, might well be able to address their common environmental concerns. A problem facing members of the EU, for example, might best be resolved in a regional organization comprised of EU members, exclusive of American or other states' influence and interference. Since environmental problems can impact on states differently, an REO may better account for variations across states within the region. Put differently, states that share similar geographic attributes often share similar concerns.[33] An REO would be better equipped to specialize in the concerns of states with shared interests that are based on a shared geography. Interest homogeneity across states in environmental issue areas is more likely when the affected states already share a common purpose in an established organization.

Second, states that cooperate on one issue area, such as trade, may be better equipped to work together on other issues. This type of spillover effect has been noted in the history of the EU, moving from cooperation and integration in relatively technical, apolitical issues areas (like coal and steel) to highly sensitive economic and political issue areas (such as self-defence forces, the euro, etc.). Moreover, the scale of environmental governance may need to mirror the scale of the problem. In other words, regional integration in one area may lead to integration, or at least cooperation, in another. This process may result from simple spillover effects or could be the result of domestic pressures on national governments for management of issues related to the core mandate of the regional organization. For instance, during the domestic debate in the USA concerning the formation of NAFTA, domestic forces and NGOs pressured the Clinton administration to support the establishment of an environmental agency as part of a side agreement. Where economic integration is occurring on a regional basis there is the potential for regional cooperation in related issues. Economic regionalization driven by state actors must be distinguished from economic regionalization that results from decisions made by private actors (such as firms).[34] These related processes are not always coterminous and the impact of variation between the two processes for environmental governance needs to be further explored.

Following Newell's[35] suggestion that the proposed WEO is too large in terms of scope and scale, an additional reason why an REO may serve as a good alternative (or addition) to a WEO is that, simply put, there would be fewer actors involved in cooperation. If environmental governance is considered a collective good, then as long as the minimum number of states needed for provision of the collective good are involved in an REO, effective cooperation may occur. Stated differently, if an

REO constitutes a "k-group" then a collective good can be possible.[36] Where trade or other regional organizations exist and are effective there is a higher chance of a k-group being formed for environmental cooperation. For instance, an REO for North America is more likely because of the presence of NAFTA. Moreover, a North American REO that is built on NAFTA would have only three members. Of course there are power differentials within NAFTA, and all three members may have the potential to be veto players. Nevertheless, regional cooperation by a handful of states may very well be easier because of the fact that there will be fewer members and hence a higher probability of consensus about burden sharing in the provision of a collective good. In other words, this "size principle" suggests REOs may be more effective because they would have fewer actors involved in decision-making, thus facilitating consensus formation or at least majoritarianism.

In addition to the three reasons discussed above, regionalism can serve as a basis of shared interests of governments, NGOs, and subnational actors within a region. Some form of "bioregionalism" might arise as state and non-state actors seek solutions to transborder environmental problems.[37] Bioregionalism can be an activity of NGOs and firms with or without state involvement. To Lipschutz and others, bioregionalism is tied to both transnational and local social structures. Environmental problems that are thought to be clearly global and presumably have only global solutions (such as climate change) do have local and regional causes and consequences.[38] In other words, most global issues are also regional, national, and local issues because the solutions to global problems rest in local, national, or regional responses. Most studies of bioregionalism focus on subnational regionalism.[39] But in many instances transnational cooperation by subnational actors is required to define and address environmental problems. An REO could be a mechanism to provide capacity to subnational responses to environmental problems, such as climate change or acid rain. In addition to capacity building, a regional coordinator of bioregionalism could establish and report on a set of environmental standards that state and non-state actors within each country must meet. This function for an REO could help integrate NGOs, firms, and private citizens into a regional environmental governance regime.[40] The next section outlines how and where REOs can fit into a larger system of global environmental governance.

Regional governance and the global environmental metaregime

The purpose of this chapter is to sketch the role for REOs in environmental governance, and it does not rule out a possible role for a WEO.

This section briefly presents how REOs can fit into an environmental governance system and serve as important links between global cooperation and domestic actors. This idealized model assumes that political obstacles to establishing such a system of multilateral environmental governance are surmountable.

In general, we can think of international organizations as manifestations of legal accords among states. The agreements entered into by governments lay the foundation for governance, as well as broad policy mandates such as development. By "governance" is meant how institutions comprised of sovereign states arrive at decisions concerning what actions will be taken and the means to implement such actions. But the documents outlining governance are the result of political negotiations and therefore reflect bargaining and compromise among members. Furthermore, the agreements are not static, in that negotiations that take place after the original compact was established can change internal governance. The institutions themselves have also evolved unique governing styles whereby the formal, constitutional governing mechanism may be circumvented for the sake of expediency or under the influence of particular members. External events also have impacted on the internal governing arrangements, and especially the policy goals and mandates of the institutions. In short, international organizations can be viewed as relatively organic entities that exist within a larger global society. The national interests of their members impact on international organizations, yet international organizations also affect the policy goals and negotiation strategies their members employ. Put differently, there is a reflexive relationship between states and global social structures. States may pursue one set of goals in a particular formal organization, and these goals can be linked to efforts in other organizations. There is in effect a nesting of states within multiple organizations. Negotiators are not playing a simple "two-level game" but instead are involved in layered bargaining games where the strategies in one setting are linked to strategies in another.[41]

Figure 4.1 depicts what the author refers to as an idealized view of multilateral environmental governance, taking into account the institutional nesting of governance. It is a model that highlights the pathways of bargaining among states and non-state actors. While there is clearly a hierarchy within the model, there is also a place for lateral pressures on organizations. The model is meant to clarify where REOs would fit into a larger environmental metaregime. As defined by Aggarwal,[42] "metaregimes represent the principles and norms underlying international arrangements, international regimes refer specifically to rules and procedures". Domestic political contexts are linked to international regimes through governmental accords. In this model, two sub-games are displayed. State action can involve unilateral, bilateral, and multilateral

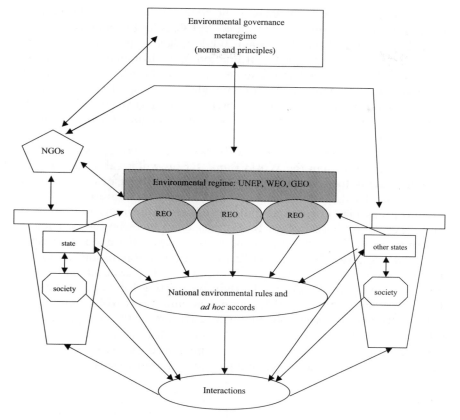

Figure 4.1 Idealized bargaining model of environmental governance

interactions. Regional organizations would fit into a larger system of environmental governance headed by a revamped UNEP or some variant of the proposed WEO/GEO. REOs would serve important roles in the international environmental regime and, as argued above, would have several advantages over a global organization. Moreover, although not displayed in this model, the overlap of regional environmental organizations with governance in other issues areas (such as trade) will potentially lead to synergies, enhancing cooperation in multiple areas.

Conclusion

This chapter has examined the question of how regional integration may serve as a stepping-stone to environmental governance. The next step is to examine the environmental policies and roles of existing regional organizations and forums (for example APEC, NAFTA, and the FTAA – Free Trade Area of the Americas). While it has argued there is a paramount role for regional-level coordination of environmental governance, there is still probably a role for some sort of WEO. While there is a role for a WEO in the management of truly global issues, REOs could fill an important position in multilateral environmental governance. Regional governance organizations, however, will have advantages over a global organization.

Just as the regional development banks cater to concerns of regional members more so than the World Bank, REOs will be able to specialize in issues facing their regional members. REOs will be positioned to accommodate local, national, and regional interests. Moreover, regional organizations may encourage spillover effects from integration in trade and other issue areas. In fact, REOs may themselves be the outcome of spillover, driven by domestic demands on states, such as in the case of the North American Council on Environmental Cooperation. REOs are more likely in regions where cooperation in other issue areas is deepening. In this sense REOs can be built on existing forms of regional integration. The simple fact the regional organizations would have fewer actors involved in decision-making suggests that REOs may prove to be efficient and effective organizations.[43] Finally, the prospects for transnational bioregionalism could possibly be improved by the presence of an REO that provides specialized and locally sentient capacity building.

Notes

1. An earlier version of this chapter was presented at the 2002 meeting of the International Studies Association, New Orleans. Shona E. H. Dodds, Peter M. Haas, and Norichika Kanie have provided helpful comments. Jessica A. McArthur provided able research assistance.
2. Vrolijk suggests that the rejection of Kyoto by Bush was potentially a positive development because it made the American position clear and Bush unwittingly made Kyoto a domestic political issue in the USA. See Vrolijk, Christiaan. 2001. "President Bush might have done Kyoto a favour", Energy and Environment Programme of the Royal Institute of International Affairs, Chatham House, London.
3. Agrawala, Shardul and Steinar Andresen. 1996. "Indispensability and indefensibility? The United States in the climate treaty negotiations", Global Governance, Vol. 5, No. 4.
4. Esty, Daniel C. 1994. "The case for a global environmental organization", in Peter Kenen (ed.) Managing the World Economy: Fifty Years After Bretton Woods. Washington, DC: Institute for International Economics; Biermann, Frank. 2000. "The case for a world environment organization", Environment, Vol. 42, No. 9, pp. 23–31.
5. There is debate amongst proponents about whether or not this new organization should have a role in only global environmental problems or if it should play a role in environmental management at all levels, even local.

6. Biermann, Frank. 2001. "The emerging debate on the need for a world environmental organization", *Global Environmental Politics*, Vol. 1, No. 1, pp. 45–55.
7. Whalley, John and Ben Zissimos. 2001. "What could a world environmental organization do?", *Global Environmental Politics*, Vol. 1, No. 1, pp. 29–34; Newell, Peter. 2001. "New environmental architectures and the search for effectiveness", *Global Environmental Politics*, Vol. 1, No. 1, pp. 35–44.
8. Esty, Daniel C. and Maria H. Ivanova. 2001. "Making international environmental efforts work: The case for a global environmental organization", Yale Center for Environmental Law and Policy, Working Paper 2/01, May.
9. Biermann, note 4 above.
10. *Ibid.*; Biermann, note 6 above; Esty and Ivanova, note 8 above; Von Moltke, Konrad. 2001. "The organization of the impossible", *Global Environmental Politics*, Vol. 1, No. 1, pp. 23–28; Runge, C. Ford. 2001. "A global environment organization (GEO) and the world trading system", *Journal of World Trade*, Vol. 35, No. 4, pp. 399–426; Runge, C. Ford, François Ortalo-Magné, and Philip Vande Kamp. 1994. *Freer Trade, Protected Environment: Balancing Trade Liberalization and Environmental Interests*. New York: Council on Foreign Relations Press; Juma, Calestous. 2000. "The perils of centralizing global environmental governance", *Environment*, Vol. 42, No. 9; Esty, note 4 above; Kennan, George. 1970. "To prevent a world wasteland: A proposal", *Foreign Affairs*, Vol. 48, No. 3.
11. Some observers call instead for major restructuring of existing international institutions (see Juma, *ibid.*). Esty and Ivanova, note 8 above, suggest a new organization that only addresses global, as opposed to regional or national, environmental problems such as climate change.
12. As Esty and Ivanova (note 8 above, p. 19) argue, "a globalizing world requires thoughtful ways to manage ecological interdependence".
13. Biermann, note 4 above, p. 24.
14. Esty and Ivanova, note 8 above, pp. 7–8.
15. Von Moltke (note 10 above, p. 23) rightly points out that the "debate about the creation of a WEO mirrors the uncertainties that have surrounded the creation of environmental ministries at the national level". He claims that national governments have been careful not to create environment ministries that have too much (enough) authority. Moreover, domestic environment governing is fragmented because, in his words, "[t]he environment is too important to be left to a single agency" (p. 24).
16. Iwama (this volume) provides a useful overview of existing multilateral environmental organizations.
17. Adapted and expanded from Hempel, Garret. 1996. *Environmental Governance: The Global Challenge*. Washington, DC: Island Press, p. 145.
18. Biermann, note 4 above, p. 25.
19. VanDeever and Dabelko discuss the problems of how the term "capacity building" is used in the environment literature – see VanDeever, Stacy and Geoffrey D. Dabelko. 2001. "It's capacity stupid: International assistance and national implementation", *Global Environmental Politics*, Vol. 1, No. 2, pp. 18–29. For a statement of capacity building as being more than a financial matter see the collection of papers in James, Valentine Udoh (ed.). 1998. *Capacity Building in Developing Countries: Human and Environmental Dimensions*. Westport, CT: Praeger. Janicke and Weidner present a collection of essays that demonstrate capacity building is also needed within developed countries – see Janicke, M. and H. Weidner (eds). 1997. *National Environmental Policies: A Comparative Study of Capacity-Building*. Berlin: Springer.
20. VanDeever and Dabelko, *ibid.*
21. On the concept of good governance in international organizations see Woods, Ngaire.

1999. "Good governance in international organizations", *Global Governance*, Vol. 5, pp. 39–61. For applications of the core ideas of good governance to existing organizations see Woods, Ngaire. 2000. "The challenge of good governance for the IMF and World Bank themselves", *World Development*, Vol. 28, pp. 823–841; Woods, Ngaire. 2001. "Making the IMF and the World Bank more accountable", *International Affairs*, Vol. 77, pp. 83–100. For a statement on good environmental governance, see Hassan, Parvez. 2001. "Elements of good environmental governance", *Asia Pacific Journal of Environmental Law*, Vol. 6, No. 1, pp. 1–11.

22. Esty and Ivanova, note 8 above, p. 9.
23. For an assessment of the GEF see Werksman (this volume). For an assessment of how the GEF's decision-making structure impacts on its ability to operate in the interests of developed and developing countries see Streck, Charlotte. 2001. "The Global Environment Facility: A role model for international governance?", *Global Environmental Politics*, Vol. 1, No. 2, pp. 71–94.
24. Biermann, note 4 above, p. 26.
25. Esty and Ivanova, note 8 above, p. 8.
26. See Biermann, note 6 above, pp. 51–54 for a response to some of the critics cited here.
27. Najam argues that instead of a WEO, UNEP should be revitalized and given a true coordinating mandate and authority – see Najam, Adil. 2001. "Why we don't need a new international environmental organization", Center for Energy and Environmental Studies, Working Paper 0104; also see Banuri, Tariq and Erika Spanger-Siegfried. 2000. *UNEP and Civil Society: Recommendations for a Coherent Framework of Engagement*, prepared for the United Nations Environment Programme. Boston: Stockholm Environmental Institute. For a useful discussion and proposed solution to the difficulties in accommodating and reconciling differences in trade and environmental laws and interests within the context of the WTO see Biermann, Frank. 2001. "The rising tide of green unilateralism in world trade law: Options for reconciling the emerging North-South conflict", *Journal of World Trade*, Vol. 35, No. 3, pp. 421–448.
28. Like Najam, *ibid.*, Von Moltke, note 10 above, p. 17 suggests a key role for UNEP.
29. Esty and Ivanova, note 8 above, make a distinction between their proposal for a global environmental organization and Biermann's proposal for a WEO. For Esty and Ivanova a GEO would only address failures in global environmental collective action and not local, national, or regional problems.
30. Lawrence, Robert Z. 1991. "Emerging regional arrangements: Building blocs or stumbling blocs?", in Richard O'Brien (ed.) *Finance and the International Economy 5. The AMEX Bank Review Prize Essays*. New York: Oxford University Press; Schott, Jeffrey J. 1991 "Trading blocs and the world trading system", *World Economy*, Vol. 14, No. 1, pp. 1–17.
31. Neumayer, Eric. 2001. "Greening the WTO agreements: Can the treaty establishing the European Community be of guidance?", *Journal of World Trade*, Vol. 35, No. 1; Sampson, Gary and W. Bradnee Chambers (eds). 1999. *Trade, Environmental, and the Millennium*. Tokyo: United Nations University Press; Esty, Daniel C. 1994. *Greening the GATT: Trade, Environment, and the Future*. Washington, DC: Institute for International Economics; Esty, Daniel C. 1996. "Stepping up to the global environmental challenge", *Fordham Environmental Law Review*, Vol. 8, No. 1, pp. 103–113.
32. Sandler, Todd. 1992. *Collective Action: Theory and Applications*. Ann Arbor: University of Michigan Press, pp. 169–177; Sandler, Todd. 1997. *Global Challenges: An Approach to Environmental, Political, and Economic Problems*. New York: Cambridge University Press. For more on environmental public goods see Heal, Geoffrey. 1999. "New strategies for the provision of global public goods: Learning from international environmental challenges", in Kaul Inge, Isabelle Grunberg, and Marc A. Stern (eds) *Global*

Public Goods: International Cooperation in the 21st Century. New York: Oxford University Press.

33. Even in a context of cooperation, however, states with similar interests can come into conflict if there is discord resulting from concern over relative capabilities. See Krasner, Stephen. 1991. "Global communications and national power: Life on the Pareto frontier", *World Politics*, Vol. 43, No. 2.

34. On this point see Higgott, Richard. 1997. "De facto and de jure regionalism: The double discourse of regionalism in the Asia Pacific", *Global Society*, Vol. 12, No. 2, pp. 165–183.

35. Newell, note 7 above.

36. Using "k-group" as defined by Schelling, Thomas C. 1978. *Micromotives and Macrobehavior*. New York: Norton.

37. Lipschutz, Ronnie D. 1999. "Bioregionalism, civil society and global environmental governance", in Michael Vincent McGinnis (ed.) *Bioregionalism*. London and New York: Routledge.

38. *Ibid.*; Feldman, David and Catherine Wilt. 1999. "Climate change policy from a bioregional perspective: Reconciling spatial scale with human and ecological impact", in Michael Vincent McGinnis (ed.) *Bioregionalism*. London and New York: Routledge, pp. 134–135.

39. One hesitates to call it "regional bioregionalism". The selections in McGinnis focus on subnational bioregionalism, but it seems possible that transnational cooperation between subnational groups (including state environmental agencies) could emerge – see McGinnis, Michael Vincent (ed.) *Bioregionalism*. London and New York: Routledge.

40. Another advantage an REO might have over a WEO is it may be less likely to suffer from the attacks by civil society that have occurred with other global institutions. One can only imagine the reaction by protesters to a global environmental organization run by states for states' interests. Without full inclusion of NGO and other civil groups (such as unions), a WEO will be subject to the same kind of demonstrations as the WTO, IMF, and IBRD. For an excellent assessment of global social movements see Fisher (this volume).

41. Kanie (this volume) provides a useful perspective on the linkage between domestic politics and global governance.

42. Aggarwal, Vinod. 1998. "Analyzing institutional transformation in the Asia-Pacific", in Vinod Aggarwal and Charles E. Morrison (eds) *Asia-Pacific Crossroads: Regime Creation and the Future of APEC*. New York: St Martin's Press.

43. On assessing effectiveness in environmental governance see Young, Oran. 1998. "The effectiveness of international environmental regimes: A mid-term report", *International Environmental Affairs*, Vol. 10, No. 4, pp. 267–289; Young, Oran. 1994. *International Governance: Protecting the Environment in a Stateless Society*. Ithaca: Cornell University Press, pp. 142–160.

5

Global environmental governance in terms of vertical linkages

Norichika Kanie

Introduction

In recent years a growing amount of scholarship in the field of international relations has emphasized the importance of the interaction between domestic and international affairs. In short, these scholars argue that what happens in the domestic arena matters in the management of international order, and vice versa. Those two arenas, domestic and international, had long been thought of as distinct in state-centric Westphalian international relations, but they have gradually been considered as closely interconnected by much of the recent scholarship, especially in the field of the political economy and global environment.[1]

In practice, after 10 years of international efforts in struggling with implementing Agenda 21, the domestic-international linkage has become even more important in global environmental governance.[2] This is even truer when many global environmental issues such as climate change and conservation of biodiversity are shifting their focus from the mere agenda-setting phase to the implementation phase. After all, unless measures are sufficiently addressed, coordinated, and implemented domestically in a concrete manner, it would be impossible to solve a complex environmental problem whatever efforts are made to address the problem internationally. One result of the development of an international agreement on tropical timber, for example, has been consequences in the dynamics of small-scale activities and the local community. Therefore, international efforts need to keep the domestic arena within their scope. Put differently, if the international community lacks the tools – either financial or educational – to recruit support from the key social, economic, and industrial actors, cooperation that entails concrete results in practice is unlikely.[3]

In the context of this collective research project, which is designed to improve insights into the strengths and weaknesses of the existing global environmental institutional structure, it is the institutional dimension of domestic-international linkage that should be given the greatest attention. Of course, this is not the only reason why institutions should be paid most attention here. Institutions are important because they can structure the relationships among actors in society, influence their preferences, and channel how ideas are brought into decision-making processes. Domestic institutions are able to mitigate the effectiveness of international efforts to alter domestic policy priorities and regulations. International institutions can influence and stimulate changes in domestic institutions.[4] Similarly, institutional change at the international level may lead to the alteration of the arrangement of institutional settings and/or the political power balance of established agencies at the domestic level. Thus, there are good reasons why institutions should be focused on.

Similarly important are other modes of domestic-international interaction and linkage. Those modes are policy interaction, interaction through non-governmental organizations (NGOs, including business/industry organizations), and interaction through the scientific community, as they have been chosen as important international players throughout this research project. Although no generally accepted taxonomy on vertical linkage exists at this stage, as Oran Young points out, at least these four modes of vertical linkages can be chosen as important modes.[5] From time to time interactions of these modes have taken place in an indirect manner, and sometimes even unconsciously or implicitly.

The purpose of this chapter is to illustrate the general character of the vertical linkages of environmental governance, and to provide ideas about what emerging forces are influencing vertical linkages. The chapter also provides consideration on what are the gaps and barriers lying between the needs and the reality of vertical linkages in order to create better global environmental governance institutions. The sections that follow first provide a brief summary of recent international relations scholarship on political interaction between domestic and international arenas. Then the chapter discusses national and international forces in environmental governance taking into account the four mechanisms of domestic-international linkage, namely policy, NGO, scientific, and institutional modes of linkages. Policy and institutional modes will be dealt with in the same subsection, because they both take a clear form at a first glance, rather than a vague and fuzzy form. The following section looks at international to national forces. The conclusion draws the implications for international environmental governance emerging from the forces and barriers narrowing the gap between domestic and international arenas.

Political interaction – International relations and the domestic arena

Until recently, most mainstream international relations scholarship has either disregarded the domestic arena as a "black box" or perceived domestic factors as a dependent variable. As represented by the arguments of Kenneth Waltz, the nature of the international system is perceived as anarchy, consisting of nation-states as units, and the nature of the anarchical international system determines the dynamics of international relations, whatever kind of domestic factors are involved.[6]

Since the late 1980s, however, growing attention has been paid to the causal relations between domestic factors and international relations, along with internationalization and globalization in many issues.[7] Broadly speaking, two modes of theoretical observation are seen in this field: "second image reversed" and "two-level games". In short, the "second image reversed" mode focuses on domestic consequences of international phenomena. Therefore, it is argued that internationalization of, for example, environmental politics affects the policy preferences of domestic economic and political actors, and then this in turn influences national policy formation and shapes the domestic institutions.[8] In this mode the impact of globalization on domestic politics is the primary concern, and therefore the main focus is on the domestic arena. Nevertheless, the linkage between domestic and international arenas is within its scope.

The "two-level games" mode, on the other hand, looks at the interplay between domestic and international arenas and deals with the international consequences of domestic institutions and the domestic political process. It challenges the conventional neo-realist view of international relations, and see domestic factors as a determinant of international relations. It is a framework that illustrates how national political leaders conduct foreign policy by simultaneously managing contending political pressures and constraints in the international (level 1) and domestic (level 2) arenas. At the international level, pressures are imposed on leaders in many different forms, such as economic considerations and commitments to international organizations. At the domestic level, leaders constantly build coalitions of support for their foreign policy initiatives. Leaders try to maximize their own ability to satisfy domestic pressures, while minimizing the consequences of foreign development. Thus, basically, the success or failure of international negotiations depends on the size of the level 2 win-set, which is defined as the "set of all possible level 1 agreements that would win, that is, gain the necessary majority among the constituents when simply voted up or down".[9]

More than a decade of development of scholarship in both of these two modes of accounts for the interaction between domestic and international arenas has shown that domestic politics and institutions do matter in international affairs, and international affairs do matter in domestic politics and institutional arrangements in a growing number of issue areas.[10] Environmental problems, which often do not respect national borders, are obviously among those issue areas. Although cooperation is necessary for dealing with global environmental problems, sometimes it is the domestic conditions of sovereign states, which continue to be the primary actors in the world politics, that do not always allow a situation where cooperation can take place. Therefore, it is necessary for us to look at the dynamics of "vertical" linkage, which means the linkage between local and the global policy-making and implementation processes, including cross-border interactions, when discussing environmental governance.

Recently Young illustrated that there are two emerging ways for what he calls "vertical interplay": one involves adjacent institutional interplay and another involves remote interplay.[11] The former is about institutional interplay located at adjoining levels of social organization, such as interaction between provincial and local governments. This type of interplay is rather obvious in the hierarchical architecture of a national government, although sometimes functional problems might exist within a bureaucratic complex. The latter kind of remote interplay needs more attention for understanding the environmental governance structure, especially when it comes to the implementation stage of global environmental policies, as globalization and international agreements have often had consequences at the operational level in small-scale local communities. Although remote at a glance, the global and the local arenas are substantially interconnected, and therefore diplomatic negotiations in the international regime-building process and the international regimes established as a result need to accommodate these emerging new dynamics. As will be seen later in this chapter and other chapters in this volume, one such attempt in the international community to create interactions among various social actors, be they international or purely domestic, is the multi-stakeholder dialogue (MSD) process of the Commission on Sustainable Development (CSD) and other international forums.

Diplomacy itself is also moving from the traditional concept of deals between states' delegates. Andrew Cooper has proposed conceptualizing

Table 5.1 Conceptualizing interactive diplomacy

Style of diplomacy	Public diplomacy (rather than quiet diplomacy)
The form of diplomatic approach	Interaction between like-minded countries and NGO, business, and industry communities
Multiple roles	State – international organs – NGO/business and industry corresponding/complementary roles create new type of coalitions
Scope	Trade, environmental, labour standards, and new concept of security

a new model of diplomacy which is drawn from observation of the diplomatic behaviour of so-called middle-power countries or like-minded countries, extending it to a more general concept of diplomacy in the era of globalization without hegemony.[12] This new mode of diplomacy is led by "interactive leadership", at the core of which is the interaction between like-minded countries and the NGO community. As Mikoto Usui argues in Chapter 11 in this volume, business/industry communities will also be a part of this interaction in the issue of environment and sustainable development. Rather than traditional, slow-speed, quiet diplomacy behind closed doors, the new diplomacy is conducted via public diplomacy to make it more open and operational. The basic elements of this interactive diplomacy are shown in Table 5.1.[13]

Forces from national to international arenas

Forces through NGOs

As has been recognized by many, NGOs link the local and the global. NGOs "simultaneously reach up to the states and their international institutions and down to the local communities", and there are several ways in which NGOs can link them.[14] They operate beyond borders, no matter whether they are business-interested or policy-interested organizations. Throughout the world they deal with micro problems in local society as well as having a voice in global negotiation settings. Furthermore, within a company there emerges a growing number of partnerships with civil society, which even have a potential to create a new type of grass-roots standards for sustainable development. Examples are given in Chapter 11 by Usui – the Unilever-led Marine Stewardship Council (since 1995) and Tea Sourcing Partnership (since 1997) as well as the Royal Dutch Shell-assigned GRI (Global Reporting Initiative, since 1997) promote standards of cross-border significance.[15] They constitute global business strategies and therefore may eventually reach the global standard platform for more official international recognition such as the ISO (International Organization for Standardization). In developing countries particularly, NGOs play the role of educators and promoters of sustainable development ideas "to a much greater extent than else-where", and therefore the NGO community (a large number of whose leaders are often academics in developing countries) "becomes the main initiator of sustainable development initiatives".[16]

Looking at international negotiation processes, NGOs participate in international negotiations through direct involvement in international negotiation processes and international institutions. In many of the MEA negotiations it is a common phenomenon that the number of NGO members registered to the conference secretariat is greater than the number of governmental delegates to the conference. Except for a few exceptional cases (such as the UNECE Regional Convention on Access to Information, Public Participation in Decision-making, and Access to Justice in Environmental Matters – the Aarhus Convention – and the Habitat II conference in Istanbul, in which NGOs were deeply involved in the official conference process and were even allowed to submit pro-posals for textual amendment in the case of the latter), NGOs cannot intervene from the floor on draft text.[17] For example, in the UNFCCC NGOs cannot intervene in negotiations from the floor. NGO interven-tion depends very much upon the character of the issues at stake, be-cause the legitimacy of NGO intervention is not yet very clear and still controversial.

Still, NGOs can comment, suggest amendments, and give ideas, based on their concrete experience and expertise at grass-roots level. In this way, the negotiated text can be better informed and more rooted in reality, so that implementation can be handled more smoothly. In this regard, notable is the CSD multi-stakeholder dialogue sessions. Created in 1993, the number of representatives from the major groups of Agenda 21 increased from 200–300 to 700–800 by 2000.[18]

The government representatives are supposed to negotiate on behalf of their governments, ideally taking into account the total balance of na-tional interests, under the current form of multilateralism. Accordingly, current institutional settings are based upon this system. However, this style of multilateral negotiation does not necessarily lead to sufficient implementation of the agreement in reality. Therefore, partnership is necessary in both negotiation and implementation.

More direct NGO/CSO participation in the international policy-making process is through government delegations – as members of a government delegation to international negotiations, or close interaction with government officials. In this way the idea and comments of NGOs may be more directly reflected in the negotiations. As part of a government delegation, they may have a chance to intervene in intergovernmental negotiations. It is not unusual in Scandinavian and some Western European states to have people from NGOs in the national delegation team to MEA negotiations. This tendency accelerated in the preparation process leading up to the World Summit on Sustainable Development (WSSD), when a growing number of countries started to recognize the importance of involvement of NGOs in order to achieve their sustainable development goals. After the Prepcom 4, even Japan, which has long neglected to include CSO delegates in its official delegation, decided to include them. Little is known, however, about the legitimacy, effectiveness, and influence of this kind of NGO participation, and more research effort is necessary to understand further the dynamics of NGO participation.

Although NGOs can represent grass-roots voices in multilateral negotiations, and such domestic to international force is beneficial to multilateral negotiations and the international regime-building process as well, one major problem is that the funding available for CSOs for them to attend is limited. Also, for NGOs in non-English-speaking countries language may be a barrier to speaking effectively in international negotiation processes.

The power of knowledge

The outcome of scientific research, no matter whether it is produced by a national laboratory or an international project, is by its nature easily disseminated beyond national borders. On the way to producing an outcome, a scientist based in a domestic research organization interacts internationally and domestically with other scientists and with policy-makers either individually or through networks. Science and scientists do not respect national borders, and therefore they may also link domestic and global forces.

The first path for science and scientists to interact with global environmental politics is through domestic institutions. Research outcomes from a domestic laboratory that could influence the domestic policy-making process may be elaborated in the form of a proposal for international environmental negotiation by national delegations. This sometimes takes the form of intellectual leadership. The case of the Netherlands' triptych approach to the European burden-sharing negotiation in climate change before the Kyoto Conference in 1997 is a good example of this. Based on the domestic climate change policy network and knowledge base in the Netherlands, the approach was formulated by a group of researchers at Utrecht University, and after scientific elaboration it was further elaborated for the Netherlands' proposal to the European GHG burden-sharing negotiations.[19]

The research team providing a basis for intellectual leadership may even not be limited to one country. It has sometimes happened, as in the case of the Club of Rome, that a like-minded international research team (of eminent people) can produce the basis for such leadership. When such a team collaborates with like-minded countries and makes a soft coalition in the given negotiation settings, it may even lead to what Andrew Cooper calls "interactive leadership" for enhanced global problem-solving.[20]

Another path for science and scientists to interact with global environmental politics is a scientist's direct involvement in a research team associated with an international institution or epistemic community. A researcher based in a certain country may bring knowledge to the international arena and influence and facilitate the international policy-making process. This path has been common in environmental policy-making since the preparation leading up to the Stockholm Conference in 1972, when the so-called "MIT group" was establised in order to find a way by which both developing and developed countries could get together to Stockholm, and when the "Founex group" was convened to create politically acceptable consensual knowledge on the environment and development.[21]

In this sense, enhancing domestic knowledge capacity and establishing solid knowledge bases at the national level in terms of problem-solving from various disciplines can enhance the forces from domestic to international arenas through the creation of well-informed and knowledgeable scientists. This may be regarded as the enhancement of "soft power". Issue-oriented strategic research programmes are important in this regard, especially when a government supports them. This can, accordingly, narrow the knowledge gap between national and international arenas. Furthermore, it should be remembered that the basis of this is capacity building through education.

Policy and institutional linkages

Forces that narrow the gap between domestic and international that come from the domestic arena are found less frequently than forces from international to domestic with regard to environmental policies. In terms of solutions, of course, implementation is primarily a local activity, so it may be ideal if bottom-up solutions can lead to the international regime. However, accumulation of *de facto* standards does not yet seem to create global regimes in the field of the environment. In the first place, once an international regime is created, the forces from international to domestic may become stronger for most countries.

The top-down characteristics of global environmental issues and policies may also be related to stronger forces from international to national arenas rather than national to international arenas. Although there still exist purely local environmental policies, and thus international cooperation is needed to solve common problems existing in each country, many environmental policies are now regarded as part of global or transboundary environmental problems such as climate change and ozone depletion which have to be dealt with and addressed internationally at one point. Even problems that were traditionally regarded as local environmental problems now have international aspects, due to a new understanding of local environmental problems. Economy and Schreurs pointed out that, for example, coal-fired power plants in China are now understood to contribute to local air pollution as well as acid rain in Japan and global climate change.[22] Another example is that a loss in species in one region is now viewed in terms of global loss of biodiversity. Local problems at first glance are now viewed, or should be viewed, from a global perspective as well in order to solve the problems fundamentally. Therefore, many environmental policies at a national, or subnational, level are now also perceived as "the consequence of international ideational and institutional forces, at times mediated by domestic politics and structures".[23]

In addition, environmental policies in a nation-state are, of course, created in domestic political and institutional contexts, and affected by international forces as the case may be. Therefore, one may argue that it is difficult to decide whether it is a policy or it is the other political factors that link the domestic and international arenas. Taking this argument into account, we can still see the policies and policy measures that can be regarded as a facilitative device linking domestic and international arenas, and these can be regarded as forces from domestic to international in order to link the two arenas.

One case of such a policy is a so-called big power's policy. Because of the amount of resources that a major country possesses, its policy (change) influences international effort in one way or another, as hegemonic theory argues. A good example is the policy change of the USA on the Kyoto Protocol. Although it was a negative change and influence in terms of the multilateral effort to combat with climate change, we have witnessed that the US domestic policy change in withdrawing its support for the Kyoto Protocol influenced the Kyoto Protocol negotiation process from COP6 through the Bonn Agreement to the Marrakesh Accord. It also changed the dynamics of the negotiation game among players. In the field of environmental policy, which is closely related to economic policy, the policy of a "big power", although it may not be called hegemony any more, is still a force that can influence the international negotiation process.

There are also kinds of policies by which domestic forces are brought into international arenas, no matter what the size or the power of countries may be. Two examples from the experience of the Netherlands are discussed below. Of course they do not provide a comprehensive picture, but what is important here is that they do illustrate that, although sometimes implicit, vertical linkage and forces that narrow the gap between different arenas do exist and do matter in some situations, and therefore need more attention when looking at the dynamics of environmental governance.

The case of the target group approach and international negotiation

The "target group approach" of Dutch environmental policy has helped to accommodate domestic consensus in a given policy area, and accordingly helped to have a certain basis of solid domestic consensus among stakeholders in preparation for international negotiation as compared with many other countries without a solid domestic consensus basis. Therefore, the policy approach can be seen as a source of position-making for multilateral negotiation – in other words, the position would have been weaker if there had not been this policy approach. In this sense, the policy approach was successful in bringing the domestic forces into multilateral negotiation.

The target group approach internalizes national policy targets into the targets of domestic stakeholders, who are simultaneously the sources of environmental problems and the ones responsible for policy implementation. Representatives of a target group participate in the process of "internalization", where negotiations with government on the policy target of each target group take place. At the same time, constituents of the target group participate in the policy-making process within the target group. This consultative approach is time-consuming, but "sustainability" of the policy may be better secured because the policy is a product of long-lasting negotiation. Taking into account that consensus by the implementing parties is vital for the sustainability of policies, this approach is very effective when it works.

An example of the target group approach influence on international negotiation can be found in a policy for the industry target group. By introducing a covenant policy between the government and industry for improving energy efficiency, the Netherlands could eliminate a potential negative influence of the industry sector on its international negotiating posture in climate change negotiation before the Kyoto Conference.[24]

The target group approach has the effect of internalizing a national policy target into the targets of domestic stakeholders. In terms of national-international linkage, the effect of the approach is to be able

to create a certain level of domestic consensus basis in a given environmental issue area, so that a solid standpoint is established in international
negotiation settings. Accommodating various interests in this manner is
more important when it comes to negotiations in which many domestic
stakeholders are supposed to have different interests, such as the case
of climate change. Having a solid domestic consensus basis while other
countries have internal struggles to accommodate the interests of various
stakeholders may even create a situation in which the country can exert
leadership in tackling the issue.

Needless to say, the success of this policy approach also depends on the
political culture of a country, public opinion, and other national-specific
situations as well. Therefore, this exact same approach may be possible
only in the Netherlands, and may not be emulated by other countries.
Yet the important point here is not whether the policy approach can
be emulated or not, but learning that there is a policy approach that
can bring domestic forces into multilateral negotiation, and that such an
approach should be applied based on each particular situation where the
country stands.

Policy integration and international negotiation

Integration of environmental policy is the characteristic of the Netherlands' environmental policy after the 1980s. Due to the policy differentiation that took place in the 1970s, the environmental policy field was
divided into several small sectors, each governed by their own laws and
regulations. Environmental policy was falling apart at the end of the
1970s, and it seemed that there was hardly any coordination between
sectors and with other policy fields such as physical planning, water
management, or agricultural policy.[25] Thus, fundamental change in policy management was urged, and in the 1980s a new integrated environmental policy was introduced. The new policy programme introduced
an "effect-oriented approach", rather than dividing issues into detailed
sectors such as waste and chemical waste, and therefore policies were integrated and formulated under six themes: acidification, eutrophication,
diffusion of substances, disposal of waste, disturbance (including noise,
odour, local air pollution, etc.), and climate change.

This policy integration made it easier to be effective in tackling
environmental issues, since many environmental issues, by their character, need an overarching holistic approach rather than a fragmented
approach. Accordingly, this effective approach helped in producing an
innovative policy and measures in some areas such as climate change and
acidification that are recognized as a frontrunner or model for policies of
other countries, and thus influenced the policies of other countries.

It also helps in initiating international negotiation by showing that particular policy measures are in fact possible and feasible. It has been argued that a certain kind of leadership in multilateral negotiation is exerted by introducing an ambitious policy domestically. This mode of leadership operates as a form of social persuasion to show "that a certain cure is indeed feasible or does work, or to set a good example for others to follow".[26] It is also argued that "the mechanism of setting an example is advocated by some groups of environmentalists who claim that by unilaterally imposing on one's own society strict standards of pollution control a government may help strengthen public demand in other countries for equally strict measures", and that "by imposing or threatening to impose unilateral environmental protection measures, a government can strengthen demand within its own society for international regulations".[27]

In fact in the eyes of many the integrated and comprehensive approach of the Netherlands' sustainable development policy is seen as one of the most successful in environmental governance.[28]

Domestic forces to narrow the gap

As seen in the Netherlands' case above, national policies can indirectly bring domestic forces into international arenas. Also, as presented in Chapter 11 by Mikoto Usui in this volume, there is some evidence in practice to show that policies within a company are able to be a source for creating a bottom-up governance structure, sometimes without noticing it. Usui points out that business and community partnerships involving civil society organizations can alter the power balance locally towards better adapted innovation and competition, thus providing a real-time policy forum raising social expectations for better than the legal minimum in practice and accountability, and then even lead to bottom-up pathways up towards regional or international standards, such as in the case of the Pan-European Certification Initiative (1999) and the African Timber Organization.

Elizabeth DeSombre also arrived at similar conclusions after the examination of various cases in American environmental policy and their impact on international relations: one way that international standards improve is "when one state takes the initiative to regulate domestically to address a problem that has international dimensions".[29] Interestingly, DeSombre has found that the cases which the USA decides to push forward internationally are "those for which there is a coalition of environmentalist and industry actors" both of whom benefit from increasing the number of actors bound by the regulation.[30]

In addition to these implicit linkages, more important mechanisms in terms of environmental governance are institutions, because they can structure the formal relationships among actors in society, influence their preferences, and channel how ideas are brought into the decision-making process. If domestic-level environmental governance is important for global environmental governance, as Agenda 21 stressed, there has to be an effective institutional linkage between domestic and international governance structures.

What we call multi-stakeholder processes now function to bring domestic forces into international arenas. Minu Hemmati has shown 20 examples of multi-stakeholder processes.[31] Among those processes the most notable and universal participation is obtained in the multi-stakeholder dialogues (MSD) of the UN Commission on Sustainable Development (CSD).[32] Started informally in 1997 and formally in 1998, CSD-MSD currently provides the most interesting institutionalized space within the United Nations to bring domestic forces into the multilateral process.[33] CSD-MSD is participated in by both NGOs and governmental organizations that are closest to their constituency (local government), thus bridging the gap between local and global.

Apart from multi-stakeholder processes, however, so far institutional, as well as implicit, vertical linkage has not been sufficiently addressed in multilateral negotiation forums, particularly in the intergovernmental negotiation process leading up to the WSSD. Issues related to governance structure have been addressed, and the discussion and subsequently negotiation have taken place since the Prepcom 2. In the Prepcom 4 finally a chapter dealing with governance was built into the "Draft Plan of Implementation for the WSSD", although the title was changed from "sustainable development governance" to "institution". However, discussion has been divided into subnational, national, regional, and global-level governance, and how to enhance the linkage between those levels was not sufficiently addressed. Implementation of the results of international negotiation cannot be realized unless vertical linkage is sufficiently addressed.[34]

Forces from international to national arenas

Forces through NGOs

NGOs participating in international negotiations have a mission to bring their experience, ideas, and expertise to the international arena. At the same time, they have a role to disseminate the information obtained in the international arena to their national or local communities. They may also be involved in national or local-level policy-making processes and provide ideas and opinions from a broader (global) perspective; thus they can bring international norms and principles into domestic policies.

There are difficulties for them in doing this. Elias[35] points out, among other things, that the information barrier and the language barrier are two of the most important barriers that hinder implementation of Agenda 21 issues. On the information barrier she sees that there is much difference in information flow between developed countries and developing countries. There are a number of success stories from developed countries where Agenda 21 principles are implemented at national and local levels, while Agenda 21 itself is not well known in many parts of the rest of the world. The low access to information and low awareness of the issues are not only a problem among the general public, but are sometimes also the case among governmental officials. Even farmers following sustainability principles in their daily activities and developing organic agriculture have never heard about Agenda 21 and its principles. Taking into account that access to the internet is still a problem in many regions, Elias argues, information provided by NGOs is often the only source that can inform people about what is happening at the global level, although funding is an urgent problem for NGOs. Such information might, in turn, bring benefits to the local society.

Related to the information barrier is the language barrier. Since official translation is usually slow in production, this is a big issue for people in non-English-speaking countries. Especially, people working with NGOs at grass-roots level can often command only their native language. The language barrier is a problem even to those who have access to the internet.

The UN's websites provide only a small number of translated documents and usually not the more recent ones. Those regions where English is not a common language are effectively cut off from accessing recent publications and documents.[36] In cases such as these, international forces cannot be brought into domestic arenas through NGOs.

The power of knowledge

Scientists directly involved in a research team attached to international institutions may be able to bring the research outcome into domestic policies. This has been common practice, and sometimes even used intentionally by a conference secretariat, in order to bring and inform international norms or international scientific consensus to national actors. In the preparation for the Stockholm Conference in 1972, Maurice Strong invited researchers from developing countries to his office as consultants to accommodate scientific consensus on the relations between environment and economic development, with the intention that they would influence national policy-makers' perspective on environment and development when they were participating in the conference.[37] Internationally recognized scientists may function to disseminate international norms to domestic decision-makers.

Internationally recognized research organizations, although not international organizations *per se*, can also bring their knowledge and expertise into national strategy-making processes. The London-based International Institute for Environment and Development (IIED) participated in the development process for national strategies on sustainable development (NSSDs) together with the OECD Development Assistance Committee (DAC), and donor and developing country partners. In order to improve understanding of the key challenges involved in developing and implementing NSSDs, the IIED was coordinating, providing guidance and support, and assisting with analysis and synthesis.[38]

As a result of recent proposals on so-called "Type 2 outcomes" of the WSSD, which are the collection of partnership initiatives to achieve sustainable development, international research organizations will be able to have more chance to work with governmental and intergovernmental organizations. Although it is obvious that the contents of the partnership and research should be the most important and one has to be careful in evaluating the intention of such partnerships, the kind of links that the Type 2 proposals are aiming at have potential to narrow the gap between domestic and international arenas through research activities.

Policy and institutional linkages

Because ultimately multilateral environmental agreements (MEAs) have to be implemented as policies at domestic level in one way or another, it is obvious that there exist "vertical" linkages in policies and forces from international to national policies. For example, upon ratification parties to the Montreal Protocol have to comply with the agreement in the protocol, and therefore implement policies domestically that could reduce the emissions of gases identified in the protocol in accordance with the time line presented in the protocol. Similarly, parties to the Kyoto Protocol, once it is ratified, are obliged to reduce greenhouse gases (GHGs). As for international non-binding norms, the likelihood of compliance depends on the capability and willingness of the state as well as on the cost of compliance.[39] After all, national sovereignty exists within a setting of international anarchy, and therefore in principle transboundary, regional, or global environmental problems cannot be solved unless the international agreements to tackle them have to be complied with by national policies, no matter whether they are legally binding or not.

International norms as well as international recommendations such as the endorsement of the "sustainable development" concept by the General Assembly of the United Nations have often been used as a rationale for introducing a national environmental policy. Since environmental ministries are often weak in the hierarchy of governmental power structures, endorsement by the international community can help introducing new policy instruments at the national level. In a situation of controversy over whether or not to introduce a particular policy measure, too, international forces may be used as (one of the) rationales to introduce the policy. In the Netherlands the coalition government collapsed in 1989 as a consequence of controversies over the financial resources to implement the new comprehensive national environmental policy plan (NEPP). After the general election the NEPP was adopted, but the necessity of a new sustainable development policy plan was described in its preamble in reference to *Our Common Future*, a report of the World Commission on Sustainable Development established by the United Nations.[40] Being able to capture the domestic political momentum, international force may be used effectively as a rationale to introduce a new policy or political agenda into a national arena.

Once international agreement is adopted, well-designed domestic policy may function as a device for compliance. For example, the "target group approach" of the Netherlands, as described in the previous section, can translate international obligation (or objectives) into the target of domestic stakeholders. In this way policy can link the international and domestic arenas.

Outcomes of international negotiation can also link the international and domestic policy arenas. The Kyoto Mechanisms in the Kyoto Protocol to mitigate climate change allow a country to conduct international projects (the Joint Implementation and Clean Development Mechanism) and international trading in GHG emissions. Therefore, domestic policies implementing the Kyoto Mechanisms inevitably facilitate cross-border environmental activities. Although officially the commitment period of the Kyoto Protocol will not start until 2008, pilot-phase projects (mainly in European countries) have shown that policies on the Kyoto Mechanisms, along with reduction targets, have great potential to bring the international agenda on climate change into a national policy arena in a concrete manner, and facilitate the industry and business sector, for example, to consider initiatives to prevent climate change.

Apart from policy mechanisms that bring international forces into the domestic policy arena, we have, as described in the previous section, the multi-stakeholder dialogues of the UN CSD as the only framework at present in the UN functioning commissions that make a direct link between international and domestic arenas by engaging various multi-stakeholders.[41] MSD-CSD has contributed to legitimizing the involvement of NGOs at national and local-level policy-making in many countries. In this sense, the existence of MSD-CSD can by itself be re-garded as an international force directed to national and subnational arenas.

Although forces have been recognized to link the domestic and in-ternational arenas, currently institutional (and non-institutional) vertical linkage has been neither sufficiently addressed in practice nor stressed in multilateral negotiation forums such as the WSSD process. Sustainable development cannot be achieved unless the internationally agreed norm is translated in the form of policy, and there seems to be an institutional gap between these two arenas. In a sense this gap is obvious in the cur-rent sovereign state system in international anarchy, but somehow the gap should be narrowed in order to achieve the sustainable development goal.

A study entitled "Global Change and Local Places: Estimating, Un-derstanding and Reducing Greenhouse Gases" by the Association of American Geographers (AAG) Global Change and Local Places (GCLP) Research Group has shown the following results.[42] Their argu-ment, based on their four case studies on US local actions to combat cli-mate change, showed that many local managers or representatives of major emitters recognized the benefits of switching fuels and upgrading technologies to emit less GHGs. And, therefore, there was a "widespread preference for state and local regulatory oversight rather than by the federal government", because emissions abatement is recognized as pri-marily a local activity.[43] However, "decisions about applications of many of the technological opportunities could not be made by local managers", and most of the political or economic decisions take place within the context of larger-scale policies.[44] More importantly, the current institu-tional framework of incentives and mandates is not designed to encour-age local actions so that local actors can act locally on global issues. Therefore, they argue, government and business leaders at national and global levels should give local communities more control over their ac-tivities and provide technology options and other tools suited for local conditions, and should develop more persuasive rewards for emission-reduction initiatives at local level in order to make full use of the poten-tial for GHG emissions reduction.

This kind of lack of authority is one of the reasons why local actors cannot produce the innovative and locally plausible responses to prob-lems that lead to a better regime design. Apart from this problem, there are also other barriers. But before going into details of the barriers, we should also pay attention to the institutional implication of the gaps. As a central part of the framework for global environmental governance, currently more than 200 multilateral environmental agreements exist.[45] Dealing with these MEAs is, however, not an easy task at a domestic level, because each MEA has requirements that cut across several governmental agencies. In other words, the responsibility for dealing with one global environmental MEA falls into more than one ministry and/or agency at a national level due to the interdisciplinary nature of an environmental issue.

This means that, first, domestic horizontal coordination is necessary in order to accommodate the vertical linkage, because MEA requirements fall into several agencies at national level (domestic coordination here includes both national and local-level coordination). The UNU's study on how MEAs are dealt with by national agencies has pointed out that institutional coordination, which includes communication and information sharing among various bodies related to MEA negotiations and implementation, is vitally important for better environmental governance. It recommends that international and regional institutions can help countries by creating tools, including models of best practice, case studies, and plans to provide examples and instructions that will guide the design of harmonized programmes.[46] Better coordination between various MEA negotiating bodies as well as implementing bodies at domestic level has central importance for creating synergies and eliminating overlap costs for a better environmental governance structure.

Secondly, non-institutionalized vertical linkage should be enhanced and facilitated in order to bring the vertical elements into the horizontal coordination procedures. In this regard, the scientific community and NGOs hold vitally important roles in realizing sustainable development governance.

As for global to local forces, there has not yet been a sufficient link between these two arenas, as the AAG-GCLP study has shown.[47] Internationally decided agreements ought to be implemented at an appropriate level of government policy, as a number of governments have recognized the value of subsidiarity since the UN Conference on Environment and Development (UNCED).[48] The fact that global to local linkages have not yet been established sufficiently means that we should look at the barriers to narrowing the gaps between the international arena and the local level that is "the sphere of government closest to the people".[49]

The International Council for Local Environmental Initiatives (ICLEI) sees that "sufficient, coordinated action has not yet taken place" in order to link local government with the global decision-making process.[50] The authority and resources required to meet the needs of citizens effectively have not yet been transferred to local authorities. Furthermore, even if a local authority does provide necessary actions, such as combating air pollution, so far gains at the local level are being undermined by the loss of local influence to multilateral bodies that make decisions on macro-level policies.[51] Therefore, there remain many spaces where better-informed policies and policies more rooted in the international norms and agreements can be implemented. The following points may account for the barriers that hinder the link between local and global policy arenas.

Lack of information network

There is a growing demand in local authorities to learn the practical experience and knowledge of other local authorities in overcoming environmental problems such as air pollution or water pollution. However, there is a lack of an information network that allows local authorities from the North and the South to obtain necessary information on possible international local-to-local cooperation. On the supply side, even though some authorities know what they can offer out of their experience and knowledge, there is no effective information network to provide other authorities with such information. The system that has been used mostly to find counterparts is the brother/sister city kind of relationship. The same problem may be said of the demand side.[52] Authorities would like to find the best place to learn the best experience and knowledge. However, since there is no effective information network, they have either to visit other places one after another, or use the relationship of brother/sister city in order to find their partners. Using the connection of brother/sister city is beneficial in the sense that there is a certain level of cooperation established between them so it is easier to get on track. Also, because a brother/sister city relationship is likely to be established on the similar strategic characteristics of the cities, such as industrial or cultural position in the country, a cooperation arrangement between brother/sister cities may easily sit within the overall strategy of the cities, and thus be supported by constituents. However, this does not guarantee that authorities can acquire the best experience and knowledge. Moreover, the information tends to be collected in the capital city, which is sometimes far from the rural people who often need such information most urgently. For them, participation in international forums such as the MSD-CSD is often not financially supported.

Furthermore, even in the case that the importance of a network is recognized, to institutionalize a network between local people and people beyond the border is difficult, due partly to human resources and language. Local people often have difficulty in speaking other languages than their own, thus even when networking is possible, it is based on individual capacity and often not institutionalized. Thus, a sustainable relationship has not been established.

Language barriers

Language can be a barrier for people in non-English-speaking countries in obtaining information, as was pointed out earlier. Local people, both officials and the public, often speak only their own mother tongue. Furthermore, in most developing countries and countries in transition there are usually no funds available for translation at national or local levels.[53]

Limits to resources

Although decentralization is explicitly pursued in documents such as Agenda 21 and Local Agenda 21, authority and resources, including human and financial resources, available to local authorities have in fact been very limited. When funding is available, it is sometimes the case that the local authority does not have control over the funding, and subsequently it can only implement short-term or *ad hoc* projects rather than projects that have the longer-term perspectives which are necessary for environmental protection. This limitation inhibits flexibility and innovation on the part of local government, and undermines its ability to provide the increased efficiency and greater equity that are necessary for the ultimate goal of decentralization. Some domestic and international funding agencies have started to fund local initiatives, but this policy has not yet taken root, partly because of the lack of dissemination of such information, and partly because of the lack of capacity within local authorities.

In addition to the lack of capacity, in many countries even the very legitimacy of the local government is questioned, and this of course causes limitation to the reliability of the local authorities. The reasons for this may be a lack of accountability to constituents, insufficient involvement of citizens in the political process, inadequate representation of all stakeholder interests, insufficient transparency in the governing process, and/or corruption.[54]

Capacity to understand problems beyond the local

A local authority is the government closest to the people. The other side of the coin is that officials in a local authority may be good at grasping problems at their own local jurisdiction but may have difficulty in understanding what happens beyond their jurisdiction. For example, an official in a developed country encountering problems with waste disposal may not only be unable to understand the global context of waste disposal, but also may not have enough scope for thinking of what happens in local communities in Tuvalu where local people are affected by the sea level rising as a consequence of climate change. Generally speaking, local people in developed countries tend to be conscious of local environmental problems whose impacts are discernible to them, but tend to be unconscious of their international contexts and other global environmental problems whose impacts tend to come out in the most serious manner in local communities in the most vulnerable parts of the earth.

Representatives to international negotiations

Although some local governments are very successful in tackling sustainable development issues, it is quite unusual that a local government representative is included in a national delegation to a global conference or an MEA negotiation. Currently they only take part in the multistakeholder dialogue. The inclusion of representatives of local governments in national delegations may bring international norms and principles into local policies.

Concluding remarks: Implications for global environmental governance

Apart from the academic literature, so far little attention has been paid to the importance of vertical linkage, or what Young calls "vertical interplay".[55] However, there are needs for enhancing vertical linkage, and there are forces emerging recently to facilitate narrowing the vertical distance, be it adjacent or remote arrangements. The emerging forces are summarized in Table 5.2. The following six points emerge out of the examination of this chapter, and may fill in the gap and create more solid vertical linkage.

- Although state representatives may continue to be the main actors in "international" negotiation, non-governmental multi-stakeholder participation (including researchers and scientists) in international negotiation should be enhanced and facilitated. This can make the negotiation text more rooted in reality and more informed, and also make the commitment to implementation stronger. Given the higher profile of NGOs and business/industry organizations these days, "interactive diplomacy" has a great potential to enrich negotiation texts in terms of the wider social backbone. Financial support for their participation, especially for those from developing countries, should be enhanced. In this regard, including them in government delegations, where relevant, may be one possibility. Their inclusion can also diversify and enhance expertise and ideas, so that they may even have the capacity for intellectual leadership.[56]
- Non-governmental multi-stakeholders participating in international negotiation should also be involved in domestic or local-level policy processes. So far, there seems to be a work division between "international people" and "domestic people", but integration can bring international perspectives and ongoing international ideas into domestic policies, which is particularly important for policies at a local level. Local policies are much more segregated into small sections than in-

Table 5.2 Forces and barriers around vertical linkages

	International relations approach	NGOs	Science	Policy and institutions
International		• Participate in domestic decision-making and implementation	• International research institutions' proposals and partnerships with government • "Type 2" • Participate in national epistemic community	• MEA (including mechanisms) • International pressure (norms, international opinion) • MSD
Interaction and barriers Local	• Two-level games • Vertical interplay • Interactive diplomacy etc.	Barrier • Information • Language • Institution (including resources and capacity) • Too many MEAs and requirements • Participate in international decision-making • Through/as delegation	• Provide research results to like-minded states • Participate in epistemic communities	• Policies with external dimensions (big power) • Innovative policies/setting an example (small/middle powers) • Regulation led by business/industry coalition with CSOs

ternational decision-makers would think. Policy segregation may be a result of the necessity for concrete policy implementation, but some extent of recognition of linkages with other issues may help improve further effectiveness in terms of both environmental integrity and economic effectiveness. Scientists and other multi-stakeholders' participation in domestic policy processes may also facilitate horizontal policy coordination, which is necessary for effective implementation of the various MEAs.

- In order to facilitate grass-roots multi-stakeholder participation in domestic and international policy processes, language and information barriers that have hindered their participation should be eliminated. In this regard, capacity building, education, and technology transfer are effective, and have great importance in terms of narrowing the vertical gap, too. The emergence of international demands to enhance environmental education during the WSSD process is welcomed in this connection.
- A domestic policy may become innovative by taking into account international perspectives, and not just taking domestic political situations into account. An innovative policy may appear to be advantageous in exerting international influence. This will be very important for developing countries, too, in the years to come. For example, when climate change negotiations start focusing on the inclusion of developing countries, what developing countries have by way of a domestic policy may turn out to have a positive (or negative) influence on the result of the international negotiation. In other cases, local-level "triangular" initiatives of business-NGO-state partnerships may turn out to create a "triangular" diplomacy.[57]
- Subsidiarity should be seriously and realistically taken into account in domestic policies, including in terms of financial resources.
- International agreements need to pay more attention to international and domestic links. At present most of the discussions deal with international and domestic arenas separately, and divide the levels into global, regional, national, and local levels, as is seen in the discussion leading up to the WSSD. Linkage has been paid less attention. Paying more attention to vertical linkages will reduce the loss of resources that is produced through friction between levels. In this connection, a possibility for improved synergy between levels may exist in enhancing the regional level as a device that bridges the gap between national and global levels, as Jonathan Strand argues in this volume.

It has been argued that the current situation around multilateralism is a contest between the "old" and the "new" forms of multilateralism. The existing state-centric multilateralim is a top-down affair that "coordinates relations among three or more states on the basis of generalized principles of conduct". The new, emerging form of multilateralism is based upon the participation of global civil society and is built from the bottom up.[58] As has been seen in this chapter, there are forces and practical actions to converge the "top" and the "bottom". In terms of domestic-international linkage, the important thing is narrowing the gap between those two arenas by accommodating the forces from both domestic and international sides in the institutional design. To date, however, systematic policy-oriented research about how vertical linkage can be effectively created and institutionally accommodated has been rare. Narrowing vertical gaps is as important as narrowing the horizontal gaps. Therefore, equal attention needs to be paid to vertical linkage as growing attention has been paid to horizontal interlinkages.

Notes

1. For example, Putnam, R. D. 1988. "Diplomacy and domestic politics: The logic of two-level games", *International Organization*, Vol. 42, No. 3, pp. 427–460; Evans, P. B., H. K. Jacobson, and R. D. Putnam (eds). 1993. *Double-edged Diplomacy: International Bargaining and Domestic Politics*. Berkeley: University of California Press; Keohane, R. O. and H. V. Milner. 1996. *Internationalization and Domestic Politics*. Cambridge: Cambridge University Press; Schreurs, M. A. and E. C. Economy (eds). 1997. *The Internationalization of Environmental Protection*. Cambridge: Cambridge University Press; Rosenau, James N. 1997. *Along the Domestic-Foreign Frontier: Exploring Governance in a Turbulent World*. Cambridge: Cambridge University Press.
2. According to the Commission on Global Governance, governance is defined as "the sum of the many ways individuals and institutions, public and private, manage their common affairs". See Commission on Global Governance. 1995. *Our Global Neighbourhood: The Report of the Commission on Global Governance*. Oxford: Oxford University Press.
3. Schreurs and Economy, note 1 above, p. 3.
4. *Ibid.*
5. Young, Oran R. 2002. *The Institutional Dimensions of Environmental Change: Fit, Interplay, and Scale*. Cambridge, MA: MIT Press, p. 85.
6. Waltz, Kenneth N. 1979. *Theory of International Politics*. Reading, MA: Addison-Wesley.
7. Of course, there had been challenges to the realist interpretation of international relations before this. See, for example, Singer, J. D. 1961. "The level-of-analysis problem in international relations", *World Politics*, Vol. 14, pp. 77–92; Rosenau, James N. (ed.). 1969. *Linkage Politics: Essays on the Convergence of National and International Systems*. New York: Free Press.
8. Keohane and Milner, note 1 above; Economy, E. C. and M. A. Schreurs. 1997. "Domestic and international linkages in environmental politics", in M. A. Schreurs and E. C. Economy (eds) *The Internationalization of Environmental Protection*. Cambridge: Cambridge University Press.
9. Putnam, note 1 above, p. 473.
10. Evans, Jacobson, and Putnam, note 1 above; Schreurs and Economy, note 1 above; Underdal, A. and K. Hanf (eds). 2000. *International Environmental Agreements and Domestic Politics: The Case of Acid Rain*. Hampshire: Ashgate.

11. Young, note 5 above, pp. 84–85.
12. Cooper, Andrew F. 2002. "Like-minded nations, NGOs, and the changing pattern of diplomacy within the UN system: An introductory perspective", in Andrew F. Cooper, John English, and Ramesh Thakur (eds) *Enhancing Global Governance: Towards A New Diplomacy*. Tokyo: United Nations University Press. Furthermore, even state delegations have begun to include non-state actors in some cases.
13. Based on Cooper, *ibid.*
14. Princen, T. and M. Finger. 1994. *Environmental NGOs in World Politics: Linking the Local and the Global*. London: Routledge.
15. For more details on the account of CSO-business/industry partnerships, see the chapter by Mikoto Usui in this volume.
16. Elias, V. 2000. "Who is aware of Agenda 21? Missing conditions: Three major barriers", in F. Dodds (ed.) *Earth Summit 2002*. London: Earthscan, p. 32.
17. Hemmati, Minu (ed.). 2002. *Multi-stakeholder Processes for Governance and Sustainability: Beyond Deadlock and Conflict*. London: Earthscan.
18. Dodds, F. 2002. "The context: Multi-stakeholder processes and global governance", in Minu Hemmati (ed.) *Multi-stakeholder Processes for Governance and Sustainability: Beyond Deadlock and Conflict*. London: Earthscan, p. 33. Major groups identified in Agenda 21 are women, youth, indigenous peoples, NGOs, business and industry, workers and trade unions, the science and technology industry, farmers, and local authorities. In this chapter the term NGO is more widely defined, and all the major groups except for local authorities are referred to as NGOs.
19. Ringius, Lasse. 1999. "Differentiation, leaders, and fairness: Negotiating climate commitments in the European Community", *International Negotiation*, Vol. 2, No. 4, pp. 133–166; Kanie, Norichika. 2001. *Chikyu Kankyou Gaiko to Kokunaiseisaku: Kyoto Giteisho wo meguru Ofanda no Gaikou to Seisaku (Global Environmental Diplomacy and Domestic Policy: The Netherlands at the Kyoto Protocol Negotiation)*. Tokyo: Keio University Press; Kanie, Norichika. 2003. "Leadership in multilateral negotiation and domestic policy: The Netherlands at the Kyoto Protocol negotiation", *International Negotiation*, Vol. 8, No. 2, pp. 339–365.
20. Andrew F. Cooper, John English, and Ramesh Thakur (eds) *Enhancing Global Governance: Towards A New Diplomacy*. Tokyo: United Nations University Press.
21. Haas, Peter M. 1990. *Saving the Mediterranean: The Politics of International Environmental Cooperation*. New York: Columbia University Press; Haas, Peter M. (ed.). 1992. *Knowledge, Power, and International Policy Coordination*. Columbia: University of South Carolina Press; Herter, C. A. Jr and J. E. Binder. 1993. "The role of the secretariat in multilateral negotiation", Foreign Policy Institute Case Studies No. 21. Washington, DC: SAIS, Johns Hopkins University.
22. Economy and Schreurs, note 8 above.
23. Haas, Peter M. 2000. "Choosing to comply: Theorizing from international relations and comparative politics", in D. Shelton (ed.) *Commitment and Compliance: The Role of Non-binding Norms in the International Legal System*. Oxford: Oxford University Press, p. 43.
24. Kanie 2001, note 19 above; Kanie 2003, note 19 above.
25. Liefferink, Duncan. 1997. "The Netherlands: A net exporter of environmental policy concepts", in Mikael Skou Andersen and Duncan Liefferink (eds) *European Environmental Policy: The Pioneers*. Manchester: Manchester University Press, p. 214.
26. Underdal, A. 1994. "Leadership theory: Rediscovering the arts of management", in I. William Zartman (ed.) *International Multilateral Negotiation: Approaches to the Management of Complexity*. San Francisco: Jossey-Bass, pp. 178–197 at p. 185.
27. *Ibid.*

28. Allenby, Branden R. 1999. *Industrial Ecology Policy Framework and Implementation.* Upper Saddle River, NJ: Prentice Hall, p. 265; De Jongh, Paul E. and Sean Captain. 1999. *Our Common Journey: A Pioneering Approach to Cooperative Environmental Management.* London and New York: Zed Books.
29. DeSombre, Elizabeth R. 2000. *Domestic Sources of International Environmental Policy: Industry, Environmentalists, and US Power.* Cambridge, MA and London: MIT Press, p. 244.
30. *Ibid.*
31. Hemmati, note 17 above.
32. The CSD was established in 1993 by ECOSOC Decision 1993/207, and accredits more than 1,000 NGOs.
33. Dodds, note 18 above.
34. Kanie 2003, note 19 above.
35. Elias, note 16 above.
36. *Ibid.*, p. 36.
37. Haas 1990, note 21 above; Haas 1992, note 21 above; Herter and Binder, note 21 above.
38. Hemmati, note 17 above.
39. Haas, note 23 above.
40. World Commission on Environment and Development. 1997. *Our Common Future.* Oxford: Oxford University Press.
41. Dodds, note 18 above.
42. Kates, Robert W. and Thomas J. Wilbanks. 2003. "Making the global local: Responding to climate change concerns from the ground up", *Environment*, Vol. 45, No. 3, pp. 12–23.
43. *Ibid.*, p. 19.
44. *Ibid.*
45. Royal Institute of International Affairs. 2000. *Global Environmental Institutions: Analysis and Options for Change.* London: Royal Institute of International Affairs, p. 30.
46. Van Toen, C. 2001. "Delegates' perceptions on synergies and the implementation of MEAs: Views from the ESCAP region", UNU Discussion Paper Series 2001–2002. Tokyo: United Nations University Global Environment Information Centre.
47. Kates and Wilbanks, note 42 above.
48. Subsidiarity means that "service delivery should be performed by the most immediate sphere of government which can best address constituent needs while maintaining economic and administrative efficiencies of scale and scope". See ICLEI. 2001. "Local government dialogue paper for the World Summit on Sustainable Development", E/CN.17/2002/PC.2/6/Add. 5.
49. *Ibid.*
50. *Ibid.*
51. *Ibid.*
52. Personal interview with a civil servant attending the Conference on International Cooperation on Sustainable Development, 18 November 2001, Kitakyushu, Japan.
53. Elias, note 16 above.
54. ICLEI, note 48 above.
55. Young, note 5 above.
56. Little is know in this field, however. The functions and effects of multi-stakeholder participation in global decision-making processes in the form of national delegation members need to be researched further.
57. Strange, S. 1992. "States, firms and diplomacy", *Foreign Affairs*, Vol. 68, No. 1, pp. 1–15; Cooper, note 12 above.
58. Regarding "new" and "old" forms of multilateralism, see Ruggie, J. G. (ed.). 1993.

Multilateralism Matters: The Theory and Praxis of an Institutional Form. New York and Chichester: Columbia University Press; Cox, R. W. (ed.). 1997. *The New Realism: Perspectives on Multilateralism and World Order.* Hampshire and London: Macmillan/United Nations University Press; Gill, S. (ed.). 1997. *Globalisation, Democratisation and Multilateralism.* Hampshire and London: Macmillan/United Nations University Press; O'Brien, R., A. M. Goetz, J. A. Scholte, and M. Williams. 2000. *Contesting Global Governance: Multilateral Economic Institutions and Global Social Movements.* London and New York: Cambridge University Press. Quote from Ruggie.

Science-policy interface for environmental governance

6

Science policy for multilateral environmental governance

Peter M. Haas[1]

The need for science policy applied to the management of transboundary and global environmental threats is now widely recognized. This chapter looks at lessons about the scientific functions that need to be performed to achieve effective multilateral environmental governance, and the institutional design by which such functions may be best performed.

Much of the current context of international environmental governance, for which policy advice is needed, is one of uncertainty. Global environmental systems are characterized by non-linear, complex behaviour associated with cumulative environmental change with both short-term and long-term consequences.[2] Funtowicz and Ravetz write:

Whereas science was previously understood as steadily advancing the certainty of our knowledge and control of the natural world, it is now seen as coping with many uncertainties in urgent technological and environmental decisions on a global scale. A new role for scientists will involve the management of the crucial uncertainties: therein lies the task of assuring the quality of the scientific information provided for policy decisions. Moreover ... "scientific evidence has a long row to hoe to have a distinctive impact on policy".[3]

Under such circumstances, decision-makers need information about the nature of threats, how each actor will be affected, and the types of arrangements that can be collectively developed to address such transboundary and global risks.

The relevant body of scientific knowledge that is needed is here termed "usable knowledge".[4] Usable knowledge is accurate information that is of use to politicians and policy-makers. It must be accurate, and politically tractable for its users. It frequently exceeds the mastery of any traditional disciplinary approach.

Clark and Majone[5] offer four criteria of usable knowledge: its adequacy, value, legitimacy, and effectiveness. Adequacy relates to including all the relevant knowledge or facts germane to the matter at hand. Value has to do with contributing to further understanding and meaningful policy. Legitimacy relates to its acceptance by others outside the community that developed it. Effectiveness relates to its ability to shape the agenda or advance the state of the debate, and, ultimately, improve the quality of the environment.

Yet science has become extremely politicized. It is often found that good science falls on deaf ears, or is met with bad science, when the politics favour neglecting it. Writers in the field of science, technology, and society investigate the implicit values and the distributional consequences of science.[6] Three challenges to its authority are often raised. Scientific consensus is often suspect because the scientists themselves are part of a broader cultural discourse, and thus lack autonomy or independent stature: scientific findings may reflect the bias of sponsors. Secondly, the use of science is mediated and thus possibly distorted by the political goals of potential users. Thirdly, science is political in its consequences, because some benefit and others suffer as a consequence of policy options that are supported by the application of scientific understanding. To the extent that those affected by the use of science in formulating policy are not consulted in its development and application, the use of science is potentially regarded by those affected as an illegitimate and exploitative set of discursive practices.

Thus the possibility for accuracy is questioned, and the political tractability is undermined by the reduced political authority of science to offer meaningful statements about the threats, their urgency, and responses. If recipients are not confident in the usefulness of scientific knowledge it will not be used.

Yet many still regard science advice as necessary, even if its philosophical expectations are somewhat reduced. Current research from comparative politics, IR, policy studies, and democratic theory suggests that science remains influential if its expertise and claims are developed behind a politically insulated wall.[7] Ravetz and Funtowicz argue for a procedural approach to developing usable knowledge by including multiple disciplines and multiple stakeholders.[8]

A new consensus is emerging amongst social scientists who study the use of science in international regimes. They suggest that science must be developed authoritatively, and then delivered by responsible carriers to politicians. The more autonomous and independent science is from policy, the great its potential influence.[9] Consensus in isolation builds value and integrity, and then its consequences should be discussed publicly. Measures of autonomy and integrity include the selection and funding of scientists by IOs rather than by governments, their recruitment by merit on important panels, and reliance on individuals whose reputation and authority rest on their role as active researchers rather than policy advocates or science administrators. Accuracy can be achieved via peer review, interdisciplinary research teams, and independence from sponsoring sources.

Political legitimacy rests on a process of knowledge development and diffusion that is scrupulously free of political interference. International institutions can help foster and disseminate information, and sanitize it so that it is not seen as compromised by potential users who may fear that the information is controlled by one country. Studies of national-level environmental policy processes have convincingly argued against relying on individual institutions for research and policy advice, because they may bias the information flow and control resources.[10]

Partial lessons are available from national experiences with the use of science policy, and their design of institutions to generate usable science. A major lesson from efforts in the USA to provide usable knowledge for domestic policy-making – the National Transportation Safety Board, the Office of Technology Assessment, and the international trade commissions – is that political impartiality is vital if technical information is to be used as the foundation for policy, in terms of leadership that does not correspond to political election cycles and recruitment on merit. The timely submission of reports according to the legislative cycle is also key.[11] While national monitoring efforts have been critiqued for their mismatch with the legislative timescales, at the international level, where regimes are administered by secretariats and COPs (conferences of the parties) that meet periodically, surprising monitoring results can be effectively introduced into the following year's agenda for addressing new threats.

While international institutions often have fewer resources and less autonomy than their national counterparts, international institutions often have a stronger influence over the supply of usable knowledge when they are not monolithic. Effective international institutions in the environmental and sustainable development domains have been those which operate through networks composed of other international institutions and elements of civil society.[12]

Scientific functions

Usable science covers a range of understandings. Dimitrov distinguishes between knowledge about the extent of the problem, knowledge about the causes of the problem, and knowledge about its consequences for human societies.[13] The Social Learning Group volumes distinguish between six different categories of knowledge as it is used in the conduct of policy formation: monitoring, risk assessment, options, goals and strategies, implementation, and evaluation.[14]

The focus here is on a smaller number of science policy functions that are widely believed to be necessary for effective multilateral environmental policy: basic knowledge, environmental monitoring, and policy advice. The data are drawn from an e-mail survey administered to MEA (multilateral environmental agreement, or regime) secretariats, secondary literature on MEAs, and the *Yearbook of International Cooperation on Environment and Development*.[15] A summary of the findings is presented in Table 6.1.

When each scientific policy function is performed well, in conjunction they can contribute to effective environmental governance. By effective governance is meant improved environmental quality that is the consequence of changed state policies influenced by international regimes. Examples where well-designed science policy functions correlate with environmental improvement include stratospheric ozone protection and European acid rain. Efforts to protect the Mediterranean Sea from pollution are a moderate example, where mobilized science informed policymaking but the quality of the monitoring remains sketchy. Efforts to protect other regional seas from pollution often lack any systematic scientific involvement, and have few accomplishments to date in terms of their ability to reverse environmental degradation.[16]

There are multiple causal links between the performance of these science functions and effective governance. Usable knowledge can influence states' political will and technical ability to address environmental threats through the provision of an institutional venue for holding cooperative meetings, by improving the capacity for environmental planning and protection, and by enhancing the concern of government officials and élites about the nature, extent, and magnitude of environmental threats. Each scientific function, if well performed, may contribute to more effective multilateral environmental governance as states learn of new threats and new ways to respond to problems that confront them.[17] Good monitoring can provide informational resources to actors who will publicize issues and contribute to agenda setting and setting collective norms and rules. Usable policy advice can educate government officials, improve the quality of environmental policies, and contribute to robust regime formation.

In addition, well-designed and well-performed scientific functions may be interactive. For instance, climate change monitoring has provoked political action to set meaningful goals for reducing greenhouse gas emissions. Stratospheric ozone monitoring encourages states to ban CFCs, and then move to accelerate the pace of their elimination as well as expanding the list of regulated substances. Ozone monitoring has also eased verification of state compliance with their obligations, as well as evaluating the effectiveness of the regime. In European acid rain regulation, monitoring led to the formulation of alternative policy responses to prevent acidification, as decision-makers became aware of new ecosystems at risk.[18] Next the chapter looks at ways to organize monitoring and policy advice better to improve effectiveness.

Basic science is the development of understanding of the behaviour of transboundary and global ecosystems, at a level of resolution that provides meaningful information to policy-makers about environmental effects at national and subnational levels. Improvements in basic science can contribute to agenda setting, early warning, and policy choice.

Monitoring is the systematic collection of information about environmental quality. Accurate monitoring may lead to prompt agenda setting, as well as to improving implementation by virtue of the shaming effect of monitoring data, and to evaluation by providing data about regime performance and observed environmental change in the target variable. Most verification, though, relies on direct information about policy implementation, rather than on indirect measures of national environmental performance.[19] This section does not discuss systems of verification, as they generally do not rely on science but on voluntary submission or observations by third-party observers.

Policy advice involves the choice of specific national and collective measures to address environmental degradation. Policy advice is likely to influence the substance of international regime obligations and national environmental policy, as well as national compliance and regime effectiveness.

Science is necessary for good policy, albeit not for cooperation. Cooperation without science occurs, but scientifically informed cooperation has been more effective. It is necessary for good regime performance and well-crafted policy. MEAs that have successfully reduced environmental degradation all had arrangements for the provision of usable knowledge, leading to the collective adoption of policies that were reasonably linked to achieving tolerable levels of environmental protection at socially acceptable costs. Moreover, supported by influential international institutions, usable knowledge helped to persuade governments

Table 6.1 Provisions for science in selected MEAs

Regime/MEA	Effectiveness	Monitoring	Science and policy	Comments
Stratospheric ozone	Very effective. Ozone-depleting substances have been eliminated and the ozone layer is significantly better than it would have been in the absence of regulations. Most CFC producers comply with the regime.	Governments monitor own emissions, and submit data to the secretariat. UNEP and NASA conduct independent monitoring of the stratospheric ozone layer.	The COP receives annual reports from the three expert panels: Scientific Assessment Panel, Technology and Economics Assessment Panel, and Environmental Effects Assessment Panel. The secretariat and chairs enjoy some discretion in appointing members to the panels based on merit.	
Acid rain/ LRTAP	Very effective at reducing emissions of sulphur and nitrogen. Most LRTAP countries comply with the regime.	Regularized monitoring programme (EMEP) of a variety of acidifying substances, with national reporting stations reporting to two national laboratories that report to the secretariat. Secretariat involves independent scientists to ensure adequacy of data.	Policies are adopted by executive body committees. Expert advice comes from the Working Group on Strategies and Review, made up of experts officially nominated by their governments. The lead country can invite additional experts. NGOs may request participation, and the choice is made by the secretariat or the executive body committee. UNECE Secretariat and IIASA work with a network of university-based modellers to provide estimates of critical loads for policy adoption.	

Biodiversity	Not effective	No monitoring entity established. Parties are obligated to develop national strategies that contain some monitoring data, and are submitted to the secretariat and then made public. NGOs follow the reports and publicize findings.	Subsidiary body on scientific, technical, and technical advice (SBSTTA), composed of nationally selected experts, provides technical advice to the COP. NGOs may be invited to participate.
CCAMLR/ Antarctica		Self-reporting, no centralized authority.	Scientific committee receives inputs from the Working Group on Ecosystem Monitoring and Management. WG considers results of national research. WG is composed of government-designated experts. Secretariat has little autonomy.
Whaling	Moratorium has reversed decline of endangered whale species. Continued whaling by Japan, Iceland, and Norway of non-endangered species threatens the legitimacy of the regime.	No formal monitoring programme. Scientific committee is developing a comprehensive assessment of whale stocks.	Moratorium applied by the COP since 1986. Scientific committee developed revised management procedure in 1994 that is not followed.

Table 6.1 (cont.)

Regime/MEA	Effectiveness	Monitoring	Science and policy	Comments
Mediterranean Sea	Governments have made efforts and quality has stabilized.	National laboratories conduct monitoring (MEDPOL) according to a common protocol and submit results to IAEA laboratory or national laboratories, but great inconsistency in national reports makes synoptic conclusions impossible. Monitoring quality is hampered by political capacity.	Secretariat has the authority to appoint scientists to standing committees. Independent panels help to develop standards for achieving reductions of land-based pollutants.	
North Sea	Governments have made efforts, unclear that the sea is much cleaner.	*Ad hoc* governmental-nominated monitoring programme.	Policy is developed by government-led panels. While membership and agendas are set by states, lead countries have incentives to publicize stronger environmental measures and technologies.	

Climate change	Low, few legal obligations have been adopted, and GHGs have increased from major parties since 1990.	Annex I (AICs) governments monitor GHG emissions and submit triennial reports to the secretariat for review by teams of government-nominated experts, coordinated by the secretariat. Reports were submitted in 1994; 1997–1998; and 2001.	The COP is composed of ministers and high-ranking officials of participating countries. It meets to consider reports from the IPCC and the subsidiary body for scientific and technical advice (SBSTA). The IPCC provides science policy advice. Its members are nominated by governments, and rely on peer-reviewed materials for their reports.	The IPCC suffers from a legitimacy crisis of governmental nomination, although formal design may allow for scientific integrity.
Baltic Sea	Governments have made efforts, unclear that the sea is much cleaner.	Regularized national laboratories conduct monitoring.	Policy is developed by government-led panels. While membership and agendas are set by states, lead countries have incentives to publicize stronger environmental measures and technologies.	Imaginative innovation of national leadership on policy committees.

that their own self-interest was associated with preserving ecological integrity.

Yet usable knowledge alone is neither necessary nor sufficient for environmental cooperation. For instance, the North Sea governments adopted a series of ministerial declarations during the 1980s to achieve 30–50 per cent reductions in the emissions of a large number of contaminants. However, in the absence of usable knowledge about the transfer and deposition of contaminants in the North Sea, the environmental effects of such regulations are unknown. In compliance with North Sea ministerial declarations, the UK government has stopped dumping sewage sludge in the North Sea, even when scientific evidence suggests that the UK contribution was marginal to North Sea environmental quality.

National ability to engage in multilateral environmental governance

Ultimately, environmental monitoring requires participation by most states. Yet many governments lack the capacity to perform most of these environmental functions effectively. Many states lack the staff and technology to monitor their environments effectively. Governments vary broadly in their administrative ability to develop and enforce environmental policies. A widespread problem facing environment ministries in developing country governments is the small number of professional staff, small budgets, and weak political influence over policy by the rest of the government. Since foreign environmental policy is generally the result of consultations amongst a number of functionally responsible agencies, a politically weak environmental body undermines the overall ability to form effective national environmental policy. Many governments could benefit from adding science assessment units to their foreign ministries.

There is a strong need for resource transfers to build national capability. A policy implication is to concentrate institution-building efforts on countries in important geographic regions facing pressing transboundary and global environmental threats, such as China, Brazil, and India. International institutions can exercise limited forms of conditionality in order to increase public resources for environmental agencies, and international institutions and NGOs can work to elevate the profile of national environmental agencies and their staffs.

Basic science

Basic science can provide a basic understanding of complex systems. Usable basic science should still be capable of expressing major threats to environmental quality, the consequences of different levels of environmental quality, and some sense of ecosystems' responsiveness to stresses. Consensual knowledge about basic ecosystem behaviour has been effectively used when it commands usable information about the behaviour of a particular ecosystem – such as the Mediterranean, stratospheric ozone, or European weather patterns – rather than a more comprehensive and fundamental understanding of global patterns (such as global biogeochemical cycles).

Keckes argues that a number of research programmes are under way that may "improve the knowledge about the physical, chemical and biological processes which form the basis for maintenance and functioning of marine ecosystems and the interaction of these processes with those taking place in the atmosphere and on land, including social and economic development".[20]

The Global Environmental Change Programme is an example of this, but has yet to provide the consensus for a systematic understanding of global ecosystems.[21] SCOPE panels, organized under the auspices of the International Council of Scientific Unions, have also tried to organize knowledge about the behaviour of core ecosystemic cycles. The current Millennium Ecosystem study focuses on living systems, and similar efforts have been made to accumulate knowledge about specific ecosystems. Much of this understanding remains to be developed. Knowledge remains concentrated on the behaviour of specific ecosystems, rather than of the earth as a whole.

Studies of global change science also address the substantive nature and the process by which such basic understanding is to be achieved. William Clark argues that:

[Substantive] knowledge systems for sustainability will require an unprecedented degree of integration. Expertise from the communities of environmental conservation, human health, and economic development will need to be harnessed in problem-solving efforts. Particularly challenging will be drawing into these collaborative endeavors the vast resources of informal expertise that comes from practical experience in grappling with particular sustainability problems in particular social and ecological settings.[22]

The organization and communication of such systematic knowledge is essential. Not only does such basic knowledge come from collaborative work of groups of scientists representing different disciplines – from both the natural and the social sciences – but they must also be skilled in communicating their knowledge to people from other disciplines, as well as to the media, politicians, and popular audiences.[23] In addition to basic science there is a need to develop better the communication skills for imparting such knowledge to various audience, and to train global change scientists in such techniques.

Monitoring

Effective environmental policy needs an overall assessment of ecosystem health, as well as monitoring of ongoing trends. These are useful for establishing baselines and early-warning systems, as well as for ongoing monitoring of existing efforts to determine if additional effort is required to achieve environmental protection. Monitoring should be impartial, comprehensive, and synoptic. Participants in monitoring programmes should be selected on merit.

Many monitoring schemes are conducted globally.[24] The open oceans are studied through UNESCO's IOC and the International Council for the Exploration of the Sea (ICES). Species-specific fisheries councils, the FAO, and the ICES monitor fisheries. Atmospheric monitoring is conducted by the WMO (World Meteorological Organization). Joint programmes of UNEP, the FAO, the WMO, and the WHO conduct some fresh water quality and urban air quality monitoring. Stratospheric ozone is monitored by UNEP, and European acid rain through LRTAP (the Long Range Transport of Atmospheric Pollution regime, administered by the United Nations Economic Commission for Europe). Biodiversity monitoring is conducted by the World Conservation Monitoring Centre and the World Conservation Union (IUCN). UNEP was initially designed to be responsible for conducting global environmental assessments through its World Watch programme, but these have taken a long time to develop and UNEP lacks the budgetary resources to perform extensive monitoring.[25] UNEP published a *Global Environmental Outlook* in 1997, 1999, and 2002,[26] summarizing trends in some of the major global ecosystems. But the degree of aggregation to achieve public recognition for such global reviews often sacrifices the kind of resolution that would make the monitoring data useful for evaluating actual change over time in controlling emissions and human activities responsible for those emissions.

Most monitoring efforts are organized regionally, within the broader institutional design of MEAs designed to address specific environmental threats, such as UNEP's many regional seas programmes. Some noticeable monitoring gaps remain, such as land use and solid waste disposal.

In practice, environmental monitoring responsibilities as stipulated in MEAs vary widely. Forty-eight MEAs call for environmental quality monitoring. Submission of monitoring reports is mandatory in 81 per cent of the cases, and voluntary in 19 per cent. Annual reports are required in 17 per cent of the MEAs, biannual reports in 19 per cent, and triennial in 2 per cent. The rest are unspecified. Governments are responsible for conducting monitoring in 69 per cent of the MEAs, international institutions are charged with conducting monitoring in 8 per cent of the cases, and governments are instructed to provide their monitoring results to international institutions in 4 per cent of the MEAs. Nineteen per cent of the MEAs have no provisions for who is responsible for performing monitoring. Some MEAs provide for free-standing monitoring committees, nominated by the secretariat based on merit. Other MEAs rely on national submissions, or defer to independent commissions (such as the global monitoring programmes discussed above). Others have rotating bodies, coordinated by the COPs or the rotating chair of the MEA. These last arrangements suffer from poor administration and poorly intercalibrated results. Diffuse national networks are capable of providing information, but suffer from political scepticism because the networks are too closely tied to governmental sources.

Still other MEAs rely on *ad hoc* committees convened periodically to study the environmental quality of a environmental resource, such as the North Sea and the Baltic environmental quality status reports. These efforts have little persistent political influence, and do not generate ongoing useful material. While they may serve a short-term agenda-setting function by publicizing environmental threats, they do not fully serve the monitoring function because assessments may only be made every five years, and the reports do not systematically monitor for the same substances, so no comprehensive picture of the health of the environment emerges. More often these surveys are conducted in order to identify "hot-spots" for policy attention. Inventorying hot-spots, rather than conducting open-ended monitoring, is growing increasingly popular. The Mediterranean, Baltic, and North Seas have all adopted hot-spots programmes. However, if such efforts are at the expense of more general monitoring they exclude the possibility of achieving early warning of new threats.

The best arrangement for organizing monitoring is through free-standing regular standing committees that report on an annual or bi-annual basis to the MEA. Standing committees provide for uniform reporting, with no loss of institutional memory. In conjunction with recruitment provisions based on merit they can confer accurate data about which decision-makers may be confident. While governments often nominate groups to participate in monitoring activities, secretariats can encourage the use of individuals or institutions based on their professional reputations. It is easier to mobilize and consolidate a policy network around standing committees than *ad hoc* ones, or independent commissions unconnected to the MEA. Such committees should also study a standard list of substances over time, so as to be able to provide synoptic information about environmental quality, and provide the data for evaluating the success of a regime at stemming environmental degradation.

NGOs sometimes serve as monitors, particularly in conservation regimes. They may suffer problems with public credibility, though, as their reports are widely suspected of not being partial. However, NGOs serve as useful counterweights to national monitoring reports to ensure accountability.

Monitoring is often insufficiently complete to provide a thorough picture of environmental quality. In addition, monitoring programmes often fail to study the same substances over time, shifting substances in order to provide an early-warning service rather than an overall monitoring function. Even UNEP's three *Global Environmental Outlook* publications treated different substances in each review.[27]

Much of the environment can be monitored remotely from satellites, and does not require the active collection and submission of data by governments.[28] Remote sensing and satellite monitoring would also enhance verification of trends in natural resource use and marine pollution from organic sources and oil, as well as helping in monitoring levels and production of greenhouse gases, although ground truthing is still necessary to confirm remote sensing data. Satellite and airplane base monitoring are less effective at monitoring inorganic marine contamination and urban air quality, for instance, which require localized sampling. More serious than such technical considerations about remote sensing are the political concerns associated with acquiring the information. Some developing countries are loath to cede access to information about their countries, which they regard as a matter of national sovereignty. Assuring intercalibrated results requires careful attention and repeated visits by training teams to assure that similar techniques and equipment are used at each monitoring station.[29]

While most monitoring appears to be subcontracted by governments to universities or government laboratories, it is important that those engaging in the monitoring be suitably trained so that the results are compatible with those from other countries. Some international institutions have provisions for evaluating and calibrating data submitted from national agencies, through some arrangements for third-party evaluation of data – as with LRTAP's two regional data-processing centres.

Funding for monitoring should come from a stable single international source, to counter the short-term political funding cycles of national governments. Some programmes may periodically have insufficient funding, or the substances they monitor may have gaps over time because the sponsors shifted the monitoring agenda to reflect immediate political concerns in their countries.

More attention could be directed to establishing indirect measures of environmental stress. Few efforts have been undertaken to monitor the social driving forces behind environmental contamination, rather than engaging in direct observation of degradation. Closer attention could be paid to human populations at risk as an early-warning sign of environmental degradation, or to patterns of human activity known to generate specific and serious environmental threats. Few examples of such anticipatory monitoring yet exist, and generally exist only for Europe, where data are better. The two Dobris Assessments released by the European Environmental Agency (in 1991 and 1995) looked at social indicators, as have OECD reports and some World Bank publications on energy use and on deforestation.

Policy advice

Scientific consensus can inform policy when groups responsible for articulating consensus have stable access to decision-makers. For instance, in the LRTAP, stratospheric ozone, and Mediterranean MEAs, stable institutional arrangements were in place to transfer scientific consensus about the source and extent of environmental threats, as well as policy responses. In each of those MEAs policy was adopted based on the scientific consensus and the quality of the environment improved, or at least the rate of degradation was slowed.

However, for consensus to be acceptable to leaders it must emerge through channels that are viewed as legitimate by the leaders. Typically these are established when the scientists have a reputation for expertise, when the knowledge was generated beyond suspicion of policy bias by sponsors, and when the information is transmitted to governments through personal networks.[30] These networks, called epistemic communities, can be supported by international institutions – such as UNEP and the Mediterranean Action Plan – and the policy advice will be disseminated from international institutions to governments, from national laboratories and networks up to governments, and from within government administrations to the top levels of decision-making when these individuals are hired as consultants or environmental agency officials. The spread of policy advice is generally through interpersonal channels.

Most science policy is provided in the context of individual regulatory regimes. Thus, different networks are mobilized for each MEA. This is generally the case because usable policy knowledge is highly issue specific: for example, experts in marine policy lack expertise in the management of other environmental media. In addition, national environmental agencies and international institutions are organized functionally to address environmental threats by media: for instance, air pollution experts do not work in the same agency as marine pollution experts and are members of entirely distinct policy networks. The Joint Group of Experts on Scientific Aspects of Marine Pollution (GESAMP) is a rare body that provides periodic reviews of the health or state of the marine environment with a high degree of policy legitimacy for decision-makers.[31] Some efforts, based on bureaucratic desperation in the face of scarce finances and on arguments of economic efficiency, have been taken to combine and cross-fertilize these policy networks by encouraging shared participation in climate change policy seminars with membership from multiple regional seas MEAs. Such consolidation of efforts may serve to broaden policy networks and share policy information, but should not substitute for building organic geographically based networks around common environmental topics.

It is important to keep the basic science and science policy functions distinct, so that the substance of policy suggestions is not tainted by potential influence from funding sponsors. Sponsors of science groups should be different from sponsors of the basic research and activities that generated initial consensus.

Policy advice should be developed and circulated by multidisciplinary international panels. Individuals should be selected by merit and serve in their personal capacity. Ideally they should be chosen by international institutions rather than by governments. The need for independent scientific advice is a matter under current discussion in the Convention on Biodiversity. Policy advice should be based upon peer-reviewed materials.

Climate change science policy is handled by the Intergovernmental Panel on Climate Change (IPCC). The IPCC's authority is hampered by governmental nomination of experts, which has the effect of limiting the perceived political autonomy of the institution. Some political integrity and authority are retained by the extensive peer-review network that scrutinizes all the IPCC publications, yet observers express concern that government nomination of experts may bias the policy analysis towards analyses of social adaptation over mitigation strategies.

Most MEAs rely on standing subsidiary policy bodies to articulate policy-relevant scientific knowledge, draft reports, and respond to queries from the secretariat and government members of the MEA. The biodiversity regime and climate change regime are arranged like this. The ozone regime relies on standing panels of experts that meet regularly. The CCAMLR has scientific experts involved in technical working groups, but the experts are nominated by member governments.

A number of less effective institutional designs for mobilizing science policy have been used as well. Some MEAs rely only on international commissions – such as GESAMP – to provide policy data. Other MEAs' policy foundations are based on *ad hoc* panels convened by MEA bureaus or by the COP chairs, such as pollution control for the South-East Pacific (SEPAC). These *ad hoc* arrangements do not provide usable policy knowledge because they lack legitimacy, and they often also lack institutional memory.[32] Rotating chairs of the COPs – the Atlantic Treaty System and the SEPAC regional seas programme – are a serious detriment to maintaining stability in the science policy network.

Lessons about mobilizing networks of scientific expertise for multilateral environmental governance

Since the Mediterranean Plan and subsequent efforts to generalize the experience to address other transboundary and global environmental threats, the following lessons are apparent about mobilizing usable policy knowledge for environmental governance.[33]

- Carefully survey the population of scientists. In the Mediterranean a UNEP consultant spent nine months visiting national laboratories to inventory national capabilities and personally build the scientific network.
- Ensure that networks and international panels have interdisciplinary representation, including the social sciences. Individuals should have high regard in their own disciplines as well as the ability to talk to experts from other disciplines.
- Recruit carefully for national and regional institutions. Base judgements on professional credentials and networking ability.
- Avoid relying on one national institution to provide research and training.
- Provide professional outlets for members through conferences and publications in refereed professional journals. This also elevates the domestic profile of individual scientists in the community of expertise, who may then be recruited to fill positions in national administrations.
- Promote scientific discussions on topics that are likely to lead to consensus, such as ripe research topics.
- Avoid government designation of scientists to international meetings.
- Try to make use of joint international panels for environmental risk assessment rather than relying on national assessments. Avoid capture by one scientific discipline or school of expert analysis.
- Assure timely submissions in advance of meetings, and avoid single-state sponsorship of collective research.
- Arrange for focused interactions between scientists and policy-makers to discuss the technical substance of the issues. In LRTAP the International Institute for Applied Systems Analysis (IIASA) arranged for two-day sessions to familiarize policy-makers with acid rain transfer and deposition models developed by scientists.

• Maintain momentum within the community by continuing to have projects and research opportunities so members do not drift away. This avoids having to reconstitute the community each time a new problem emerges.

Broader consideration of the proper institutional design of science policy entails timing. When consensus has been achieved before an issue reaches the agenda and policy discussions begin, then scientists can merely be introduced as experts, following the lessons above. However, at times it is necessary simultaneously to develop scientific consensus and advance policy debates. For such issues, as was the case in the Mediterranean and ozone regimes, the development of science policy must be kept insulated from ongoing policy debates, with the two streams united only when consensus has been achieved. In other cases, where consensus remains elusive and policy debates have already attained their own momentum, as in climate change and biodiversity, it may be best if the two activities can be kept as separate as possible.

Financing science

Most secretariats of MEAs responsible for performing various aspects of science policy complain of financial limitations. The budgets of most MEAs, paid by member states, are meagre, and no international institutions have suitable financial resources to perform all the science functions by themselves. The Global Environment Facility (GEF) provides some support for the climate change regime, biodiversity, deforestation, desertification, and stratospheric ozone protection. UNEP helps administer the Montreal Ozone Fund, which also contributes financial support for the transition to non-CFC-based substances. These institutional arrangements are insufficient to provide enough money to pay for environmental protection, much less sustainable development, and secretariat officials are leery of becoming overly reliant on one funding source. The UNDP, World Bank, or private foundations could exercise a profound influence on improving usable knowledge and disseminating it by supporting research programmes and convening conferences and panels to apply basic knowledge to environmental policy.

Conclusion and recommendations

In preparation for Rio+10 many policy analysts pondered what to do with the existing haphazard arrangement of international institutions handling various aspects of science policy and environmental governance.[34] Aspiring institutional designers considered how to streamline and enhance synergies between regimes. Some urged the creation of a new global environmental organization that would centralize all science policy functions, as well as performing policy analysis, centralizing the administration of all the current existing MEAs, and verifying compliance with the MEAs. In principal a GEO would be the single authority – consolidating all existing arrangements – for monitoring the environment and collecting monitoring data.

UNEP was created in 1973 to serve such a centralizing role. But this was in a period when no organizations performed any significant environmental governance functions. In the intervening years other institutions have assumed environmental responsibilities, so the administrative design question is whether to reform the current array of responsibilities or to create a new, centralized organizational structure.

Current thinking in organizational theory seems to run counter to a centralized authority, though. The best-designed institutions for dealing with complex and uncertain policy environments are loose, decentralized, dense networks of institutions that are able to relay information quickly back and forth, and where there are sufficient redundancies in the performance of functions such that the elimination or withdrawal of funding for one institution does not jeopardize the entire network.[35]

Rather than centralizing science policy functions, it may be better to reform many of the existing arrangements and build a centralized source for coordinating information flow between the institutions responsible for performing the different science policy functions. Recruitment patterns should be reformed, so they are uniformly based on merit. Each MEA should have a standing monitoring and science policy body. Open-ended basic research should be conducted, possibly supported by UNEP, in order to anticipate new threats. Greater attention should be focused on the existing gaps in the present science policy structure: waste disposal, fresh water quality, and land-use practices. Concerted efforts should be taken to recruit and train a generation of science advisory experts, capable of working at the interstices of interdisciplinary environmental research while remaining experts in their own domain, and also capable of communicating effectively to people outside their domain. Institutionalized monitoring efforts could be clustered by environmental medium. More generally there is a clear need for expanding and extending capacity-building efforts to include the former centrally planned economies and the newly industrialized countries.

Notes

1. The author is grateful to Kelly Craven for research assistance and to Ron Mitchell and Kathryn Harrison for comments on the questionnaire. Edward Parson provided valuable

information on institutional arrangements for the stratospheric ozone protection regime.

2. Kasperson, Roger E., Jeanne X. Kasperson, and Kirstin Dow. 2001. "Introduction: Global environmental risk and society", in Jeanne X. Kasperson and Roger E. Kasperson (eds) *Global Environmental Risk*. Tokyo: United Nations University Press/ London: Earthscan, pp. 2–5.

3. Funtowicz, Silvio O. and Jerome R. Ravetz. 2001. "Global risk, uncertainty, and ignorance", in Jeanne X. Kasperson and Roger E. Kasperson (eds) *Global Environmental Risk*. Tokyo: United Nations University Press/London: Earthscan, p. 178.

4. For an earlier and slightly different usage, see Clark, William C. (ed.). 1990. *Usable Knowledge for Managing Global Climatic Change*. Stockholm: Stockholm Environment Institute.

5. Social Learning Group. 2001. *Social Learning and the Management of Global Environmental Risks*, 2 volumes. Cambridge, MA: MIT Press, Vol. 1, p. 15; Clark, William C. and Giandomenico Majone. 1985. "The critical appraisal of scientific inquiries with policy implications", *Science, Technology and Human Values*, Vol. 10, No. 3, pp. 6–19.

6. Jasanoff, Sheila, Gerald E. Markle, James C. Petersen, and Trevor Pinch (eds). 1995. *Handbook of Science and Technology Studies*. Thousand Oaks, CA: Sage Publications; Miller, Clark A. and Paul N. Edwards (eds). 2001. *Changing the Atmosphere*. Cambridge, MA: MIT Press.

7. Botcheva, Liliana. 2001. "Expertise and international governance", *Global Governance*, Vol. 7, pp. 197–224; Andresen, Steiner, Tora Skodvin, Arild Underdal, and Jorgen Wettestad. 2000. *Science and Politics in International Environmental Regimes*. Manchester: Manchester University Press; Social Learning Group, note 5 above.

8. Funtowicz, Silvio O. and Jerome R. Ravetz. 1991. "A new scientific methodology for global environmental issues", in Robert Costanza (ed.) *Ecological Economics*. New York: Columbia University Press; Ravetz, Jerome R. 1986. "Usable knowledge, usable ignorance", in William C. Clark and Ted Munn (eds) *Sustainable Development of the Biosphere*. Cambridge: Cambridge University Press, pp. 415–434.

9. Andresen *et al.*, note 7 above; Botcheva, note 7 above; Haas, Peter M. 2001. "Epistemic communities and policy knowledge", in *International Encyclopedia of Social and Behavioural Sciences*. Oxford: Elsevier.

10. Skoie, Hans. 2001. *The Research Councils in the Nordic Countries – Developments and Some Challenges*. Rapport 10/2001. Oslo: Norsk Institutt for Studier av Forskning og utdanning.

11. Brown, George. 1997. "Environmental science under siege in the US Congress", *Environment*, Vol. 39, No. 2, pp. 12–20, 29–31; Morgan, M. Granger and Jon M. Peha (eds). 2003. *Science and Technology Advice for Congress*. Washington, DC: Resources for the Future.

12. Haas, Peter M. and Ernst B. Haas. 1995. "Learning to learn", *Global Governance*, Vol. 1, No. 3, pp. 255–285; Reinicke, Wolfgang H. and Francis Deng. 2000. *Critical Choices*. Ottawa: International Development Research Centre.

13. Dimitrov, R. S. 2003. "Knowledge, power, and interests in environmental regime formation", *International Studies Quarterly*, Vol. 47, No. 1, pp. 123–151.

14. Social Learning Group, note 5 above.

15. *Yearbook of International Cooperation on Environment and Development*, www.greenyearbook.org/.

16. Haas, Peter M. 2001. "Environment: Pollution", in P. J. Simmons and Chantal de Jonge Oudraat (eds) *Managing Global Issues*. Washington, DC: Carnegie Endowment for International Peace.

17. *Ibid.*; Haas, note 9 above.

18. Social Learning Group, note 5 above, Vol. 2, chs 16 and 21.
19. Victor, David, Kal Raustiala, and Eugene Skolnikoff (eds). 1999. *The Implemenation and Effectiveness of International Environmental Commitments.* Cambridge, MA: MIT Press; Weiss, Edith Brown and Harold Jacobson (eds). 1998. *Engaging Countries.* Cambridge, MA: MIT Press.
20. Keckes, Stjepan. 1997. "Review of international programmes relevant to the work of the Independent World Commission on the Oceans", mimeo prepared for the Independent World Commission on the Oceans, p. 1.
21. Global Environmental Change Programme. 2001. *Global Change and the Earth System: A Planet Under Pressure.* Stockholm: IGPB.
22. Clark, William C. 2001. "Knowledge systems for sustainable development", *Environment*, Vol. 43, No. 8, p. 1.
23. National Oceanographic and Atmospheric Administration, www.oar.noaa.gov/education/.
24. Keckes, note 20 above; Tsai-Koester, Li-Hsin. 1995. *A Survey of Environmental Monitoring and Information Management Programmes of International Organizations.* Bonn: Information Highway to the Global Environment (IHGE), www.gsf.de/UNEP/blue1.html.
25. Gosovic, Branislav. 1992. *The Quest for World Environmental Cooperation.* London: Routledge; Fritz, Jan Stefan. 1998. "Earthwatch twenty-five years on", *International Environmental Affairs*, Vol. 10, No. 3, pp. 173–196.
26. UNEP. 1997. *Global Environmental Outlook.* New York: Oxford University Press; UNEP. 1999. *Global Environmental Outlook 2000.* Nairobi: UNEP; UNEP. 2002. *Global Environmental Outlook 3.* London: Earthscan.
27. *Ibid.*
28. Gurney, R. J., J. L. Foster, and C. L. Parkinson. 1993. *Atlas of Satellite Observations Related to Global Change.* Cambridge: Cambridge University Press; Sheehan, Molly O. 2000. "Satellites boost environmental knowledge", in World Watch Institute *Vital Signs 2000.* New York: W. W. Norton, pp. 140–141; Chagas, Carlos and Vittorio Canuto (eds). 1987. *Study Week on Remote Sensing and Its Impacts on Developing Countries.* Rome: Pontificia Academia Sceinteiarium; Rodenburg, Eric. 1992. *Eyeless in Gaia.* Washington, DC: World Resources Institute.
29. de Sherbinin, Alex, Kasren Kline, and Kal Raustiala. 2002. "Remote sensing data", *Environment*, Vol. 44, No. 1, pp. 20–31.
30. Haas, note 9 above.
31. Taylor, Peter. 1993. "The state of the marine environment", *Marine Pollution Bulletin*, Vol. 26, No. 3, pp. 120–127; Windom, Herbert L. 1991. *GESAMP: Two Decades of Accomplisments.* London: International Maritime Organization.
32. Kimball, Lee. 1996. "Treaty implementation: Scientific and technical advice enters a new stage", ASIL Studies in Transnational Legal Policy No. 28. Washington, DC: American Society of International Law.
33. Haas, note 16 above; Tolba, Mostafa and Iwona Rummel-Bulska. 1998. *Global Environmental Diplomacy.* Cambridge, MA: MIT Press; Hordijk, Leen. 1991. "Task force on integrated assessment modelling", *Monitair*, Vol. 4, No. 6, pp. 8–11; Eckley, Noelle. 1999. "Drawing lessons about science policy institutions", Belfer Center for Science and International Affairs Paper E-99-11 September; Haas, Peter M. 1990. *Saving the Mediterranean.* New York: Columbia University Press.
34. United Nations University. 1999. *Inter-Linkages: Synergies and Coordination between Multilateral Environmental Agreements.* Tokyo: United Nations University, www.geic.or.jp/interlinkages/aide.html; Pocantico Dialogue Site, www.yale.edu/gegdialogue/dialogues.htm; German Advisory Council on Global Change. 2001. *World in Transition:*

New Structures for Global Environmental Policy. London: Earthscan; Haas, note 16 above, pp. 345–346; Von Moltke, Konrad. 2001. "The organization of the impossible", *Global Environmental Politics*, Vol. 1, No. 1, pp. 23–28; Whalley, John and Ben Zissimos. 2001. "What could a world environmental organization do?", *Global Environmental Politics*, Vol. 1, No. 1, pp. 29–34; Newell, Peter. 2001. "New environmental architectures and the search for effectiveness", *Global Environmental Politics*, Vol. 1, No. 1, pp. 35–44; Biermann, Frank. 2001. "The emerging debate on the need for a world environmental organization", *Global Environmental Politics*, Vol. 1, No. 1, pp. 45–55.

35. Aggarwal, Vinod (ed.). 1998. *Institutional Designs for a Complex World.* Ithaca: Cornell University Press.

7

The IPCC: Its roles in international negotiation and domestic decision-making on climate change policies

Yasuko Kameyama

Purpose

Climate change is a global problem that has only started to attract political attention at international level since the late 1980s. Two international agreements have been adopted so far to respond to this complicated global environmental problem. The Framework Convention on Climate Change (FCCC), adopted in 1992 and entered into force in 1994, urges the industrialized countries and economy-in-transition countries (EITs, including the former Soviet Union and East European countries) to take measures aiming at returning their greenhouse gas (GHG) emissions to 1990 levels by 2000. The FCCC was followed by the Kyoto Protocol, adopted in 1997, that called for achieving legally binding targets for GHG emissions during a five-year period from 2008 to 2012. For instance, annual average GHG emission from 2008 to 2012 is to be 6 per cent less than that of the 1990 level for Japan, 7 per cent for the USA, and 8 per cent for the EU as a whole.

These commitments by the parties are not free from obstacles. In 2001 the USA officially publicized its intention to withdraw from the Kyoto Protocol regime, and announced its own climate change programme in the following year. There were several reasons why the USA left the Kyoto Protocol, one of which was scientific uncertainty regarding human-induced climate change and its impact.

Since the climate change problem is of a scientific nature, international negotiation on climate change has always been affected by opposites that emphasize the vast uncertainty of the issue. Thus, the negotiation has been supported by a group of scientific experts called the Intergovernmental Panel on Climate Change (IPCC). It is an organization established in 1988 that supports policy-makers by reviewing relevant scientific activities around the globe on climate change. It has published three assessment reports so far, in 1990, 1996, and 2001. The latest report states that without relevant climate policies, global mean temperature is expected to increase 1.4–5.8°C between 1990 and 2100.[1] Such temperature change is likely to cause adverse effects for agricultural production, biodiversity, human health, etc. The IPCC statements are referred to at various levels, from international negotiating levels to national policy levels.

The role of scientific knowledge or of academic groups in global environmental regime is a matter of interesting debate by itself,[2] and the role of the IPCC has also been debated in a substantial number of academic papers.[3] There are, however, still several reasons for reviewing the IPCC's role at this moment. First, there may have been a shift in the expected role of the IPCC. The IPCC today may be expected to do something different from the time when it was first set up 14 years ago. Second, the IPCC may have been expected to play different roles by various stakeholders. Political processes within and surrounding the FCCC as a whole may seek for one thing in the IPCC while negotiators from each country may look for another. Scientists may be another group of players who are involved in the IPCC process, seeking for another type of fruit. This means that the IPCC may have played additional roles that were originally not expected when it was first established. The purpose of this study is to review the role of the IPCC in the last 14 years and assess what kind of role it has, or has not, played for various stakeholders. The outcome of this study is then introduced to give suggestions for a possible scientific organization that may work for a world environmental organization (WEO).

The chapter concludes that the role of the IPCC has expanded over the last 14 years. Originally, the IPCC was established to collect and assess scientific studies relevant to climate change, as other aspects of the problem were assumed to be determined by the FCCC and other relevant political processes. The late 1980s was an agenda-setting period, in which the IPCC was expected to signal climate change as a global issue. As two international agreements were adopted, however, the main concern of countries became more political as well as technical. The IPCC, as an intergovernmental organization, needed to answer additional demands from various stakeholders in order to maintain its legitimacy.

It has undergone several revisions to fulfil such a requirement. In other cases, the IPCC is still struggling to find a satisfying goal.

In order to maintain or increase the legitimacy of the IPCC, it is important to continue reflecting political needs to support future negotiation, and at the same time reject individual political preference. This may be achieved, or improved at least, by restructuring the election process of leading authors and the drafting process of reports from the point of equity of participation, as well as from the point of the independence of science from politics. Inviting more leading authors from developing countries and securing travel costs for those participants is an example of such improvement from an equity perspective. Involving more scientists outside of the IPCC regime for the peer-review process is another example to gain more scientific legitimacy for the IPCC. Publishing two types of reports, namely assessment reports and summaries for policy-makers, is a good way to maintain scientific quality while giving policy-makers enough opportunities to reflect their intention. It is worthwhile for the IPCC to continue this two-type report approach.

If a WEO were to be established, the IPCC is a good example of a new scientific organization that may be established under the WEO. In that case, there are lessons to be learned from the IPCC.

History of the IPCC and its structure

Initial development before the establishment of the IPCC goes back to the early 1980s. In 1985 a major international review of the issue formed the basis of the third Villach Conference organized by the World Meteorological Organization (WMO), UNEP, and the International Council of Scientific Unions (ICSU). This was said to be the time when the problem of anthropogenic climate change was moved on to the political agenda.[4] The first appearance of the climate change problem as a significant issue on the international political agenda was in 1988. Over 300 individuals attended the Conference on the Changing Atmosphere: Implications for Global Security held in Toronto, Canada, in June 1998. In its final statement, it was stated that an emission goal of a 20 per cent reduction of carbon dioxide levels by the year 2005 would be necessary to prevent anthropogenic global warming. The IPCC was set up in the autumn of the same year.

Structurally, the IPCC was established under the auspice of two international bodies, UNEP and the WMO. The IPCC was set up not as an "international" panel but an "intergovernmental" panel under the auspices of the United Nations. This brought about one characteristic of the IPCC that made it different from other international scientific organizations such as the ICSU and the International Geographic-Biological Programme (IGBP) – the IPCC was expected from the very beginning to be not a purely scientific organization, but an interface between politics and science.

The core decision-making bodies of the IPCC are the plenary, the bureau, three working groups (WGs), and, from 1989 to 1992, a special committee for the participation of developing countries. The scientific/administrative distinction runs through the WG level, between WG plenary (as distinguished from panel plenary) and task force establishments, and lead- and contributing-author meetings, which constitute the "scientific core".[5]

Publications of the IPCC are categorized into six types. The best known IPCC publication is its assessment report. The panel, at its tenth session, decided that an approximately five-year interval would be reasonable; three assessment reports had thus been published by 2001. Executive summaries and summaries for policy-makers (SPMs) are relatively short reports with the status of "reports approved by working groups and accepted by the panel". They are subject to line-by-line approval by the WG plenary. As the panel consists not only of scientists but also of government officials, SPMs are most likely to be influenced by politics. Special reports (SRs) assess literature in one specific field, and are subject to review, acceptance, and approval procedures. Technical reports (TRs) are reports on technical issues, but no acceptance and approval procedures are necessary. Finally, the IPCC also publishes synthesis reports.

The IPCC and its reports are expected to support negotiators in making judgements based on the best available scientific and technical knowledge. They are also likely to contribute to dissemination of information at a domestic level. The reality, however, seems to be more complex, and the IPCC is observed from various angles in different ways.

The roles of the IPCC: What has been expected by stakeholders

Officially, at the UN level, the IPCC was given a mandate of providing "internationally coordinated assessments of the magnitude, timing, and potential environmental and socio-economic impact of climate change and realistic response strategies".[6] It is necessary to establish a clearer distinction of the needs of the stakeholders, however, to assess the IPCC by considering its potential roles. For negotiators, evaluation of the IPCC would be made according to "how much could inputs from the IPCC help us to come to an agreement?". At the same time, another

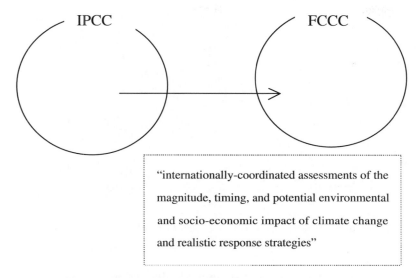

Figure 7.1 Role of the IPCC: Official mandate

measurement of their evaluation may be "how much could our government utilize the IPCC in order to incorporate our position into the final text of the agreement?". On the other side, scientists would feel the IPCC was useful if "our arguments were incorporated into the final text of the agreement" or "it helped us collect more research funds".

The plausible roles of the IPCC (as a scientific organization) for the FCCC (and relevant political arenas) and for other stakeholders are described in Figures 7.1 and 7.2. Arrows in the figures express directions in which benefit is given. The mandate of the United Nations only expected the IPCC to give benefit to the FCCC and its relevant political process in order to achieve an international agreement that is most effective in mitigating climate change (Figure 7.1). The reality is, however, more complex. By institutionalizing "science", the IPCC was asked to play more than one role (Figure 7.2). In addition to the formally given mandate, scientists involved in the IPCC process and negotiators involved in the FCCC process were expecting something more from the IPCC. One way of categorizing the different roles of the IPCC that was found in relevant studies is according to whom the benefit of the IPCC is destined.

- Benefit that is given to the FCCC process:
    (1) IPCC as a provider of scientific knowledge
    (2) IPCC as a body to legitimate what is written in reports
    (3) IPCC as a forum to reach political agreements that would not be achievable only by political argument, such as those in the FCCC.

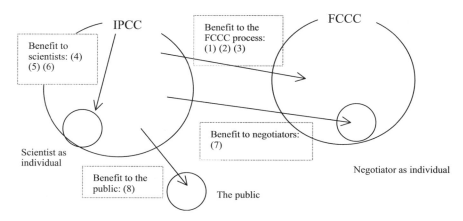

Figure 7.2 Role of the IPCC: Perceptions of different actors

- Benefit that is given to scientists individually and as a group:
  - (4) IPCC as a corridor for the epistemic community to influence politics
  - (5) IPCC as a forum to reach an agreement (if not consensus) in scientific findings
  - (6) IPCC as a tool for researchers to obtain constant research funds.
- Benefit that is given to negotiators in terms of governmental officials:
  - (7) IPCC as a tool for negotiators to justify their governments' positions.
- Benefit that is given to the public in general:
  - (8) IPCC as an organization that disseminates information concerning climate change to the public.

In this section, each of these eight roles of the IPCC is further reviewed one by one.

IPCC as a provider of scientific knowledge to the political process

The provision of scientific knowledge is the role that is the closest to the IPCC's original mandate. A question that may arise concerns the implication of the term "assess". Is the IPCC merely a provider of scientific knowledge, or is it given a full authority to evaluate scientific findings and to say some findings are more reliable than others?

The objectives of the IPCC, given by itself according to its first assessment report (FAR), are twofold.[7] They are, first, to assess the scientific information related to the various components of the climate change issue and the information needed to evaluate the environmental and socio-economic consequences of climate change; and, second, to formulate "realistic response strategies for the management of the climate change issue". The FAR was introduced to the Second World Climate Conference in 1990, and it was accepted as an adequate basis upon which to initiate international negotiation on the FCCC. The report actually became an impetus for nations to take action on climate change.

On the other hand, it should be noted that the FCCC does not explicitly recognize the IPCC as the basis of its judgement. The chapeau of the FCCC[8] acknowledges analytical works conducted by various actors, without explicitly referring to the IPCC: "conscious of the valuable analytical work being conducted by many States on climate change and of the important contributions of the WMO, UNEP and other organs, organizations and bodies of the United Nations system, as well as other international and intergovernmental bodies, to the exchange of results of scientific research and the coordination of research". The FCCC convention requests only the subsidiary body for scientific and technological advice (SBSTA) to "provide the Conference of the Parties and, as appropriate, its other subsidiary bodies with timely information and advice on scientific and technological matters relating to the Convention". In this context, the IPCC voluntarily produces reports, and it is up to the SBSTA whether or not to refer to the IPCC reports.

Five years after the adoption of the FCCC, the Kyoto Protocol gave a slightly more significant role to the IPCC. It seeks for the IPCC's determination to establish some of its technical procedures. For instance, in Article 5 the protocol states that the parties are to use methodologies that were accepted by the IPCC for estimating anthropogenic emissions by sources and removals by sinks of all greenhouse gases not controlled by the Montreal Protocol. This mandate is, however, still rather technical and requires relatively few political decisions. On the whole, both in the FCCC and the Kyoto Protocol, the IPCC is referred to as an organization with only academic information relevant to climate change.

IPCC as a body to apply legitimacy to what is written in its reports

The mechanism of climate change due to the increase of greenhouse gases in the atmosphere had been suggested by scientists even before the establishment of the IPCC. Scientific knowledge on climate change in general would have existed today even without the IPCC. One of the IPCC's roles is to legitimize those scientific findings by referring to them in its reports. The final conclusions of the SPMs are considered to be the most influential part of the reports. The IPCC strives to secure legitimacy of its reports by involving wide participation from around the world, as well as by organizing a repetitive peer-reviewing process by both scientists and government officials. The higher the legitimacy, the stronger the influence of the IPCC reports in the political process.

One example of IPCC legitimacy in the FCCC process was seen during the Second Conference of the Parties to the Convention (COP2). The IPCC's second assessment report (SAR) was accepted late in 1995, during the process of negotiation for the Kyoto Protocol. At COP2, parties took note of the result of the ministerial round table called the Geneva Ministerial Declaration.[9] In the declaration there is a reference to the IPCC SAR:

Recognize and endorse the SAR of the IPCC as currently the most comprehensive and authoritative assessment of the science of climate change, its impacts and response options now available. Ministers believe that the SAR should provide a scientific basis for urgently strengthening action at the global, regional and national levels, particularly action by Parties included in Annex I to the Convention (Annex I Parties) to limit and reduce emissions of greenhouse gases ...

This declaration was not accepted by the parties by consensus, but it was incorporated in the report of COP2. Ministers would not have referred to specific scientific findings if it were not for the IPCC legitimacy attached to them.

The level of legitimacy seems to differ according to the type of work undertaken by each WG of the IPCC. Themes such as "mechanism of climate change and its impact", a theme of WG1, are more likely to achieve higher legitimacy than other themes such as "policy required to mitigate climate change", a main theme of WG3. Reports from WG3 seem to have had more controversial topics than the other two WGs. The divergence of level of legitimacy among the three WGs in the IPCC seems to have occurred chiefly not by difference of procedure taken in each WG but by the nature of the themes. WG3 mainly dealt with policies that lead to the most controversial issue, the parties' actions and commitments.

Some of the drafting processes were said to hamper the legitimacy of the IPCC. The quality of the reviews in the FAR and SAR "was degraded by omissions or inadequately defined error assignments, unlabeled graphical scales, missing references and cross-references, reference to material unavailable to the general reader, comparisons involving disparate cases, and an absence of overall result summaries and discussion".[10]

Another issue that led to a decrease of IPCC legitimacy was insufficient participation from developing countries. Agarwal and Narain suggested there were those who would use "one-world" discourses about the environment to dilute responsibility for climate change by spreading it evenly among industrialized and developing countries.[11] Not enough participation from developing countries was indicated most strongly during the process of the FAR. Many suggested restructuring of the IPCC process,[12] and it has been improved to a certain extent in subsequent activities. It was decided that in the SAR process there should be at least one expert from a developing country in each lead author's team. The IPCC has received some support from the Global Environment Facility (GEF) to increase such broad participation. It has also been suggested that more articles written in languages other than English should be reviewed in the future reports.

IPCC as a forum to reach political agreements that would not be achievable in the political arena

Negotiators may wish to manipulate scientific inputs in order to control the FCCC and other political processes. This tendency increases when the legitimacy of the IPCC is high enough to influence the FCCC and other political processes. On the other hand, the IPCC reports would lose legitimacy if negotiators could easily rewrite them. There would always be a concern for the IPCC to maintain its legitimacy by preventing political argument by negotiators.

It could be said that this is a role that deals with "trans-science" in contrast to "science".[13] Processes of knowledge creation, community formation, and expert institutionalization are themselves highly political exercises, with substantial implications for broader debates concerning how people of vastly unequal technological capacity and means are going to live together on the planet.[14]

Efforts to avoid politicization of the IPCC process are difficult, as the IPCC involves participation of government officials, and also as the IPCC actually intends to deal with political themes. The IPCC has dealt with this problem by publishing two different types of reports. Assessment reports are bulky documents that review best available studies concerning climate change. These reports are intended to maintain the quality of academia of experts. On the other hand, the SPMs are more or less interpretation of scientific findings. They leave room to allow reflection of the interests of policy-makers. Arguments that are seen in the FCCC process mainly refer only to SPMs. Since SPMs are likely to give political preference to selective scientific findings, the drafts are often subject to political debate by themselves before they are referred by the FCCC and other negotiating meetings.

There are occasions where some governments try to use the IPCC for political purposes. Requests from governments to the IPCC concerning what should be taken up by the IPCC are an initial step of political influence on scientific activities. For example, in the sixteenth subsidiary body meeting to the FCCC in 2002, there was a discussion in the SBSTA about whether or not to request the IPCC to deal with Article 2 of the FCCC, which is the ultimate objective of the FCCC, about a level of atmospheric concentration of greenhouse gases that would prevent dangerous anthropogenic interference with the climate system. This was denied by a number of countries, as such studies are too political and may lead to suggestions that more action should be taken by certain governments.

Among different types of IPCC reports, SPMs are recognized as "consensus" achieved among participants in the IPCC process. This, however, is not always convincing. The SAR concluded: "the balance of evidence suggests that there is a discernible human influence on global climate".[15] This sentence, however, had not been in the final draft of the IPCC. It was incorporated during the final process of drafting the SPM. Industry lobby groups that were sceptical of the IPCC findings immediately attacked the report, asserting that IPCC participants had violated rules of procedure.[16]

Another possibility for politicization of the IPCC is extracting different messages from the IPCC main documents by different interpretation of climate change and its impact. Political power could shift the outcome of knowledge by altering the direction of discourse.[17] For instance, there might be a question of whether to discuss emission sources of greenhouse gases or to focus more on enhancement of sinks – these have the same effect on concentration of greenhouse gases in the atmosphere, but the consequences for necessary policies would be quite different. To focus more on one specific aspect of a problem than on other aspects is a political process. In order for the IPCC to continue dealing with political agendas without being politicized by governments, it is necessary to recognize such drawbacks and consider ways to prevent them. Some ideas are given in the last section of this chapter.

IPCC as a corridor for the epistemic community to influence politics

The role of the epistemic community is best known from the works of Haas[18] regarding conservation of water quality in the Mediterranean Sea. Benedick[19] also stressed the importance of the role of scientists in international negotiations to agree the Montreal Protocol to limit ozone-depleting substances. Peterson, on the other hand, concluded that in the case of the International Whaling Commission (IWC), a group of cetologists did not determine outcomes either by the indirect method of defining the terms of debate so that only their preferred policy appeared reasonable or by the direct method of placing members or former students into enough decision-making and implementing posts.[20]

Have scientists working on climate change been able to influence international negotiations on climate change? Some of the success stories of climatic scientists are those in the early days of the IPCC and/or before the IPCC was established. The Villach Conference in 1985 and the Advisory Group on Greenhouse Gases (AGGG) set up by the conference are regarded as the starting point where researchers began to send out messages to the public and managers of political power.[21] Another development of the power of scientists was observed during 1989–1990. At the 1989 Noordwijk Conference in the Netherlands, the USA, as well as some other countries like the UK and the Soviet Union, brought scientific scepticism to the international negotiation, claiming that there was insufficient scientific evidence to know by how much emissions of greenhouse gases needed to be cut.[22] Such a claim, however, left these countries in a disadvantageous position after the FAR was published in 1990. The IPCC acknowledged that a number of uncertainties remained, but still it considered the report as an authoritative statement of the views of the international scientific community at this time.[23] In May 1990 the UK officials changed their position on the science, and announced the UK's national emission target for CO_2.

The USA had used the "uncertainty" of the IPCC results as one of the reasons for the USA not to agree to ambitious emission reduction targets. The Bush (senior) administration never accepted the scientific assessments of the IPCC and felt they were too uncertain. This position of the US government was changed during the Clinton administration. It accepted the findings of the IPCC, which say that climate change is a real problem and is caused at least in part by human activities.[24] In the new Bush (junior) administration, the USA rejected the Kyoto Protocol in March 2001, but at the same time it recognized a need for some action to be taken. In the long term, the USA had to change its position on the science because of what has been written in the three assessment reports of the IPCC.

On the other hand, there were times when science could not take a role during important decision-making. International negotiation up to COP3 dealt little with sequestration of CO_2 by activities related to land use, land-use change, and forestry. Just before COP3, at the eighth Ad Hoc Group on the Berlin Mandate (AGBM8), some countries such as New Zealand and Finland proposed to consider such activities as well. The key question in their proposal was how actually to count the amount of sequestration of CO_2 by forestry and other human activities related to sequestration. Countries were aware of a lack of methodology and data to incorporate forest-related activities at the same level as emissions. In the final round, however, it was agreed to consider certain types of activities referred to in Article 3.3 of the Kyoto Protocol, and request the IPCC to prepare a special report on land-use change and forestry by 2000.[25] Emission targets in the Kyoto Protocol for Annex B countries also had little to do with the IPCC or any other scientific evidence, but were a result of hard negotiation within the field of politics.[26]

It may be said that groups of scientists were able to give impetus to policy-makers in the early days in the 1980s, but their influence decreased as negotiations drew close to an agreement.

IPCC as a forum to reach an agreement (if not consensus) concerning scientific findings

Could it be said that the IPCC played a role of finding a single, converged answer among the divergent results of scientific findings? Or was it possible for scientists to come to a consensus by utilizing the forum of the IPCC? The first chair of the IPCC, Bert Bolin, emphasizes the role of the IPCC as achieving a kind of consensus among scientific experts by saying that "hardly any articles published in scientific journals which apply a peer-review procedure reject the IPCC's conclusion that continued atmospheric emissions of greenhouse gases will lead to a significant increase of the global temperature and associated changes in regional climate".[27]

This, however, is not always convincing. Some argue there is a problem of participation in the IPCC, not in terms of developing countries this time, but in terms of scientists who have different views from those in the IPCC. Although the IPCC involves thousands of participants, there are scientists who are marginalized by core group members of the IPCC. For example, during the drafting process of the FAR, a study that based analysis of response options on environmental targets was excluded by IPCC WG3 as basis for the formation of emission scenarios as its effects-based logic ran counter to the IPCC's cost-based assessment of strategies.[28]

There are also others who do not wish to participate in the IPCC process and are sceptical of conclusions in the IPCC SPMs. They are especially active in the USA.[29] Debate between the scientists on both sides became more popular in the process of the third assessment report (TAR) of the IPCC. It thus seems difficult to state that consensus exists among scientists – it may even be said that the scientists do not mind lack of consensus, only negotiators do.

IPCC as a tool for researchers to obtain constant research funds

From the point of scientists, participation in the IPCC may be a convincing reason for getting research funds. Boehmer-Christiansen suggests that "the scientific bodies set up in the 1980s to advise governments on climate change policy emerged from the globally coordinated research community which acted primarily as a lobby for its own research agendas dedicated to the modeling of planet Earth and the development of alternative energy sources".[30]

Not quite the same but a more productive way of interpretation is viewing this as the development of scientific activity relevant to climate change. With more people getting interested in the issue and scientific outcomes related to the issue, more researchers and money would be invested in studies relevant to climate change, and would thus create more output. This may result in unexpected results (more researchers might come to prove that climate change would not occur) but it is still a progression of science itself. The institutionalization of science by the IPCC has come to support researchers in this field.

There is also competition among researchers. The IPCC is increasing its interest in policy-relevant studies, such as those of social/human dimensions. As more attention is given to those fields of study, funding for natural sciences might decrease. Even with the continuation of the IPCC as a whole, researchers will remain restless to get more funding.

IPCC as a tool for negotiators to justify their governments' positions

Another way of explaining the relation between science and politics is an aspect that puts heavier weight on politics, at both domestic and international levels.

Modes of interaction between scientific and political cooperation articulated by American foreign policy-makers and institutionalized in organizations like the WMO provide a normative framework against which policy-makers could define and articulate states' interests as well as an institutional model for how states could pursue those interest through specific kinds of activities.[31] Countries in the EU referred to the IPCC report at COP2 to justify their positions to aim for CO_2 atmospheric concentration of 550ppm.

Governments could also use the IPCC reports to convince opponents in their respective countries to implement climate-relevant policies. British politicians found the threat of climate change useful as "greenwash" for unpopular energy and taxation policies.[32] Certain ministries, especially environment-related ministries, are likely to refer to the IPCC conclusions to convince other ministries.[33] In any policy-making at national and subnational levels, the IPCC is a good institution to justify policies that reduce emissions, even if the original purpose of the policy was not relevant to climate change.

IPCC as an organization that disseminates information concerning climate change to the public

Although this is not a mandate given to the IPCC, the IPCC contributes to raising public awareness in some countries.

In an interview survey of policy-makers and others involved in the decision-making process for the FCCC, the IPCC was said to contribute to informing the public of climate change in Japan.[34] The media dealt with the results of the IPCC as scientific consensus at international level, and this type of information (whether it is correct or not) educated ordinary citizens.

Little influence of the IPCC was observed in public awareness of climate change in other countries. During the 1900–1992 period, the Netherlands and Germany were countries that were proposing the most ambitious emission reduction targets. Governments of both countries were supported by the public with high awareness, but interviews suggested that such awareness was not motivated by the IPCC. It may be said that the IPCC does not consider ordinary public individuals as target readers of its reports.

Should there be such a role in international organizations? Education and training is actually a different type of task, but it is also an important task. The FCCC has training programmes organized by its secretariat, and thus it may be concluded that the IPCC does not require such task management. On the other hand, the IPCC reports are the most effective for such training and education. The IPCC seeks to translate as many as possible of its reports into other UN official languages. This is an important step to diffuse the latest information on climate change.

Ideas for a scientific organization under the WEO

The role of the IPCC was reviewed in the previous section, and some conclusions may be drawn from it.

First of all, this review of the IPCC's role suggests there is enough evidence to say the IPCC has more or less fulfilled its mandate – set by itself – to "assess on a comprehensive, objective, open and transparent basis the scientific, technical and socio-economic information relevant to understanding the scientific basis of risk of human-induced climate change, its potential impacts and options for adaptation and mitigation".[35] The IPCC played a major role in directing political processes to reach international agreements that would contribute to mitigation of climate change.

There were other indirect roles of the IPCC that were perceived by various actors, and the weight of those roles shifted over time. First, the power of scientists to influence decision-making directly has decreased over the last 14 years. This can be seen from the IPCC's role 4 (see pp. 146–148). Second, on the other hand, the legitimacy of the IPCC has increased during the same period. This is due to restructuring the IPCC process in order to reflect requests from the FCCC process, and can be drawn from role 2 (pp. 143–145). Third, in order to maintain the legitimacy of the IPCC, it is important to continue reflecting political needs that increase legitimacy, and at the same time reject individual political preference. This will be achieved by reflecting political needs only by restructuring the process from the point of equity, and not by rewriting the content of reports.

This conclusion of the IPCC is a message to a future WEO. Establishment of a body of highly qualified scientific experts similar to the IPCC will contribute to a WEO becoming an influential organization. The scientific organization would work most effectively if it considered some of the important aspects that could be learned from the IPCC.

- The scientific organization affiliated to the WEO should involve broad participation, from both developed and developing countries. Enough funding should be secured for participants from developing countries. Papers written in languages other than English should be fully reflected in the review process.
- The scientific organization should be able to involve scientists who disagree with the core group of experts in the organization. It is important to have opportunities for a free discussion by those who agree and disagree with scientific issues raised.
- The peer-review process should be as open as possible. Closed-door sessions should be limited to a minimum. There are critical views on the IPCC process for its sometimes redundant review process. One option for a new scientific body is to invite more involvement of experts for reviews so that the focus would be on scientific/technical matters.
- Involvement of government officials (negotiators) in the scientific body should be limited to a minimum. It is seen that the IPCC process is overly politicized by the involvement of government officials. On the other hand, such involvement was effective for the IPCC to attract much attention from countries during negotiations. The IPCC's

approach, to have two types of reports, assessment reports and summaries for policy-makers, is one good example that may be followed by the new scientific organization if it were to allow participation of governmental officials. It is also effective to divide an issue into several working groups according to the level of relevance to politics. Some fields of study, such as mechanisms of an environmental problem or monitoring, would have less danger of politicization than studies of other areas such as policy analysis. It is also an option to establish another body similar to the SBSTA of the FCCC that limits participation of scientists and links political processes with scientific activities.

- The scientific organization may have a subgroup that focuses on education of the public and dissemination of scientific knowledge. The IPCC lacked a means to inform ordinary citizens. Such activity may lead to greater support from the public for the organization itself.
- If the WEO is to be an organization that aims to solve interlinkage issues among different environmental conventions, the scientific body for the WEO should also play a role as a forum for respective scientific/technical bodies under those environmental conventions to exchange views. The present (year of writing: 2003) Millennium Ecosystem Assessment organized by UNEP is a kind of activity that could be undertaken regularly by the scientific organization under the WEO.

With the points raised above, the WEO will be able to consolidate its relevant scientific views under one organization, and make use of it to consolidate views to build action programmes based on the knowledge. Such a scientific basis will contribute to reaching political agreement at both international and domestic levels.

Notes

1. IPCC. 2001. *Climate Change 2001: The Third Assessment Report of the IPCC*. Cambridge: Cambridge University Press.
2. Haas, Peter M. 1989. "Do regimes matter? Epistemic communities and Mediterranean pollution control", *International Organization*, Vol. 43, No. 3, pp. 377–403; Hajer, Maarten. 1995. *The Politics of Environmental Discourse*. New York: Oxford University Press; Jasanoff, Sheila and Brian Wynne. 1998. "Science and decision-making", in Steve Rayner and Elizabeth Malone (eds) *Human Choice and Climate Change. Vol. 1: The Societal Framework*. Columbus: Battelle Press, pp. 1–87.
3. Boehmer-Christiansen, Sonia. 1994. "Global climate protection policy: The limits of scientific advice. Part 1", *Global Environmental Change*, Vol. 4, No. 2, pp. 140–159; Boehmer-Christiansen, Sonia. 1994. "Global climate protection policy: The limits of scientific advice. Part 2", *Global Environmental Change*, Vol. 4, No. 3, pp. 185–200; Alfsen, Knut and Tora Skodvin. 1998. "The Intergovernmental Panel on Climate Change (IPCC) and scientific consensus: How scientists come to say what they say about climate change", CICERO Policy Note 1998:3. Oslo: Center for International Climate and Environmental Research.

4. Jaeger, Jill and Tim O'Riordan. 1996. "The history of climate change science and politics", in Tim O'Riordan and Jill Jaeger (eds) *Politics of Climate Change*. London: Routledge, pp. 1–31.

5. Skodvin, Tora. 1999. *Structure and Agent in the Scientific Diplomacy of Climate Change*. Oslo: Center for International Climate and Environmental Research, Oslo.

6. United Nations. 1988. General Assembly Resolution 43/53.

7. IPCC. 1990. *Climate Change: The IPCC Scientific Assessment*. Cambridge: Cambridge University Press.

8. United Nations. 1992. Framework Convention on Climate Change.

9. United Nations. 1996. Document FCCC/CP/1996/15/Add.1.

10. Ritson, D. M. 2000. "Gearing up for IPCC-2001", *Climatic Change*, Vol. 45, No. 3, pp. 471–488.

11. Agarwal, Anil and Sunita Narain. 1991. *Global Warming in an Unequal World*. New Delhi: Center for Science and the Environment.

12. Dowdeswell, Elizabeth and Richard Kinley. 1994. "Constructive damage to the status quo", in Irving Mintzer and Michael Chadwick (eds) *Negotiating Climate Change: The Inside Story of the Rio Convention*. Cambridge: Cambridge University Press.

13. Weinberg, Alvin. 1972. "Science and trans-science", *Minerva*, No. 10, pp. 209–222.

14. Miller, Clark and Paul Edwards. 2001. "Introduction: The globalization of climate science and climate politics", in Clark Miller and Paul Edwards (eds) *Changing the Atmosphere*. Cambridge, MA: MIT Press, pp. 1–30.

15. IPCC. 1996. *Climate Change 1995: The Science of Climate Change*. Cambridge: Cambridge University Press.

16. Edwards, Paul and Stephen Schneider. 2001. "Self-governance and peer review in science-for-policy: The case of the second assessment report", in Clark Miller and Paul Edwards (eds) *Changing the Atmosphere*. Cambridge, MA: MIT Press, pp. 220–246.

17. Litfin, Karen. 1994. *Ozone Discourse*. New York: Columbia University Press.

18. Haas, note 2 above; Haas, Peter M. 1992. "Banning chlorofluorocarbons: Epistemic community efforts to protect stratospheric ozone", *International Organization*, Vol. 46, No. 1, pp. 187–224.

19. Benedick, Richard. 1991. *Ozone Diplomacy*. Cambridge, MA: Harvard University Press.

20. Peterson, M. 1992. "Whalers, cetologists, environmentalists, and the international management of whaling", *International Organization*, Vol. 46, No. 1, pp. 147–186.

21. Thomas, Caroline. 1992. *The Environment in International Relations*. London: Royal Institute of International Relations.

22. Rowlands, Ian. 1995. *The Politics of Global Atmospheric Change*. Manchester: Manchester University Press.

23. IPCC, note 7 above.

24. Harris, Paul. 2000. "Climate change: Is the United States sharing the burden?", in Paul Harris (ed.) *Climate Change and American Policy*. New York: St Martin's Press, pp. 29–50.

25. Oberthür, Sebastian and Hermann Ott. 1999. *The Kyoto Protocol: International Climate Policy for the 21st Century*. Berlin: Springer.

26. Grubb, Michael, Christiaan Vrolijk, and Duncan Brack. 1999. *The Kyoto Protocol: A Guide and Assessment*. London: Royal Institute of International Affairs/Earthscan.

27. Bolin, Bert. 1997. "Scientific assessment of climate change", in Gunnar Fermann (ed.) *International Politics of Climate Change*. Oslo: Scandinavian University Press, pp. 83–109.

28. Haas, Peter M. and David McCabe. 2000. "Amplifiers or dampeners: International institutions and social learning in the management of global environmental risks", in

Social Learning Group (ed.) *Learning to Manage Global Environmental Risks*, Vol. 1. Cambridge, MA: MIT Press, pp. 323–348.

29. Gelbspan, Ross. 1995. *The Heat is On*. Cambridge, MA: Perseus Books.
30. Boehmer-Christiansen, note 3 above.
31. Miller and Edwards, note 14 above.
32. Boehmer-Christiansen, Sonia. 1995. "Britain and the International Panel on Climate Change: The impacts of scientific advice on global warming. Part 1: Integrated policy analysis and the global dimension", *Environmental Politics*, Vol. 4, No. 1, pp. 1–18.
33. Kawashima, Yasuko. 2000. "Japan's decision-making about climate change problems: Comparative study of decisions in 1990 and in 1997", *Environmental Economics and Policy Studies*, Vol. 3, No. 1, pp. 29–57.
34. Kawashima, Yasuko. 1997. "Comparative analysis of decision-making processes of the developed countries towards CO_2 emissions reduction target", *International Environmental Affairs*, Vol. 2, No. 2, pp. 95–126.
35. IPCC. 1998. "Principles governing IPCC work", approved at the Fourteenth Session, Vienna, 1–3 October.

NGOs and environmental governance

8

Institutionalization of NGO involvement in policy functions for global environmental governance

Satoko Mori

Introduction

Debate on global environmental governance has resurged because various efforts in the past several decades have been ineffective in halting environmental degradation. Indeed, data from various sources reveal that the environmental situation has worsened. Many observers point out that part of the explanation for environmental degradation lies in the institutional and structural problems of the United Nations Environment Programme (UNEP), such as small budgets and narrow mandates. Others conclude that scattered, overlapping, and even conflicting mandates among the more than 500 multilateral environmental agreements (MEAs) have hindered opportunities for coordinated responses. Based on these arguments, several proposals, which include strengthening the mandate of UNEP, clustering of MEAs, strengthening the UN Commission on Sustainable Development (CSD), and creating a world environmental organization, might provide a more integrated environmental framework.

No matter what new framework for global environmental governance is designed, it should not be another organization mandated solely by states. As the Commission on Global Governance defines it, governance is "the sum of the many ways individuals and institutions, public and private, manage their common affairs".[1] It is vital to ensure the engagement of non-governmental organizations (NGOs) in any new institutional framework because NGOs enhance the policy-making function of global environmental governance by increasing its transparency and accountability.

This chapter seeks to raise two major questions in terms of NGO involvement in global environmental governance. What are the necessary arrangements to ensure meaningful participation of NGOs to enhance their policy-making function? Secondly, how and to what extent should NGO involvement in global environmental governance be institutionalized? Related to this second question is whether institutionalization is appropriate in the age of networking. To answer these questions, the chapter first presents an overview of NGO access in the UN system. Second, it examines the existing institutional arrangements for NGO involvement at the international level, and compares and contrasts the strengths and weaknesses of these arrangements. In this section, three types of institutional arrangement for NGOs are selected as case studies. The first case study concentrates on the institutional arrangements adopted by the CSD, which attempts to integrate both development and environmental goals and policies. To enable a focus on the environment field, the second case study examines the institutional arrangements adopted by the UN Framework Convention on Climate Change (FCCC), which is an MEA. Finally, the international financial institutions, which have financed environmental projects and programmes, are looked at through a study of the World Bank. After identifying strengths and weaknesses within the current systems, this chapter will propose possible ways of establishing an ideal and practical system of involving NGOs to enhance their policy functions in global environmental governance.

Overview of NGO access in the UN system

The first formal provision for relations between NGOs and the United Nations is outlined in Article 71 of the UN Charter:

The Economic and Social Council may make suitable arrangements for consultation with non-governmental organizations, which are concerned with matters within its competence. Such arrangements may be made with international organizations and, where appropriate, with national organizations after consultation with the Member of the United Nations concerned.

Based on Article 71, in 1946 the UN Economic and Social Council (ECOSOC) adopted Resolution 1296, and provided consultative status to 41 NGOs through its own screening in 1948. The NGOs with consultative status (hereafter ECOSOC/NGOs) acquired certain rights to submit written statements, participate in intergovernmental meetings as observers, and have access to information. However, the role of NGOs was confined to consultation, not negotiation.

Parallel to ECOSOC, specialized UN agencies such as the UN Children's Fund (UNICEF), the UN High Commissioner for Refugees (UNHCR), and the UN Development Programme (UNDP) introduced their own accreditation procedures, developing their relationships with NGOs, particularly at the operational level. During the 1970s and 1980s, the involvement of NGOs in the work of these organizations and programmes grew significantly, while at the same time they expanded their political space to improve their activities and increase their influence.

A series of UN-sponsored world conferences in the early 1990s widened and deepened the involvement of NGOs in the UN system. The UN Secretariat welcomed the participation of not only ECOSOC/NGOs but also national-based NGOs, which did not have accreditation status with ECOSOC. The United Nations attempted to strengthen and revitalize the General Assembly through broader participation of NGOs, since this would enhance the political legitimacy of the United Nations. In particular, the secretariat of the UN Conference on Environment and Development (UNCED) promoted broader participation of NGOs both in the preparatory process and at the conference. The secretariat relaxed accreditation policy and provided accreditation status to non-ECOSOC/ NGOs. The increasing number of NGOs and their access to formal and informal meetings at world conferences went beyond the standard set by ECOSOC. By June 1992 more than 1,400 NGOs were accredited (hereafter UNCED/NGOs), most being national-based and/or issues-based organizations from developing countries. This unprecedented measure was followed by successive world conferences. Each UN conference organized by the General Assembly provided NGOs with their own accreditation status, since there were no formally integrated rules of procedure for NGOs participating in world conferences. The 1995 World Summit for Social Development at Copenhagen accredited 1,299 NGOs, of which 811 were represented by a total of 2,315 non-governmental participants.[2] The 1995 Fourth World Conference on Women in Beijing accredited 2,607 organizations, and a total of 4,010 representatives from 1,700 NGOs participated in the conference itself. A parallel NGO forum, which has been introduced since the 1972 UN Conference on the Human Environment, became an integral part of official events.[3] NGO representatives were invited to address the plenary session at the World Conference on Human Rights in 1993. NGOs participated in the informal drafting groups that drew up the Declaration and Programme of Action in the preparatory process for the 1996 UN Conference on Human Settlements. Thus, in the early 1990s, these UN-sponsored conferences expanded NGO participation in terms of both quantity and quality, and confirmed a new level of NGO dynamism and influence in global governance.

The substantial expansion of NGO involvement in world conferences also demonstrated that the existing rules and procedures for NGO participation provided in ECOSOC Resolution 1296 were outmoded and needed to be revised. Consequently, increasing pressure from the NGO community led to a major review of ECOSOC Resolution 1296. However, the new consultation arrangement, adopted as Resolution 1996/31, remained virtually unchanged from the previous arrangements despite the NGOs' expectations that their rights would be expanded and their access made more flexible. This review process revealed a backlash amongst many member states. Governments were unwilling to allow broad NGO participation because they suspected it would undermine state sovereignty. One of the few improvements was the establishment of a new principle that allowed national, regional, and subregional NGOs to seek consultative status.

Not satisfied with their continuing consultative role, NGOs tried to extend their roles as negotiators. In recent years, for example, NGOs have called for member states to grant them formal consultative rights with the General Assembly and the Security Council. However, these attempts were met with considerable and increasing resistance from member states. Some governments feared changes that might compromise their sovereignty or weaken their monopoly on global decision-making, while others obviously opposed any expansion of the scope of NGO activities.[4] Since the late 1990s, the political environment surrounding NGOs has become much less friendly for them than it was in the late 1980s and early 1990s. Hence, the holding of world conferences ceased in the late 1990s. This backlash against NGOs can be attributed not only to the hardened attitudes of nation-states, but also to the financial difficulties of the United Nations and to divisions within the NGO community, namely between the "established NGOs" and "new NGOs". According to James Paul, the established NGOs, which have a long history of access to the United Nations, claimed that the flood of new and purely national NGOs would downgrade the NGOs' position, whereas the new NGOs viewed the established group as a privileged élite.[5]

Institutional practices of NGO involvement in the CSD

Accreditation process and participation modalities

After UNCED, the CSD was set up in 1993 as a functioning commission of ECOSOC to continue policy discussion and monitor the implementation of Agenda 21, the action plan for implementing sustainable development. Agenda 21 identifies nine "major groups" of civil society,[6] and recommends promoting greater involvement in the CSD's work by a wide range of organizations. In particular, Chapter 27 of Agenda 21 clearly states that NGOs have well-established experience, expertise, and capacity, and recommends that the UN system and governments initiate a process to review formal procedures and mechanisms for the involvement of NGOs at all levels from policy-making and decision-making to implementation.[7] In order to reflect these ideas, the CSD Secretariat followed the flexible and inclusive accreditation rules adopted at UNCED, which went beyond the then-existing ECOSOC rules. UNCED/NGOs were readily granted accreditation to attend sessions of the CSD after they had again submitted applications for accreditation to the secretariat.[8] A total of 570 NGOs out of the 1,400 that participated in UNCED were placed on the roster in the CSD (hereafter CSD/NGOs).[9] The full list of NGOs with consultative status numbered about 3,000 organizations in 2001.[10]

As observers, CSD/NGOs were allowed the same rights provided by ECOSOC. These are the right to participate in the meetings of the CSD, to submit written statements at their own expense, and to address meetings briefly at the discretion of the chair. For example, NGOs at the first CSD could have unprecedented access and involvement through *ad hoc* arrangements at the discretion of the chair, Rasali Ismile. Accredited NGOs were also allowed to set up informal side events and exchange their views with governments. The CSD Secretariat facilitated and coordinated these NGO activities.

NGO staff members, who had been involved in the CSD process from an early stage, evaluated NGO involvement as follows:

The CSD has seen large involvement of the major group organizations in its work. About 200 to 300 major group representatives have attended each Commission meeting at some point during the three-week period. The CSD has pioneered a greater involvement of the Major Groups in the work of an ECOSOC Commission. None of the sessions is now closed – even the small working groups are held open for major group representatives to attend and in many cases to speak. Their increased involvement in implementing the UN conference agreements has also meant increased involvement in framing them in the first place.[11]

Coordination of activities among NGOs

In order to coordinate activities for the CSD, in 1994 representatives of NGOs and other major groups formed the CSD NGO Steering Committee. Two co-chairs were elected from the North and the South, respectively. Members of the steering committee, who were elected by region,

issues, and major groups, served as focal points to ensure equal participation of issues and regional networks within the NGO community. The
committee facilitated the sharing of information and arranged for NGO
input into official processes. Its mandate was to coordinate the development of common NGO positions rather than to represent the NGO
community or make policy. Unfortunately, however, in 2000 intense disputes between caucuses within the steering committee resulted in the
majority of the Northern NGOs and issue caucuses absenting themselves
from the committee.

As a result, parallel to the CSD NGO Steering Committee, the Sustainable Development Issues Network (SDIN) was set up in 2001 as a
collaborative effort among civil society networks and non-governmental
issue caucuses engaging in the World Summit on Sustainable Development (WSSD) process.[12] The SDIN, which was facilitated by three
networks – the Northern Alliance for Sustainability (ANPED), the Third
World Network (TWN), and the Environmental Liaison Center International (ELCI) – aimed to improve communication among NGOs working
towards the WSSD in 2002.[13] The SDIN prepared a draft paper and circulated it through various list-servers. Anyone interested could contribute thoughts, alterations, and points through a website discussion forum.
Taking into account comments contributed through the internet as well
as discussions, three network NGOs of the SDIN developed an NGO
position paper, which would be delivered to the secretariat.

Multi-stakeholder dialogue as a new NGO-government forum

In response to a decision taken by the General Assembly at its nine-
teenth special session in 1997, that the CSD should strengthen its interaction with representatives of major groups through greater and
better use of focused dialogue sessions and round tables,[14] the multi-
stakeholder dialogue (MSD) was introduced as a unique participatory
model.[15] The purpose of the MSD is to engage major groups and governments effectively in a dialogue on specific sustainable development
issues.[16] It also aims at providing an opportunity for representatives
of major groups to share their views on progress that has been achieved.
At the MSD segment, multi-stakeholders exchanged views and discussed
specific issues with government representatives.

Starting at the CSD in 1998, the MSD segment has been held over two
days at the beginning of each session. Specific themes have included the
role of industry in sustainable development (1998); tourism (1999); sustainable agriculture (2000); and energy and transport (2001). The MSD
segment precedes the "high-level" segment in which final decisions are
issued by the CSD and submitted through ECOSOC to the General

Assembly for approval. The MSD segments initially involved five key stakeholders from major groups: business and industry, trade unions, NGOs, local authorities, and scientific and technological communities. Later, all nine major groups were involved in the segment.

In general, NGOs regarded the MSD segment as an opportunity to formalize NGO involvement in the CSD process, to take their voices to a wider audience, and to contribute constructively to the improvement of global decisions. They also regarded the MSD as an occasion to exchange views and experiences directly with government representatives on an equal footing. The increasing number of major groups' representatives attending the CSD shows their growing expectations of MSD.[17] To assist the major group participation in dialogue, a multi-stakeholder steering group composed of network organizations from the five key major group sectors was set up. These network organizations facilitated the preparation of dialogue papers and consulted with their networks to identify representatives and prepare them for participation in the dialogue. For example, the representatives of NGOs were selected on the basis of gender, age, experience, constituency, issues for MSD, geography, and so on. The SDIN posted the set of criteria on its website in order to make the selection process open and transparent.[18]

For the organizers, the MSD has been assessed as a unique way to involve major groups in reviewing the progress of Agenda 21 implementation, as it was designed to build consensus on possible future actions and generate new partnerships for sustainable development.[19] Based on these practices at the CSD, the MSD segments have become a standard part of the official work programme of the CSD and the preparatory committee meetings for the WSSD in 2002.[20]

Strengths and weaknesses

The CSD has been providing a basis for new ways of involving NGOs in UN processes. In general, the NGO community seems to welcome the MSD segment, pointing out that the CSD has developed an innovative participatory model with the major groups.[21] It can be said that MSD is an innovative mechanism for formalizing increasing NGO participation in a part of the official process.

However, several claims need to be addressed. First, many participants indicated that the effectiveness of NGO participation in the dialogue was very much in doubt.[22] Some are disappointed with the consistent lack of government attention to the dialogue,[23] doubting that their input will be used or acknowledged. This is because proposals made by major groups at the MSD are not guaranteed inclusion in the chair's summary, which is part of the CSD's final report on the session. The decision on what will be included in the chair's summary still depends on the interests of the government delegations. In practice, at the CSD in 2002 the recommendations of stakeholders were not reflected in the final decision.[24]

Second, the selection process of stakeholder representatives varies considerably because the multi-stakeholder steering groups identify their participants through their own processes. For example, NGOs selected their representatives through consultation, using criteria such as expertise, gender, and the regional balance set up by the SDIN.[25] In contrast, trade unions decided on the basis of case studies submitted, and on gender and regional balance.[26] In addition, each stakeholder group employed its own mechanism for drafting and developing papers and consulting with their constituencies.[27] This inconsistency might engender some serious questioning of the legitimacy of representatives.

Third, the NGOs' traditional independence of thought and action might be threatened, because NGOs are obliged to integrate their diverse viewpoints through the MSD process. It is also of concern that NGOs might be exposed to the influence of other influential participants, namely the business sector, thereby reducing their opportunity to take their message to a wider audience.[28]

Institutional practices of NGO involvement in the FCCC

Accreditation process and participation modalities

Regarding the accreditation of NGOs, Article 7 of the FCCC provides that:

Any body or agency, whether national or international, governmental or non-governmental, which is qualified in matters covered by the Convention, and which has informed the secretariat of its wish to be represented at a session of the Conference of Parties (COP) as an observer, may be admitted unless at least one third of the Parties present object. The admission and participation of observers shall be subject to the rules of procedure adopted by the Conference of Parties.[29]

In order to be accredited as observers, NGOs must be legally constituted entities and competent in matters related to the FCCC. Almost 400 NGOs at COP5 and 270 NGOs at COP6 were accredited. As observers, NGOs are allowed to attend convention meetings such as COPs and meetings of subsidiary bodies without the right to vote. At COP4 it was formally decided to allow observers to attend open-ended contact groups, subject to the same provisos.[30] Observers are permitted to intervene during meetings, subject to the approval of the chair. NGOs have been given the opportunity to address statements to plenary meetings of the COP and its subsidiary bodies. The FCCC Secretariat encourages NGOs to make their statements on behalf of a broad constituency.[31]

The NGO members have another route by which to gain access to the policy-making process. Some NGO members have attended official meetings as appointed members of government delegations. For example, Australia and Canada placed members of NGOs on their delegation to the FCCC. In some cases, governments of developing countries have provided delegate status to NGO representatives from other countries.[32] This is beneficial to NGOs because, as government delegates, NGOs could have the opportunity to access diplomatic processes and information necessary for policy-making. Also, during sessions of the COPs, an increasing number of governments have held regular meetings with NGOs to exchange opinions and information in very interactive ways. Moreover, some NGO members are working as FCCC Secretariat staff and play an important role as a filter between NGOs, the state members, and scientific groups.

Coordination of activities among NGOs: Transnational NGO network

Besides these formal processes, NGOs have influenced negotiations on climate change by forming a transnational network, the Climate Action Network (CAN), which is a principal umbrella group facilitating information exchange and coordinating activities among environmental NGOs. CAN, created in 1989, has been actively involved in the negotiating process of the FCCC from its earliest stages by lobbying government delegations, issuing statements, conducting research, organizing campaigns, and so on. This well-organized network has increased dramatically in size from its original 47 member organizations to more than 320 in 2000.

During conferences, CAN members hold daily meetings to exchange information on the responses of the various governments and decide lobbying strategies for the following day. Some NGOs, mainly the core members of CAN, have developed good relationships with government delegations over the years, enabling them to collect up-to-date information. Such information is particularly useful for NGOs which have little access to government delegations. CAN members also select those NGO representatives who will speak on behalf of other members. CAN has a role in ensuring transparency in intergovernmental negotiations by publishing *ECO*, a newsletter issued every day during the conference. *ECO* is an influential lobbying tool for NGOs, and CAN members also use it as a political tool for expressing their positions.

Strengths/weaknesses

NGO participation in the meetings of the FCCC has gone far beyond the formal provision of the ECOSOC statute, since the member states of the COP attempted to include diverse opinions from among the various actors. This inclusive approach has resulted in the participation of more than 3,000 representatives of non-governmental and non-profit organizations.

However, NGOs participating in the climate policy debate are now facing a number of problems. First, NGOs are wondering about their potential role in enforcing the Kyoto Protocol. In the case of the Convention on International Trade in Endangered Species (CITES), NGOs have been active in monitoring violations of the provisions of CITES and in bringing these to the attention of the convention secretariat. These NGO activities have contributed to a decline in the trafficking of African elephants. To enable NGOs to play a monitoring function in the climate change issue, it will be necessary to incorporate provisions into the Kyoto Protocol that give NGOs further monitoring rights.

Second, the greater the opportunity for NGOs to participate in the official process as government delegates, the less the freedom they will have to act and speak independently. Peter Willetts explains:

When NGOs do participate on the inside, they have to decide whether constraints on their freedom of action and the dangers of being co-opted outweigh the benefits of closer access and the potentiality for direct influence. Usually a satisfactory compromise is made. The insiders accept some personal constraints. They can encourage other NGO representatives to take action they cannot undertake themselves.[33]

Third, according to the inclusive approach taken by the FCCC Secretariat, a broad spectrum of non-state actors, representing different and sometimes conflicting interests, are lumped together in one category as "NGOs". In the climate change negotiation process, three main constituency groupings have emerged: environmental groups; business and industry associations; and local government and municipal authorities. It is difficult even for environmental groups to distinguish citizens' groups from other non-state actors. In addition, the attempts to promote NGO participation inclusively have inevitably increased the lobbying activities of the business community. Therefore, environmental NGOs have become frustrated at being treated together with business and industry associations.

Institutional practices of NGO involvement with the World Bank

Participation modalities

Over the past few decades, specialized agencies at the United Nations have developed their own arrangements with NGOs. These vary considerably depending on the particular history of the agency and the issues in its mandate. Among these agencies, UNICEF, the UNHCR, and the UNDP have a long history of working with NGOs, and thus they permit the greatest degree of NGO access.

In contrast to these organizations, the World Bank, an independent specialized agency with no obligation to follow ECOSOC provisions, originally had no interest in making any arrangement for formal relations with NGOs. Its collaboration with NGOs began in the mid-1970s when it began providing grants to NGOs. The Bank became interested in drawing NGO experience and expertise into Bank-supported lending operations after adopting a new development strategy focusing on basic human needs in 1974. It perceived NGO and community involvement as a tool to facilitate project completion, preferably at a low cost. The Bank's arrangements with NGOs were generally informal and applied only to field operations, not policy-making. According to the Bank's statistics, operational collaboration between the Bank and NGOs showed a steady increase from 1974. However, as the Bank had no fixed internal provisions for NGO participation, throughout the 1970s Bank-NGO relations were traditionally *ad hoc* and informal, varying from project to project. The Bank neither consulted with the public nor had a filing system.

The gradual but increasing operational collaboration with NGOs made it necessary for the World Bank to prepare a manual to clarify relations. In 1988, after consultation with NGOs, the Bank issued Operational Manual Statement 5.30 titled "Collaboration with NGOs". In this, the Bank stated that civil society was to be involved in the design, implementation, and evaluation stages of a project cycle, but not the decision-making stage. In 1989 the Bank issued Operational Directive 14.70, which instructed Bank staff to involve NGOs in projects. The Bank regarded NGOs as private organizations engaged in operational works to relieve suffering, promote the interests of the poor, protect the environment, provide basic social services, and undertake community development.[34]

Faced with strong criticism from developmental, environmental, and human rights NGOs against the structural adjustment policy, the World Bank dramatically increased the involvement of NGOs in 1989. According to a social development report, the ratio of Bank projects with NGO involvement increased from about 20 per cent in 1990 to over 70 per cent in 2000.[35] It seems that NGOs have come to be more involved in Bank projects quantitatively. However, these figures do not always indicate the improved quality of NGO involvement. Covey points out that there is little evidence that NGO involvement is making a substantial difference.[36]

Coordination of activities among NGOs

The first attempt to institutionalize Bank-NGO relations was the establishment of the World Bank-NGO Committee in 1981. This committee's aim was to facilitate dialogue through exchanging information and promoting collaboration between Bank staff and NGOs at the project operation level. It originally comprised 14 NGO members from particular development organizations from Africa, Asia, Europe, Latin America, and the Caribbean, and 15 Bank staff from its regional offices and its policy and planning departments.[37] The members met twice a year, in Washington and in a third world location.

However, NGO committee members were criticized for their lack of accountability to the wider NGO community, for the method of selecting committee members, and for the confidentiality of discussions.[38] The committee was also strongly condemned for transforming the responsibility of the Bank and its operations into a public relations exercise. As a result, the committee could not fulfil its function as an official consultative forum between NGOs and the Bank. Consequently, in 1984 NGO members disapproving of the committee established the NGO Working Group on the World Bank (NGOWG) as an autonomous and parallel body. The mandates of the NGOWG are to act as a pipeline, transmitting information and analyses and offering access to information on the Bank; to represent a constituency rather than act as individuals; and to feed grass-roots experiences and information effectively into the Bank and its processes.[39] The members of the NGOWG are self-selected from interested organizations. Hence, the World Bank-NGO Committee was restructured and is currently composed of NGOWG members and Bank staff. Since 1994, the NGOWG has shifted its emphasis towards decentralization and regionalization, based on the idea that the direct engagement of Southern NGOs is vital in tackling the issue of poverty reduction.[40] The regional assemblies have now become one of the principal modes for dialogue between NGOs and Bank officials on matters pertaining to the design, implementation, and evaluation of Bank-supported projects at national and regional levels. The dialogue between the NGOWG and the Bank also opened an opportunity to examine the introduction of a participatory development approach.

Non-institutionalized pressures of NGOs on the Bank

The NGO community has comprised mainly two groups, depending on their attitude towards the World Bank. One group, consisting mainly of European and Southern NGOs and operational NGOs, is attempting to reform the behaviour of Bank staff. This group tries to make an impact on Bank policy through constructive dialogue with the Bank by participating in the World Bank-NGO Committee. The other group, consisting mainly of US NGOs and advocacy NGOs, is seeking to change institutional aspects of the Bank radically or even to close it down. This group attempts to influence Bank policy externally by organizing public campaigns and by lobbying activities directed toward the US Congress.

In the early 1990s, NGO criticisms of the World Bank for failing to alleviate poverty and implement environmental protection increased. In 1990 the latter group, which sought radical restructuring of the Bank, launched a campaign against India's Narmada Dam project; and in 1994 it launched the "50 Years Is Enough" campaign at the 50th Bretton Woods anniversary. These NGOs argued that Bank-financed projects created poverty while destroying the environment. More than 200 NGOs participated in the "50 Years Is Enough" campaign and criticized the Bank's undemocratic structure. They called for institutional reforms to create openness, full public accountability, and the participation of affected populations in decision-making procedures of the Bank.[41]

Both internal and external pressures, in other words institutionalized and non-institutionalized pressures, from NGOs have led the Bank to reform its relationship with NGOs in two substantial ways.[42] The most noticeable change was the establishment in 1994 of a public information centre under a new information disclosure policy. The creation of this centre was an acknowledgement by the Bank of the need for greater transparency and accountability. The centre provided documents, such as project information documents, project appraisal reports, environmental impact assessments for projects with the most severe and irreversible impacts on the environment, and country-based reports, which had previously been classified. The Bank's growing commitment to increasing transparency was reinforced when it revised its information disclosure policy in 2001. It is expected that documents such as implementation completion reports, performance assessment reports, operational policy papers, and sector strategy papers will be available to those who are interested in the workings of Bank-financed projects.

The other reform was the establishment in 1993 of an independent inspection panel. This panel, one of several measures designed to increase the World Bank's accountability, was created in response to the international NGO campaign against the Narmada Dam in India. It is a three-member body that provides an independent forum for private citizens who believe that they or their interests have been or could be directly harmed by a Bank-financed project. This is the first system put in place by the Bank to receive requests for a complete investigation from directly affected people or from NGOs representing adversely affected people.[43] The system allows NGOs to scrutinize the activities of the Bank and ascertain whether the Bank has complied with its own operational policies and procedures with respect to the design, appraisal, or implementation of Bank-financed projects.[44] The panel has been successful in bringing problems concerning project implementation, which are concerns of NGOs, to the attention of the Bank's board of directors. In other words, the panel has brought about a significant change in NGO-government relations, because the affected borrowing-country citizen is now able to lodge complaints with the panel without consulting his or her borrowing national government. In addition, the panel enhances the position of NGOs *vis-à-vis* the international institution of sovereign state members.

While the creation of the panel has been judged a significant step forward in relation to formalizing the role of NGOs in the inspection process, it has been claimed that the nation-states still retain their power on the panel. Large borrowing countries such as India and Brazil, which have large Bank-funded infrastructure projects, see the panel as an infringement on their sovereignty.[45] There are many instances where the board of directors of the Bank did not permit the panel to conduct a full investigation of the claims. Instead, the board sought a political compromise to save borrowing countries, even after the panel submitted preliminary reviews.[46] In fact, only one claim has resulted in a full investigation, although 14 claims were filed during 1994–1998. Also, it has been pointed out that the panel has not succeeded in institutionalizing sanction measures in the case of non-compliance.[47]

Strengths and weaknesses

The interaction between NGOs and the World Bank started from the operational level and later extended gradually to the policy level. NGO staff members are now involved in the Bank's team that prepares country-based reports on poverty. Also, dialogues between NGOs and Bank staff, including senior Bank managers, on Bank-financed projects have been instituted and expanded to the regional level. Moreover, local NGOs now have the opportunity to enter into discussions with the Bank's resident representatives. This increasing transparency and accountability of the Bank has been brought about by the mutually reinforcing interaction between institutionalized pressure and the non-institutionalized pressure of NGOs on the Bank.

However, these changes in Bank policies are slow at best, and the performance does not always match the promise. Thus, NGOs must keep pressure on the Bank in the following areas. First, as NGOs have claimed, the extent of the release of information under the new disclosure policy is problematic and controversial. For example, the Bank Information Center, one of the NGOs providing information to other NGOs on projects and policies of the Bank, pointed out that the Bank rejected the NGOs' recommendations for meaningful progress in the release of documents during the preparation and implementation of project or investment loans.[48] In addition, the Bank Information Center claimed that the unwillingness of the Bank's board to release details of the board's activities to the public would undermine the credibility of the Bank's governance process, although the information disclosure policy has contributed to a gradual increase in the Bank's transparency.[49]

Second, the inspection panel should be vested with enforcement power. Although the establishment of the inspection panel contributes to the increase in transparency and accountability of the Bank, unfortunately it is weakened because of the lack of a sanction measure.

Third, although NGO involvement in Bank projects has been increasing, the quality and type of participation are under question. The meaningful participation of NGOs will not be realized by the provision of one-way information, nor by their involvement only at the implementation stage after the Bank has already made decisions. Rather, NGOs' meaningful participation would be attained by creating a dynamic two-way communication system, and by providing them with the information necessary to enable them to participate in policy-making.

Conclusion: Prospects of NGO involvement in global environmental governance

By comparing the existing arrangements for NGOs in the above sections, the following policy implications can be drawn regarding the arrangements necessary to ensure meaningful participation of NGOs and to increase the extent of NGO involvement in global environmental governance.

Institutionalization of public policy dialogue

NGO involvement has been expanding from the operational level to the policy level over the past few decades. In particular, a growing phenomenon is the institutionalization of NGO-government dialogue in the official process, as seen in the MSD at the CSD. While enhancing policy dialogue in the official process, it is necessary to clarify how NGO inputs are incorporated into the main decision-making process in order to enhance the policy-making function of NGOs. Otherwise, the public policy dialogue would be merely a forum for non-state actors simply to speak out. This would undermine efforts to secure public support, which is a necessary condition for legitimizing global governance.

The FCCC case suggests that the introduction of an inclusive approach involving a broad range of non-state actors is a desirable arrangement for non-state actors. However, such an arrangement results in treating environment NGOs together with business associations. At the conferences of MEAs, the convention secretariats must make some arrangements to distinguish diverse non-state actors as multi-stakeholders, like the provisions at the CSD. In addition, it is necessary to integrate into clusters the individual rules of procedure adopted by the COPs of respective MEAs so that NGOs can participate efficiently and effectively.

Both the CSD and the FCCC cases present the expansion of NGO involvement from the agenda-setting stage to the decision-making stage, whereas the Bank case shows a gradual but important shift of NGO involvement through public dialogue from operational level to policy-making level. The creation of the public information centre and the inspection panel contributed to the increasing transparency and accountability of the Bank, thereby ensuring meaningful participation of NGOs. The right of access to justice would be fully ensured if the panel gained enforcement power. These arrangements must be expanded to the policy-making level.

Extent of NGO involvement

So, to what extent should NGO involvement be institutionalized while retaining the NGOs' policy-making function in global environmental governance? More formal and structured NGO involvement would provide the NGO community with many more opportunities to influence policy-making. However, at the same time it can also create unintended consequences for the NGO community, for the following two reasons. First, with more structured NGO involvement, NGOs are in danger of being coopted by governments or intergovernmental actors. In recent years, NGOs have been asked by UN bodies or the convention secretariats to organize themselves and to select representatives to make statements, as the number of accredited NGOs has been growing rapidly while the physical space and available time remain the same. Second, a full institutionalization of NGO involvement impedes the comparative advantages of the NGO networks over conventional hierarchy. The cases of the CSD, the FCCC, and the World Bank demonstrate that non-institutionalized activities in the form of networks, including caucuses, working groups, and campaigns, could have an impact on government policy making by mobilizing public opinion. For example, the advocacy campaign "50 Years Is Enough" was operated without any form of institutional access to the Bank. Therefore, it is necessary to leave certain choices to NGO networks, including the selection of representatives to participate in or speak at meetings, and the coordination of diverse opinions and activities among their member organizations.

In conclusion, it would be desirable for NGOs to select their own representatives through NGO networks rather than by government control. The important mission for these NGO networks is the establishment of internal self-governance, which will show transparency and accountability not only to member NGOs but also their constituencies. The cases of the CSD NGO Steering Committee, the SDIN, and the WB-NGO Committee illustrate the necessity of clarifying the criteria for selecting representatives and making the selection process transparent. The institutionalization of NGO involvement by keeping a balance between external and internal self-governance is the key for NGOs to exercise their policy functions in global environmental governance.

Notes

1. Ramphal, Shiridath and Ingvar Carlsson. 1995. *Our Global Neighbourhood: The Report of the Commission on Global Governance.* New York: Oxford University Press, pp. 2–3.
2. United Nations, Department for Policy Coordination and Sustainable Development. 1996. "Role of major groups", Background Paper No. 2, prepared by the Division for Sustainable Development for the CSD Fourth Session, 18 April–3 May 1996. New York: United Nations, p. 8, fn. 5.
3. Over 25,000 people from 11,000 organizations participated in the 1992 global forum at Rio, while over 300,000 people attended the Beijing NGO forum.
4. Paul, James A. 1999. "NGO access at the UN", Global Policy Forum, www. globalpolicy.org/ngos/access/index.htm.
5. *Ibid.*
6. According to Section III of Agenda 21, "Strengthening the role of major groups", the following nine groups are identified as major groups: women, youth, indigenous people and their communities, NGOs, local authorities, workers and their trade unions, business and industry, the scientific and technological community, and farmers.
7. United Nations. 1992. *Agenda 21: Programme of Action for Sustainable Development.* New York: United Nations.
8. ECOSOC/NGOs did not have to register and automatically had observer status.
9. CSD/NGOs are presently on ECOSOC's roster as a result of ECOSOC decision E/1993/215 para. 2 (C). See United Nations, note 2 above, p. 33.
10. Consensus Building Institute. Undated. "Multi-stakeholder dialogues: Learning from the UNCSD experience", Working Paper. Cambridge, MA: Consensus Building Institute, p. 14.

11. Bigg, Tom and Felix Dodds. 1997. "The UN Commission on Sustainable Development", in Felix Dodds (ed.) *The Way Forward: Beyond Agenda 21*. London: Earthscan, p. 31.
12. Issue caucuses evolved as a women's caucus at the Beijing Conference, then spread to other issues. Issue caucuses at the CSD include the corporate accountability caucus, the energy and climate change caucus, the fresh water caucus, and the sustainable production and consumption caucus.
13. The three NGO networks were invited by the WSSD Secretariat as the organizing partner of the MSD for NGOs.
14. UN General Assembly Special Session Resolution S-19/2: Programme for Future Implementation of Agenda 21 (A/RES/S-19/2, annex, para. 133 (e)), 19 September 1997.
15. The idea of the dialogues was taken up by the CSD NGO Steering Committee, which wrote to the Under-Secretary-General Nitin Desai in 1996 requesting his support for the introduction of dialogues at the CSD in 1997. Dodds, Felix. 2002. "The context of global governance: Multi-stakeholder processes and global governance", in Minu Hemmati (ed.) *Multi-stakeholder Processes for Governance and Sustainability*. London: Earthscan, p. 35.
16. UN Document E/CN.17/2001/6, "Multi-stakeholder dialogue on sustainable energy and transport", para. 5.
17. The number of NGO participants increased from around 200–300 in 1993 to between 700 and 800 by 2000. See Hemmati, Minu (ed.). 2002. *Multi-stakeholder Processes for Governance and Sustainability*. London: Earthscan, p. 33.
18. See website www.rio10.dk.
19. UN Document E/CN.17/2001/6, note 16 above, para. 8.
20. At Johannesburg the dialogue sessions are planned to include representatives from all nine major groups.
21. Willetts, Peter. 1999. "The rule of the game: The United Nations and civil society", in John W. Foster and Anita Anand (eds) *Whose World is it Anyway?*. Ottawa: UNA in Canada, p. 269.
22. UNED Forum. 2001. "Count us in, count on us", co-chairs summary presented at UNED Forum, International Workshop on Multi-stakeholder Processes, New York, 28–29 April 2001, p. 3.
23. Consensus Building Institute, note 10 above, p. 23.
24. *Ibid.*, p. 6.
25. The criteria, guidelines, and time schedule for NGO candidates for MSD are posted on www.rio10.dk.
26. Report of UNED Forum, "CSD multi-stakeholder dialogues", www.earthsummit2002.org/msp/examples/ex-csd.htm.
27. *Ibid.*
28. *Ibid.*
29. The COP to the FCCC has not yet formally adopted its rules of procedure, owing to differences of opinion over the voting rule. Since all other rules have been agreed to, the draft rules of procedure are applied at each session, with the exception of the rule on voting.
30. However, the contact groups' chairpersons retained the discretion to close the groups to observers at any time. Informal closed meetings are not open to observers.
31. Depledge, Joanna. 2000. *A Guide to the Climate Change Process*. Bonn: FCCC Secretariat, p. 19.
32. Lawyers of the Foundation for International Environmental Law and Development (FIELD) were placed on the delegation on behalf of the Alliance of Small Island States (AOSIS), or helped the governments of AOSIS as advisers.

33. Willetts, note 21 above, p. 267.
34. World Bank. 1988. "Collaboration with NGOs", Operational Manual Statement 5.30. Washington, DC: World Bank; World Bank. 1989. "Involving non-governmental organizations in Bank-supported activities", Operational Directive 14.70. Washington, DC: World Bank.
35. "Social Development, World Bank, World Bank-Civil Society Collaboration, Progress Report for Fiscal Years 2000 and 2001." Washington: World Bank. See website wbln0018.worldbank.org/esd.nsf/NGOs/home.
36. Covey, Jane G. 1998. "Is critical cooperation possible? Influencing the World Bank through operational collaboration and policy dialogue", in Jonathan A. Fox and David Brown (eds) *The Struggle for Accountability: The World Bank, NGOs, and Grassroots Movements*. Cambridge, MA: MIT Press, p. 87.
37. Over time the number of NGO participants has increased to 25.
38. Cleary, Seamus. 1996. "The World Bank and NGOs", in Peter Willetts (ed.) *The Conscience of the World: The Influence of Non-Governmental Organisations in the UN System*. Washington, DC: Brookings Institution, pp. 71–72.
39. *Ibid.*, p. 79.
40. World Bank. 2000. Proposal by the NGO Working Group on Future Relations with the World Bank, August. See www.worldbank.org/devform/forum_ngowg/html.
41. Cleary, note 38 above, p. 88.
42. Dana Fisher examines the relationship between protesters who have demonstrated outside specific international meetings and representatives of NGOs who have participated inside these meetings. See Chapter 9 in this volume.
43. World Bank. 1994. "The panel's operating procedures", www.worldbank.org/html/inspanel/operating procedures.html.
44. Cameron, James and Ross Ramsay. Undated. "Integrating dissident voices through international institutional law: Participation by non-governmental organizations in the World Trade Organization", paper posted on website www.gets.org/, p. 9.
45. 50 Years Is Enough. "The World Bank's inspection panel: Background and an update", *Economic Justice News* online, www.50years.org/ejn/v2n3/panel.html.
46. Fox, Jonathan A. 2000. "The World Bank inspection panel: Lessons from the first five years", *Global Governance*, Vol. 6, No. 3, pp. 291–294.
47. *Ibid.*, p. 310.
48. Bank Information Center. Undated. "Bank Information Center update: The ongoing struggle for World Bank transparency – The outcome of the information disclosure policy review", www.bicus.org/mdbs/wbg/Info%20Disclosure/infodiscupdate.htm.
49. *Ibid.*

9

Civil society protest and participation: Civic engagement within the multilateral governance regime

Dana R. Fisher[1]

Introduction

In recent years, civil society protests have taken place around the world in response to the meetings of international institutions and international regimes. These protests, which are responses to aspects of globalization and expressions of civic dissatisfaction with global governance, bring about a relatively new type of citizen mobilization: international demonstrations that focus on different aspects of globalization. Although significant differences exist between demonstrations against economic institutions and those in support of the formation of multilateral environmental regimes, they are similar in that they include participants from many countries who are affiliated with international non-governmental organizations and, in many cases, the participants in these protests are mobilized around issues related to the global environment.

As a result of such international protest, questions arise about the role that civil society can play in the global agenda-setting process. Although scholars have pointed to civil society as the social sphere from which pressure must come for the state to develop the political will to create successful multilateral environmental governance regimes,[2] it is unclear whether civil society is capable of that level of mobilization. In order to understand the role that it can and should play in the possible formation of a world environment organization, this chapter explores civil society's involvement in the recent meetings of international institutions and multilateral regimes. By developing an understanding of the relationship between protesters who have demonstrated *outside* specific international meetings and the representatives of NGOs who have participated *inside* these particular meetings, we can learn about opportunities for civil society engagement with international institutions and identify ways that a world environment organization should interact with civil society actors.

The sections that follow explore the relationship between civil society protest and NGO participation in the international meetings of economic institutions and multilateral regimes by looking at civil society engagement at particular meetings in recent years. First comes a brief summary of the dynamics of civil society and the growing literature on the multiple civil society actors who engage in social protest at these international meetings. Second, the chapter looks at the overall relationship between the size of the protests and level of NGO participation at particular international meetings: those of the World Bank/International Monetary Fund and the UN Framework Convention on Climate Change. Third, it explores the organizational affiliation of the citizens protesting outside specific international meetings. Finally, it suggests opportunities for multilateral environmental governance regimes and a world environment organization to engage with civil society, rather than isolating it.

Understanding the dynamics of civil society

As a first step in comprehending the multiple roles that civil society actors are playing at the meetings of international institutions and multilateral regimes, it is necessary to describe the social sphere that has come to be known as civil society. Originally, civil society was seen as a relatively residual category within which social actors outside of the state and the market were placed. With an increased concern for democracy and social movements, the sphere of civil society became of central interest to scholars. In fact, the notion of civil society has its roots in some of the mainstream theories of contemporary sociology.[3] Within this vast literature, the notion and roles of civil society are derived and discussed. Much of the literature focuses on conceptualizing the evolving role of the citizen in society. To date, civil society continues to be seen as a social sphere that is separate "from both state and economy".[4]

Not only do civil society actors continue to be considered distinct and outside of other social spheres, but civil society is viewed as consisting of a separate and distinct institutional complex. Emirbayer and Sheller contend that:

the state, economy and civil society are realms of social life whose relative independence from one another constitutes one of the principal hallmarks of modernity. Many of the dynamics of contemporary society are captured in the relations among these empirically interpenetrating and yet analytically distinct institutional domains ... [Civil society is] the institutional sector that, metaphorically speaking, lies "in between" the state and economy.[5]

Although the sphere of civil society in developing countries does not have the level of institutional sophistication of developed countries, protests at the meetings of international organizations in the developing world have increased. At the World Summit on Sustainable Development (WSSD) in Johannesburg, South Africa, for example, "thousands of protesters from within and outside South Africa took to the streets, marching from the poor residential area known as Alexandra to the official WSSD".[6]

Perhaps, in its most general form, civil society has come to be defined as involving a "self-organized citizenry".[7] Inside this social sphere lie social movements, civic associations, non-governmental organizations, and citizens who voice their political preferences through their demonstrations, votes, and wallets. In other words, NGOs that participate in international meetings and the citizens who demonstrate outside of them are both specific civil society actors.

The recent literature on civil society has centred around two main themes. On the one hand, scholars have looked at civil society's role in newly emerging democracies.[8] Much of this work has focused on the contributions of civil society to the democratic legitimacy of the nation-state. On the other hand, research has tended to focus on understanding and explaining the levels of civic engagement in advanced nations, with the majority of the focus being on engagement within the USA.[9] This work tends to pay less attention to the role that civil society can play in overthrowing governmental regimes and more to the role that citizens play through traditional democratic avenues in industrialized countries. Within this chapter, both of these conceptions of civil society are appropriate: citizens have responded to the meetings of international institutions and multilateral regimes using the tactics that can be seen in the literature on newly emerging democracies, but they have also joined in the conversations taking place at these meetings by using more institutionalized action forms such as lobbying inside the actual conference halls as NGO observers.

International NGOs, transnational social movements, and protest

In addition to the growing literature on the complex of civil society, in recent years scholars have begun to study the role that civil society organizations are playing within transnational social movements.[10] Perhaps Smith[11] best describes the extensive array of work conducted by international NGOs that are involved in transnational social movements today:

By facilitating flows of information across national boundaries, organizations with transnational ties helped cultivate movement identities, transcend nationally defined interests, and build solidary identities with a global emphasis.

This summary aptly describes the work of many NGOs at international meetings. These organizations communicate the interests of their constituents to the representatives of governments and economic institutions, and report the progress of the meetings to their members. In addition, many civil society organizations involved in international meetings have also played a role in organizing protests that take place outside the conference halls during the meetings.

With the increasing frequency of large protests at international meetings, scholars have looked towards these international and transnational social movements to understand citizen resistance to globalization.[12] These authors look at many different types of social movement organizations and protest. One such example can be seen by the stark differences between the 1999 anti-globalization protests in Seattle[13] and the 20,000-person demonstration in Kyoto, Japan during the UN Framework Convention on Climate Change negotiations in 1997.[14] Although these cases are very different, they both provide examples of social movements responding to specific aspects of globalization: economic integration and multilateral environmental governance.[15] Generally, social movements have demonstrated *against* the former and *in support of* the latter. This distinction is very important to bear in mind when looking at the tactics and messages promoted by the protests presented in this chapter, which will be discussed in more detail in the sections that follow. At the same time, as will also be discussed in further detail, these different types of protest are similar in their initial organization and structure.

Although scholars have just recently begun to study protests at international meetings, sociologists had been studying social protest well before the literature on transnational social movements emerged.[16] The general goal of this research has been to understand who protests and why. In the beginning, scholars interpreted protest as collective behaviour stemming from the irrational action of emotional masses.[17] More recently, however, sociologists have dispelled what McPhail[18] calls the "myth of the madding crowd", finding instead that protest participants tend to behave rationally. Beyond the question of the behaviour of protesters, research has looked into the relationship between the organizational forms and action forms of social movements.[19] In other words, these scholars have studied what tactics are more or less likely to be used by particular social movements based on the level of organization of their members.

Perhaps the organizational forms associated with protest have been most clearly addressed in the work of Staggenborg. In her analysis, she goes beyond the basic organization/non-organization dichotomy presented in much of the literature by looking more clearly at social movement organizations (SMOs) involved in the pro-choice movement and discussing levels of formalization and centralization. She also points out the difficulty associated with classifying SMOs. In her own words, "some SMOs look formalized on paper, but are informal in practice".[20] Similarly, within his research on the women's movement, Buechler also adds to the simple dichotomy between organization/non-organization.[21] By presenting the notion of the social movement community, the author describes a type of social movement organization that is made up of "informally organized networks of movement activists".[22] In other words, social movement communities lie in between the institutionalized social movement organization and the non-institutionalized social movement. Koopmans[23] goes beyond these classifications in his attempt to disaggregate different types of organizational support for protest. He identifies four types of organizational support: terrorist, communist vanguard, other SMO, and external ally.

The discussion of action forms within the sociological literature tends to follow this research on organizational/institutional forms. After disaggregating organizational forms, the authors come to similar results as those of Piven and Cloward, who say that "Protest is indeed 'outside of normal politics' and 'against normal politics' in the sense that people break the rules defining permissible modes of political action".[24] Staggenborg, for example, says that formalized SMOs "tend to engage in institutionalized tactics and typically do not initiate disruptive direct action tactics".[25] In Buechler's work on social movement communities, he says that "formal organization cannot be assumed to be the predominant or even the most common form for mobilizing collective action".[26] Koopmans also finds similar results in his analysis of protest waves in West Germany. He reclassifies action forms into disruptive, confrontational, light violence, and heavy violence, and looks at the relationships between these different action forms and organizational support. The study concludes that "the involvement of organizations has a moderating influence rather than a disruptive influence".[27]

More recently, scholars have begun to discuss the internationalization of social movements and protest. Meyer and Tarrow, for example, write about what they call a "movement society". With the emergence of transnational social movements, the authors find that social protest, protest behaviour, and the professionalization and institutionalization of social movements have become more common.[28] In contrast to Piven and Cloward's finding that protest is not a part of normal politics,[29] these new movements have "often acted *within* institutional politics and movement activists have learned to combine institutional modes of action with non-institutional convention".[30] In many cases, protests at the meetings of international institutions and multilateral regimes represent this type of combination, as has been previously noted, in that civil society organizations work both *inside* the meetings as NGO participants and simultaneously organize protests to take place *outside* the conference centres that were housing the meetings.

In order to understand the differences between the civil society actors participating inside these meetings and those protesting outside them, it is useful to refer to the definitions provided by Tarrow in his work on transnational politics.[31] Although civil society includes many types of organizational forms, to restate once again, this chapter specifically focuses on social actors within civil society that are working inside and outside of these international meetings. As such, the difference between international non-governmental organizations and transnational social movements is of particular interest to this chapter.[32] Many of the civil society actors who are working on issues related to the environmental effects of international institutions and multilateral regimes are international non-governmental organizations, which Tarrow defines as "organizations that operate independently of governments, are composed of members from two or more countries, and are organized to advance their members' international goals and provide services to citizens of other states through routine transactions with states, private actors, and international institutions".[33] Also in attendance at the meetings of international institutions are non-governmental organizations that represent members from only *one* country.[34] International and domestic NGOs, as defined above, tend to be the only civil society actors who participate in the meetings of international institutions and multilateral regimes and they tend to use more institutionalized forms of action. Although these types of organizations are the only ones that participate *inside* these international meetings, other civil society actors are involved in discussions surrounding the meetings; but they tend to participate *outside*. Particularly, transnational social movements have organized around these meetings to stage protests and demonstrations. In Tarrow's words, transnational social movements are "socially mobilized groups with constitutents in at least two states, engaged in sustained contentious interaction with powerholders in at least one state other than their own, or against an international institution, or a multinational economic actor".[35] The "50 Years is Enough" campaign against the World Bank and the Climate Action Network's campaign to pressure states to ratify the Kyoto Protocol provide clear examples of transnational social movements that have actively demonstrated at international meetings in recent years.

The difference between international non-governmental organizations and transnational social movements can be seen in the action forms that they use. Turning once again to the work of Tarrow, he restates the difference between the different types of civil society action:

Transnational social movements engage in sustained contentious interaction with states, multinational actors, or international institutions, whereas INGOs [international non-governmental organizations] engage in routine transactions with the same kinds of actors and provide services to citizens of other states.[36]

In other words, NGOs participate inside international meetings while transnational social movements protest outside them.

Perhaps beginning with the demonstrations against the World Trade Organization in Seattle in November 1999, protests against international institutions and multilateral regimes have become more common. Since Seattle, international protests have taken place in cities around the world including Washington, DC, Prague, Genoa, Quebec, and New York. Although it is clear that international non-governmental organizations and transnational social movements have both participated in these international meetings, it is unclear how these two civil society actors are related to one another. In other words, what is the relationship between protesters and NGO participants at these international meetings? The sections that follow will incorporate two different approaches to understanding this relationship. First, the chapter will look at the overall levels of civil society participation at these international meetings by analysing the relationship between the number of protesters outside specific international meetings and the number of NGO observers inside the meetings. Second, it will look more clearly at the relationship between the protesters outside international meetings and those NGO observers inside the meetings by presenting data on protesters' affiliation to social movement organizations[37] at two specific demonstrations – one that was held to show support for international environmental policy-making and one that protested against economic globalization.

Protests and participation at international meetings

A first step to understanding the characteristics and levels of civil society participation and engagement at international meetings is to look at the relationship between NGO participation and civil society protesters at recent international meetings. As has been previously stated, civil society actors have protested against aspects of economic globalization and in support of aspects of political globalization. Therefore, this chapter includes analyses of civil society participation and protest at the meeting of an economic institution and a multilateral environmental regime. This section presents data from meetings of the World Bank/International Monetary Fund (IMF) and the Conferences of the Parties of the UN Framework Convention on Climate Change (UNFCCC). Due to the timing of the recent meetings and data availability, it presents data from two meetings of each: the annual meeting of the World Bank/IMF in Prague in September 2000 and the spring meeting in Washington, DC, in April 2000; and the two sixth Conference of the Parties meetings of the UNFCCC climate change negotiations in November 2000 (COP6) and July 2001 (COP6bis). Before presenting the analysis, it is important to restate one of the significant differences between the kinds of civic responses to these different conferences: civil society actors participated in protests *against* certain aspects of the practices of international economic institutions such as the World Bank/IMF, and civil society actors participated in protests *in support of* strong policies being accepted at the meetings of environmental regimes such as the climate change negotiations. It is important to keep these differences in mind as we look at data from these international meetings.

Data and methods

This section looks at the differences between protesters and NGO participants at recent meetings of the World Bank/IMF and the UNFCCC climate change negotiations. NGO participation is operationalized by the number of people affiliated with NGOs that are registered as participant observers at these different meetings. NGO participants are included in the participant directories of the UNFCCC climate change negotiations that are made available to the public by the UNFCCC Secretariat at every round of the negotiations.[38] Lists of NGO participants registered for the meetings of the World Bank/IMF, in contrast, are not publicly available. Approximations of the number of NGO participants at recent meetings were provided by representatives of both the World Bank and the IMF. In the cases where the approximations were different, the numbers were averaged.

It is also important to note the difference between the levels of NGO representation permitted at these different meetings. As long as a person can provide a letter stating that he/she is affiliated with an NGO, participant observer status is granted by the UNFCCC Secretariat to attend the

Table 9.1 NGO observers versus protesters at international meetings

	NGO observers		Protesters	
	World Bank/IMF	UNFCCC	World Bank/IMF	UNFCCC
2001		1,587 people		3,000
Autumn 2000	425 people	3,144 people	7,500	5,000
Spring 2000	200 people		15,000	

climate change negotiations. As a result of this policy, most NGOs that participate in the negotiations bring multiple participants – some even send more than 20 members. The World Bank/IMF, in contrast, only allows one representative for each NGO that registers.[39] Representatives of the World Bank and IMF state that the NGO registration process is *pro forma* and almost all NGOs that register in time are approved to send a representative.

Data on the demonstrations at each of these meetings were provided by both NGO accounts and mainstream media sources of articles on the protests.[40] In cases where the media and NGO accounts of protest participation were different, the numbers were averaged. Table 9.1 provides the number of people registered as NGO participants and estimates of the number of protesters at the recent meetings of the World Bank/IMF and the UNFCCC climate change negotiations.

The disassociation index

In order to understand the types of civil society participation taking place at these meetings, this section looks at the relationship between civil society engagement inside and outside of these international meetings. The author has created a "disassociation index" that measures the extent to which civil society is disassociated from what is taking place at these international meetings. The index compares the levels of civil society protesters to participants; it is the ratio of the protest population to the NGO participant observers.[41] As might be expected, the disassociation indices were very different for these international meetings; in particular, they were significantly higher for the World Bank/IMF meetings than the UNFCCC negotiations. The annual meeting of the World Bank in 2000 yielded an index of 17.65 and the spring meeting in 2000 yielded an index of 75. In contrast, both of the climate change negotiations generated a disassociation index of less than 2 (1.59 in the autumn of 2000 and 1.89 in summer 2001). Table 9.2 provides the disassociation indices for these international meetings.

Table 9.2 Disassociation indices for international meetings

	World Bank/IMF	UNFCCC
2001		1.89
Autumn 2000	17.65	1.59
Spring 2000	75.00	

The disparities between the disassociation indices point to significant differences in the characteristics of the types of civil society participation at these international meetings. It is likely that because of the limitations to NGO participation in the World Bank/IMF meetings and the negative responses by civil society to the financial institutions themselves, there were significantly more citizens protesting outside these meetings than participating in the discussions that were taking place inside the meetings. Once again, it is important to note that this research points to the difference between protests *against* meetings of international institutions and those that are *in support* of a meeting that is taking place. The disassociation index, in fact, provides a useful way to quantify these differences. Most of the demonstrations that involve tens of thousands of citizens and lead to violence tend to be associated with the meetings of international organizations that do not include a large amount of NGO involvement or transparency. Meetings that include the active participation of NGOs and provide opportunities for citizen engagement inside the meeting have not experienced the same levels of protest and score much lower in the disassociation index.

Protests and social movement organizations

Although the disassociation index helps us to understand the relationship between protests and participation at international meetings, it does not provide any information about the protesters themselves or their connection to NGOs. In order to understand the organizational affiliation of the protesters at these international meetings, the chapter will now turn to look at how protests are organized and how people come to attend civil society protests. The pages that follow present a study of the characteristics of civil society protesters at protest events at two separate international meetings: the Human Dike at the UNFCCC negotiations in autumn 2000, and the Another World is Possible rally during the World Economic Forum in winter 2002. The demonstrations studied represent examples of the different types of international meetings being discussed within this chapter: international economic institutions and multilateral environmental regimes. It is the hope that by analysing data collected at these protests, we will gain a deeper understanding of the relationship between social movement organizations and protest at international meetings.

Data and methods

In order to understand this relationship, the author studied the protests at two international meetings that received a lot of public attention: the COP6 meeting to negotiate the Kyoto Protocol for global climate change, and the World Economic Forum, a meeting of the "world's most powerful policy makers and entrepreneurs".[42] Background data for the different protests were collected in different ways: data for the Human Dike were collected through in-depth qualitative interviews with protest organizers representing the local and international organizations sponsoring the demonstration, and information about the protests from the organizers and media sources was collected; data for the Another World Is Possible protest were collected through the compilation of background information from the internet and the popular press. Information on the protest was also collected from protest organizers. The bulk of the data about the protesters at these two events, however, were collected in the same way: 204 protest participants were randomly selected and answered the survey at the Human Dike and 316 protest participants were randomly selected and answered the survey at the Another World Is Possible rally.

The Human Dike

On Saturday 18 November 2000 protesters were surveyed while they filled sandbags and piled them to form a dike around a section of the conference centre within which the climate change negotiations were being held. Because eight people refused to answer questions and four people were unable to respond to questions in the languages spoken by those conducting the surveys,[43] 204 participants from 25 countries completed the entire survey. The participants were randomly selected: the fifth person in each of the many lines of dike-builders that made up the protest was interviewed. All of the people were asked the same questions regarding how and why they had attended the protest.

The purpose of the Human Dike was, in the words of Ilse Chang, the local coordinator for the event from the Dutch environmental organization Milieudefensie, to "show that people are concerned [with the issue of global climate change] and want action now".[44] The international coordinator of the protest, Tony Juniper of Friends of the Earth International, further explained: "the goal of public demonstrations [such as the

Human Dike] is to shift the discussion ... the countries at the negotiation are defending their domestic interests but they are not terribly interested in their citizens".[45]

It is important to note that this protest had the stated purpose of trying to show support for the states participating in the meeting so that they negotiated and consented to a strong multilateral environmental agreement; the goal of the protest was not to disturb or stop the negotiations. Tony Juniper of Friends of the Earth International compared this protest to the protest that took place during the meeting of the World Trade Organization in 1999: "In Seattle, they were trying to stop the meeting ... we are trying to make climate policy better."[46] Consistent with this purpose, the protest organizers respected the boundaries maintained by the security for the UN-sponsored conference. In order to increase participation the protest was scheduled for a Saturday, when citizens would be off work and when most NGO observers to the negotiations would be free to participate. The organizers of the demonstration had worked through their social networks to recruit citizens from all over the world who were involved in this transnational social movement.

The Another World Is Possible protest

On Saturday 2 February 2002 approximately 7,000 people took to the streets of New York City to protest the practices of the World Economic Forum that was holding its annual meeting inside the Waldorf-Astoria hotel.[47] The purpose of the protest was summarized by Another World Is Possible (AWIP), a coalition of more than 100 social movement organizations, that organized protests to take place during the five-day event: "Tell the 'Masters of the Universe' that they don't have the answers to our problems. Join us in the streets as we visualize solutions that build a better world where the people are in control."[48] A march was planned from the south-eastern corner of Central Park down to the Waldorf-Astoria hotel. All interested organizations and individuals were invited to join the march. Before the march began, a rally was held on the edge of Central Park in Grand Army Plaza. Protesters were surveyed during the rally. Surveyors entered the rally from the four corners of the plaza on which the rally was taking place.[49] The participants were randomly selected and every fifth person in the crowd was interviewed.[50] Everyone was asked the same questions regarding how and why they had attended the protest. Because 27 people refused to answer questions and one person did not complete the full survey, 316 participants from four countries completed the entire survey. These questions were worded identically to those on the English-language survey for the Human Dike.

Unlike the Human Dike protest, it is important to note here that the Another World Is Possible march was organized to protest *against* the practices of the World Economic Forum and against economic glob-alization more generally. Although groups interested in different types of protest joined, the organizers asked that participants honour their request that the protest be completely non-violent and exclude direct action, or what is called in the parlance of these demonstrations "green". In the words of a flyer that was handed out, "many local activists would prefer not to alienate our local heroes right now, especially since so many of them are feeling screwed by the same system we are protesting".[51] Even with the plea from the protest organizers, 36 people were arrested during the protest.[52]

Results

Who protests at an international meeting?

The first question in the survey looked at the diversity of protesters. Roughly one-third of the protesters came from the country in which the Human Dike protest was held: the Netherlands. Although Dutch par-ticipants were the largest percentage of the population, the protesters surveyed represented 25 countries. Table 9.3 presents the distribution of protesters and the countries from which they came. The majority of par-ticipants involved in the protest were from Europe. Given the prohibi-tively expensive cost of travel to the Hague from outside Europe, it is not a surprise that the overwhelming majority of protest participants were European.

In contrast to the participants at the Human Dike protest, most of the people protesting the World Economic Forum came from the country within which it was staged: the USA. That said, it is important to note the significant differences in size between the USA and the Netherlands. Given this difference, participants were asked from which state or coun-try (if outside of the USA) they had come. Table 9.4 presents these data. Over 97 per cent of the protesters surveyed came from the USA and more than 67 per cent of them came from within New York itself.

How do protesters hear about a demonstration?

The second question in the survey addressed a significant issue of interest to social movement theorists who study protests.[53] Specifically, the ques-tion asked how people came to learn that the demonstration would be taking place. Table 9.5 summarizes how the protesters learned about the Human Dike protest. Over 70 per cent of the protest participants learned about the demonstration from an organization. Over 18 per cent of the people who attended the protest heard about it through their social net-work: a friend or family member who was attending the protest. Televi-

Table 9.3 Participant distribution at the Human Dike protest

Country	Frequency	%
Austria	3	1.5
Belgium	15	7.4
Canada	1	0.5
Columbia	1	0.5
Croatia	1	0.5
Czech Republic	1	0.5
Denmark	4	2.0
Estonia	1	0.5
Finland	1	0.5
France	23	11.3
Germany	24	11.8
Hungary	1	0.5
Italy	3	1.5
Lithuania	1	0.5
Netherlands	67	32.8
Nigeria	1	0.5
Norway	1	0.5
Poland	1	0.5
Slovak Republic	4	2.0
Spain	2	1.0
Sweden	1	0.5
Switzerland	1	0.5
Turkey	1	0.5
UK	41	20.1
USA	4	2.0
Total	204	100

sion, radio, and other media sources recruited about 6 per cent of the participations.

Table 9.6 summarizes how the protesters learned about the Another World is Possible protest against the World Economic Forum. Over 28 per cent of the protest participants learned about the demonstration from an organization. Over 32 per cent heard about it through their social network. In contrast to the Human Dike protest, one-quarter of the people who attended the protest heard about it through the traditional media. In addition, almost 10 per cent of the protesters said that they heard about it through the internet.

With whom do protesters come to demonstrations?

The third question in the survey focused on the issue of how people mobilize to attend a demonstration. Of particular interest in this question is whether participants travelled to the protest alone, with friends, or with an organization. Table 9.7 presents the distribution of how people came

Table 9.4 Participant distribution at the Another World is Possible protest

Country or state	Frequency	%
Argentina	1	0.3
California, USA	4	1.3
Canada	7	2.2
Colorado, USA	1	0.3
Connecticut, USA	9	2.8
Washington, DC, USA	7	2.2
England	1	0.3
Florida, USA	1	0.3
Georgia, USA	1	0.3
Illinois, USA	1	0.3
Indiana, USA	1	0.3
Massachusetts, USA	13	4.1
Maryland, USA	1	0.3
Maine, USA	1	0.3
Michigan, USA	4	1.3
Minnesota, USA	2	0.6
North Carolina, USA	8	2.5
New Hampshire, USA	1	0.3
New Jersey, USA	16	5.1
New York, USA	212	67.0
Ohio, USA	3	0.9
Okalahoma, USA	1	0.3
Pennsylvania, USA	9	2.8
Puerto Rico, USA	1	0.3
Rhode Island, USA	5	1.6
Vermont, USA	3	0.9
Washington, USA	2	0.6
Total	316	100

Table 9.5 How do protesters hear about a demonstration? The Human Dike

Source	Frequency	%
Media	13	6.4
Other	10	4.9
Social movement organization	144	70.6
Social network	37	18.1
Total	204	100

to the Human Dike protest. The majority of the people attending the protest travelled with members of an organization. The rest of the participants at the protest were split almost equally between those who came with friends and/or family and those who came alone.

In contrast to the Human Dike, the majority of people who attended

Table 9.6 How do protesters hear about a demonstration? The Another World is Possible protest

Source	Frequency	%
Media	79	25.0
Other	16	5.1
Social movement organization	89	28.2
Social network	102	32.3
Internet	30	9.5
Total	316	100

Table 9.7 With whom do protesters come to demonstrations? The Human Dike

	Frequency	%
Alone	33	16.2
Friends or family	45	22.0
Social movement organization	126	61.8
Total	204	100

Table 9.8 With whom do protesters come to demonstrations? The Another World is Possible protest

	Frequency	%
Alone	62	19.6
Friends or family	162	51.3
Social movement organization	92	29.1
Total	316	100

the Another World is Possible protest did not travel with members of a social movement organization but came with friends or family members. Over 50 per cent of the participants accompanied friends and/or family members, compared to the almost 30 per cent who came with an organization. Almost 20 per cent of the protest participants at the protest against the World Economic Forum came alone. Table 9.8 presents the data for this protest.

What percentage of protesters received funding to attend?

In addition to questions about how people learn that a demonstration is taking place, and with whom they travel to the protest, the survey included a question about whether support was provided by organizations to protest participants. The goal of this question was to explore whether participants received financial compensation for attending the protest.

Table 9.9 What percentage of protesters received funding to attend? The Human Dike

	Frequency	%
Received funding	52	25.5
Did not receive funding	152	74.5
Total	204	100

Table 9.10 What percentage of protesters received funding to attend? The Another World is Possible protest

	Frequency	%
Received funding	19	6.0
Did not receive funding	297	94.0
Total	316	100

Table 9.9 provides the distribution of people attending the Human Dike protest who received funding. About 25 per cent of the protesters acknowledged receiving a reimbursement to cover travel costs. The Dutch environmental organization which sponsored the Human Dike, Milieudefensie, offered to reimburse Dutch participants for their train fares, but most participants surveyed stated that they would not take advantage of that offer. Similarly, Friends of the Earth organized reductions in the price of a ferry ticket for participants coming from the UK, and arranged buses to bring participants from France. Since many who received support in the form of subsidized travel did not perceive it as "funding", it is probable that the survey results underestimate the percentage of the protesters who received support from organizations to attend the protest.

In contrast to the Human Dike, which was held during an international negotiation that involved a high number of NGO observers who subsequently participated in the protest during the weekend, the World Economic Forum involved very few if any non-governmental organizations. This situation contributed to the fact that only 6 per cent of the people surveyed at the Another World is Possible protest received any funding to attend. Table 9.10 presents these data.

Discussion

The data collected through the surveys of protesters at the Human Dike demonstration at the climate change negotiations in the Hague and the

Another World is Possible protest at the World Economic Forum in New York add a level of understanding to the relationship between civil society organizations and international protest. As Meyer and Tarrow[54] suggest in their work, civil society actors work both *within* international institutional structures by lobbying members of national delegations as NGO participants, and by organizing protests *outside* of the meetings of such international institutions and multilateral regimes. In other words, these international meetings bring about the involvement of both international non-governmental organizations and transnational social movements. It is, perhaps, because NGOs are included in the negotiations of multilateral environmental agreements and receive unrestricted official observer status for their members from the United Nations to attend meetings like the one in the Hague that protests at such international meetings tend to be orderly and supportive of what is going on inside the conference centre. In contrast, very few NGOs were allowed to participate in the meeting of the World Economic Forum. As mentioned earlier, the Another World is Possible protest – even though organizers requested that the protest be "green" – was less orderly and 36 people were arrested. The differences between the Human Dike and the Another World is Possible protests may be a product of the lack of non-governmental organization involvement and engagement in the World Economic Forum itself. The people protesting in New York were doing so, at least to some degree, because they were not permitted inside the Waldorf-Astoria. Many of the protesters at the Hague, in contrast, were actually registered participants in the climate change negotiations. To restate the results presented earlier, the climate change negotiations in 2000 and 2001 yielded a disassociation index of 1.89 and 1.59 respectively. In other words, there were less than twice as many protesters as there were NGO participants at the climate change negotiations. The meetings of the World Bank/IMF in 2000, which are similar to the World Economic Forum (WEF) in their interests and levels of engagement with civil society, yielded disassociation indices that are much larger (17.65 and 75 respectively). It is also important to note that the protest against the WEF was the first large-scale protest to take place in the USA after 11 September 2001. Thus it is likely that there was lower attendance at this protest, and those who did attend engaged in less civil disobedience because of the recent events.

Contrary to protests against economic globalization, the Human Dike protest was so legitimized by political élites involved in the negotiations that Jan Pronk, the Environment Minister of the Netherlands and President of the COP6 negotiations, appeared at the demonstration and had the honour of placing the final sandbag on the Human Dike in front of members of the international press. Of more significance to this study, however, is the relationship between the protesters and the civil society organizations which coordinated the protest. Organizations informed the public about the protest, participants travelled to the demonstration with the organizations themselves, and some organizations even coordinated financial assistance to cover participant travel to the protest. Even though fewer of the Another World is Possible protest participants received funding from organizations and learned about the protest from the organizations, they still played an important part in mobilizing participants: over a quarter of the participants reported that they had heard about the protest from an organization and came to the protest with the organization itself.[55]

Even with the differences between the goals of protests at these very different international meetings, civil society organizations played a significant role in organizing and coordinating both the Another World is Possible and the Human Dike protests. In some ways, unlike Piven and Cloward's well-known statement about social protest being outside of normal politics,[56] these types of international protest have become a part of normal global politics. At the same time, demonstrations that support what is going on inside the meetings and also include the involvement of NGO observers who are participating inside the meeting are qualitatively different to demonstrations at meetings where most civil society actors are kept outside of the events.

These data give us the opportunity to begin to compare the participants at a protest in support of the global governance of the environment and those against the meeting of an international institution involved in economic integration that has been criticized for its effects on the global environment. Although protest in response to different aspects of globalization may take distinctly different action forms, as was discussed earlier, these data support the notion that the role of civil society organizations – both transnational and domestic – is strong in organizing protests. Gaining a better understanding of the relationship between different civil society actors – international non-governmental organizations and transnational social movements – will contribute to our overall knowledge about how and in what ways institutions should respond to citizens' environmental concerns within this increasingly globalized world.

Implications for multilateral governance regimes

With these results, one can now turn to the question of how a world environment organization and multilateral environmental governance regimes should engage with civil society actors in an effective manner.

As the disassociation index clearly shows, the more NGOs there are involved in the political process itself, the less transnational social movements mobilize to protest. In addition, demonstrations at meetings where multiple members of NGOs can participate are designed to contribute to the policy-making process and do not aim to stop the meeting. By allowing multiple members of organizations to participate *inside* the halls of the meetings – if not inside the rooms themselves – while at the same time providing a certain level of transparency to their activities, it is likely that there will be less civic dissatisfaction with the process itself. When there are high levels of civic dissatisfaction, it tends to be expressed by transnational social movements in the form of protests – many of which turn violent.

Although the level of civil society dissatisfaction with international meetings can be altered through transparency and increased levels of NGO participation, civil society organizations will continue to organize protests outside international meetings until civil society's role in international meetings of all types becomes institutionalized.[57] The types of protests that take place and the amount of dissatisfaction that will be expressed by protesters are directly correlated to their access to information and to what is going on inside the meetings. Multilateral organizations should keep these recommendations in mind for effectively engaging civil society.

Another way of further engaging civil society actors is to hold smaller, regional meetings that provide opportunities for input from civil society organizations. Civic dissatisfaction with international meetings tends to occur when there is no place for input and grievances to be heard. As one thinks about how to develop an effective world environment organization, it is very important that NGOs and civil society are more broadly and actively involved in the process – at both regional and global levels. It is these civil society actors which are the bridge from multilateral regimes to civil society that is geographically rooted. If the bridge is closed, civil society actors will continue to make their voices heard, often in disruptive and potentially violent ways. In addition, if the political will for multilateral environmental regimes and a world environment organization is expected to be the product of pressure from civil society actors, then they must be involved in all aspects of the process of environmental regime formation.

The following are a summary of lessons learned from the protests at the meetings of international institutions, and recommendations for ways to increase the levels of civil society engagement for a world environment organization or any other multilateral institution.

- Transparency of the actions of the organization through the internet and other educational documents.

- Unlimited non-governmental organization participation as registered observers in meetings.
- Support of demonstrations outside of meetings with involvement of institutional representatives.
- Non-governmental organization participation throughout the process, including a role within the organization's development, perhaps in the form of an advisory council.

Notes

1. The author would like to thank Simone Pulver of the University of California at Berkeley and Anne Janssen at Wageningen University for assistance in surveying protesters at the Human Dike protest and David Berman, Jessica Green, and Gina Neff of Columbia University and Andrea Boykowycz of the New School for their assistance in surveying protesters at the World Economic Forum protest. Also, the author would like to thank Professor Sidney Tarrow and the Transnational Contention Workshop at Cornell University for helpful comments on earlier drafts of this chapter.
2. Bhagwati, Jagdis. 2001. "Why globalization is good", *Items: Social Science Research Council*, Vol. 2, Nos 3–4, pp. 7–8; Charnovitz, Steve. 2002. "A world environment organization", presentation at the World Summit on Sustainable Development PrepCom, 27 March, New York.
3. Calhoun, Craig. 1992. *Habermas in the Public Sphere*. Cambridge, MA: MIT Press; Cohen, Jean L. and Andrew Arato. 1994. *Civil Society and Political Theory*. Cambridge, MA: MIT Press; Dewey, John. 1927. *The Public and Its Problems*. New York: Holt Rinehart and Winston; Gramsci, Antonio. 1971. *Selections from the Prison Notebooks of Antonio Gramsci*. New York: International Publishers; Habermas, Jurgen. 1989. *The Structural Transformation of the Public Sphere*. Cambridge, MA: MIT Press; Habermas, Jurgen. 1998. *Between Facts and Norms*. Cambridge, MA: MIT Press.
4. Cohen and Arato, *ibid.*, p. ix.
5. Emirbayer, Mustafa and Mimi Sheller. 1999. "Publics in history", *Theory and Society*, Vol. 28, pp. 143–197 at p. 151.
6. http://allafrica.com/stories/200209010002.html.
7. Emirbayer and Sheller, note 5 above, p. 146. For a complete discussion, see Cohen and Arato, note 3 above; Hann, Chris and Elizabeth Dunn. 1996. *Civil Society: Challenging Western Models*. London: Routledge.
8. Arato, Andrew. 2000. *Civil Society, Constitution, and Legitimacy*. Lanham: Rowman and Littlefield; Cohen and Arato, note 3 above.
9. Putnam, Robert D. 2000. *Bowling Alone*. New York: Simon and Schuster; Skocpol, Theda and Morris P. Fiorina. 1999. *Civic Engagement in American Democracy*. Washington, DC: Brookings Institution.
10. Hanagan, Michael. 1998. "Irish transnational social movements, deterritorialized migrants, and the state system: The last one hundred and forty years", *Mobilization*, Vol. 3, No. 1, pp. 107–126; Keck, Margaret E. and Kathryn Sikkink. 1998. *Activists Beyond Borders: Advocacy Networks in International Politics*. New York: Cornell University Press; Lewis, Tammy L. 2000. "Transnational conservation movement organizations: Shaping the protected area systems of less developed countries", *Mobilization*, Vol. 5, No. 1, pp. 105–123; Meyer, David S. and Sidney G. Tarrow. 1998. *The Social Movement Society: Contentious Politics for a New Century*. Lanham: Rowman and Littlefield, pp.

ix, 282; Risse-Kappen, Thomas. 1995. *Bringing Transnational Relations Back In: Non-state Actors, Domestic Structure and International Institutions.* Cambridge: Cambridge University Press; Rothman, Franklin Daniel and Pamela E. Oliver. 1999. "From local to global: The anti-dam movement in southern Brazil, 1979–1992", *Mobilization*, Vol. 4, No. 1, pp. 41–57; Smith, Jackie, Charles Chatfield, and Ron Pagnucco. 1997. *Transnational Social Movements and Global Politics: Solidarity Beyond the State.* Syracuse: Syracuse University Press; Tarrow, Sidney. 2001. "Transnational politics: Contention and institutions in international politics", *Annual Review of Political Science*, Vol. 4, pp. 1–20.

11. Smith, Jackie. 2001. "Globalizing resistance: The battle of Seattle and the future of social movements", *Mobilization*, Vol. 6, No. 1, pp. 1–21 at p. 5.

12. Ayres, Jeffrey M. 2001. "Transnational political processes and contention against the global economy", *Mobilization*, Vol. 6, No. 1, pp. 55–68; Caniglia, Beth S. 2002. "Elite alliances and transnational environmental movement organizations", in Jackie Smith and Hank Johnston (eds) *Globalizing Resistance.* New York: Rowman and Littlefield; Keck and Sikkink, note 10 above; Maney, Gregory M. 2001. "Transnational structures and protest: Linking theories and assessing evidence", *Mobilization*, Vol. 6, No. 1, pp. 83–100; Nepstad, Sharon E. 2002. "Creating transnational solidarity: The use of narrative in the US-Central American peace movement", in Jackie Smith and Hank Johnston (eds) *Globalizing Resistance.* New York: Rowman and Littlefield; Reimann, Kim. 2002. "Building networks from the outside in: Japanese NGOs and the Kyoto Climate Change Conference", in Jackie Smith and Hank Johnston (eds) *Globalizing Resistance.* New York: Rowman and Littlefield; Smith, *ibid.*; Tarrow, Sidney. 2002. "Towards a sociology of transnational contention", in Jackie Smith and Hank Johnston (eds) *Globalization and Resistance.* New York: Rowman and Littlefield; Ayres, Jeffrey and Sidney Tarrow. 2002. "The shifting grounds for transnational civic activity", available on the Social Science Research Council website at www.ssrc.org/sept11/essays/ayres.htm.

13. Smith, *ibid.*

14. Reimann, note 12 above.

15. These two characteristics are not meant to represent an exhaustive list. Rather, they represent aspects of political and economic globalization that are particularly relevant for this study.

16. Koopmans, Rudd. 1993. "The dynamics of protest waves: West Germany, 1965–1989", *American Sociological Review*, Vol. 58, No. 5, pp. 637–658; McAdam, Doug. 1982. *Political Process and the Development of Black Insurgency, 1930–1970.* Chicago: University of Chicago Press, p. 304; McPhail, Clark. 1991. *The Myth of the Madding Crowd.* New York: A. de Gruyter; Piven, Frances Fox and Richard A. Cloward. 1977. *Poor People's Movements: Why They Succeed, How They Fail.* New York: Pantheon Books; Piven, Frances Fox and Richard A. Cloward. 1992. "Normalizing collective protest", in M. A. Mueller (ed.) *Frontiers in Social Movement Theory.* New Haven: Yale University Press; Oliver, Pamela. 1989. "Bringing the crowd back in: The non-organizational elements of social movements", *Research in Social Movements, Conflict and Change*, Vol. 11, pp. 1–30; Staggenborg, Suzanne. 1988. "The consequences of professionalization and formalization in the pro-choice movement", *American Sociological Review*, Vol. 53, No. 4, pp. 585–606; Tarrow, Sidney. 1998. *Power in Movement: Social Movements and Contentious Politics.* Cambridge: Cambridge University Press.

17. For a full discussion of the collective behaviour literature see Smelser, Neil. 1962. *Theory of Collective Behavior.* New York: Free Press; Turner, Ralph H. and Lewis M. Killian. 1972. *Collective Behavior.* Englewood Cliffs, NJ: Prentice Hall.

18. McPhail, note 16 above.

19. Buechler, Steven M. 1997. "Beyond resource mobilization?", in Steven M. Buechler

and F. Curt Cylke (eds) *Social Movements: Perspectives and Issues*. Mountain View, CA: Mayfield Publishing, pp. 193–210; Koopmans, note 16 above; Oliver, note 16 above; Staggenborg, note 16 above.

20. Staggenborg, note 16 above, pp. 426, 590.
21. Buechler, note 19 above; see also Buechler, Steven M. 1990. *Women's Movements in the United States*. New Brunswick, NJ: Rutgers University Press.
22. Buechler, note 19 above, p. 199.
23. Koopmans, note 16 above.
24. Piven and Cloward 1992, note 16 above, p. 303; see also Piven and Cloward 1977, note 16 above.
25. Staggenborg, note 16 above, p. 599.
26. Buechler, note 19 above, p. 199.
27. Koopmans, note 16 above, p. 652.
28. Meyer and Tarrow, note 10 above; see also Tarrow, note 16 above.
29. Piven and Cloward 1992, note 16 above, p. 303.
30. Meyer and Tarrow, note 10 above, p. 5.
31. Tarrow, note 10 above.
32. For more specific information on NGO participation in multilateral governance, see Chapter 8 of this volume.
33. Tarrow, note 10 above, p. 12.
34. One such example can be seen by the case of the American Global Climate Coalition, which represented a number of US economic interests at the climate change negotiations.
35. Tarrow, note 10 above, p. 11.
36. *Ibid.*, p. 12.
37. Social movement organizations include international non-governmental organizations and other less institutional organizations.
38. For example, UNFCCC Secretariat. 1999. *Provisional List of Participants – Conference of the Parties Fifth Session*. Bonn: UNFCCC; UNFCCC Secretariat. 2000. *Provisional List of Participants – Conference of the Parties Sixth Session*. The Hague: UNFCCC; UNFCCC Secretariat. 2000. *Provisional List of Participants – Conference of the Parties Sixth Session Part II*. Bonn: UNFCCC.
39. In some cases different branches of the same organization, such as the European and American sections of an NGO, are allowed to send one representative each to the same meeting.
40. Houlder, Vanessa. 2001. "Peaceful protest thrown a lifeline Friends of the Earth", *Financial Times*, 23 July, p. 6; Kahn, Joseph. 2000. "Protests distract global finance meeting", *New York Times*, 27 September, p. A8; Kifner, John and David E. Sanger. 2000. "Financial leaders meet as protests clog Washington", *New York Times*, 17 April, p. A1; McDonald, Frank. 2000. "Protesters at the Hague demand deeds not hot air", *Irish Times*, p. 4.
41. The equation for the disassociation index is "number of protesters/number of participants".
42. Sanger, David E. 2002. "Economic forum shifts its focus to new dangers", *New York Times*, 3 February, p. A1.
43. Interviewers conducted the surveys in English, French, Dutch, or German, depending on the protester's language of choice.
44. Interview with author, 16 November 2000.
45. *Ibid.*
46. *Ibid.*
47. *New York Times*. 2002. "Drawing a line", *New York Times*, 3 February, p. A1.

48. www.anotherworldispossible.com/convergenceA.html.
49. The rally took place on the small square that is located at Fifth Avenue between 59th and 60th Streets.
50. Although the protesters were not standing in formal lines like those at the Human Dike, the crowd was so dense that it was possible to weave through the demonstration surveying every fifth person.
51. Another World Is Possible (AWIP). 2002. Protest flyer, 2 February.
52. *New York Times*, note 47 above.
53. McPhail, note 16 above; Oliver, note 16 above; Smelser, note 17 above; Turner and Killian, note 17 above; Meyer and Tarrow, note 10 above.
54. Meyer and Tarrow, note 10 above.
55. Anarchist affinity groups have been included under the classification of civil society organization.
56. Piven and Cloward 1992, note 16 above, p. 303.
57. For example, Gemmill, Barbara and Abimbola Bamidele-Izu. 2002. "The role of NGOs and civil society in global environmental governance", in D. C. Esty and M. H. Ivanova (eds) *Global Environmental Governance: Options and Opportunities*. New Haven: Yale Center for Environmental Law and Policy, pp. 1–24.

Business/industry and
environmental governance

10

Balancing TNCs, the states, and the international system in global environmental governance: A critical perspective

Harris Gleckman[1]

Transnational corporations are unavoidably part of the dialogue on global environmental governance. One aspect of environmental governance is to strike the correct balance in environmental protection between global market forces and international public needs. In political science terms, one of the functions of governance is to set rules to neutralize the imperfections in a market and ensure that legitimate public concerns are incorporated appropriately in the operations of the marketplace. Most of the chapters in this book examine the role of international environmental governance between states. This chapter examines the role of interstate bodies, firms, and civil society in global environmental governance.

The chapter opens with a reflection on the way governments engage in the environmental management of their domestic business enterprises and how this has changed over time. At the domestic level, there is no doubt that there is an ongoing power alignment and realignment between a state-driven environmental regime, on the one hand, and a private-sector-driven environmental system, on the other. The should-the-state-decide or should-the-manufacturer-decide debate has a long history, going back at least to the days when environmental regulations were principally local zoning rules.[2] The chapter offers an overview of domestic practices in OECD countries and presumes that these long-standing domestic histories will affect how interstate actors and transnational corporations at the international level will approach and understand international environmental governance.

The argument here is that the power balance in national environmental governance has shifted within the last 15 years, from a system that is mainly state-driven to one that is increasing market-driven. Internationally, things are a little different. The chapter looks at some special characteristics regarding the international environmental governance of business activities; the rationale underlying the recent evolution of international private environmental rule-making; and the role that a world environment organization would need to play. It concludes with a number of policy recommendations that can redress the current imbalance in the international environmental arena and give greater weight to government and public participation in global environmental management.

Domestic markets

Current government environment regulatory systems affecting business activities can best be seen as having four major components:[3] laws, regulations, enforcement, and public engagement. What is unique in each OECD country is the variety of ways in which these four components are combined and the relative importance given to each element in daily practice. In the OECD context, "laws" are those governmental regulatory activities made through a parliamentary process; "regulations" are those governmental regulatory activities made by an administrative process; "enforcement" denotes those government regulatory activities performed by administrative agencies in conjunction with judicial bodies; and the "public engagement" components are those governmental activities that obligate the state to keep citizens informed on environmental matters.

Table 10.1 presents some of the endogenous and exogenous factors

Table 10.1 Selected factors that create differences between national environmental regimes

- Differences in range of ecological realities
- Different choices in different historical experiences
  - different accidents affect public consciousness
  - different issues get broadcast media attention
  - different cultural concerns and environmental values
  - differences in the scope and conception of the "environment"
- Different underlying legal regimes
- Different existing administrative systems
- Different history of external impositions and political battles (e.g. colonial history, civil war)

that affect the particular combinations in different OECD countries. The different combinations of these four components also reflect the relative political power of citizen groups, the state, and corporate interests at any given time.

A state regulatory system affecting business activities is needed by "civil society" and the "business sector", but in different ways. The former needs the state to provide protections that individual consumers and nature cannot, on their own, effect. The latter needs the state to provide legitimacy of standards, to minimize the advantages of environmental free corporate riders, and occasionally to restrict market entry that could challenge the existing market shares.

The business need for legitimacy of its standards and the associated enforcement of these standards is widely recognized in the business press. In order to garner public trust, individual businesses recognize that they benefit from state regulation whenever they proclaim "we are law-abiding corporate citizens" and "our emissions meet government standards". Business also endorses governmental standards when they provide a legal ceiling on civil liability matters and opportunities for effective advertising campaigns ("government reports that XX is the best in its class").[4]

Corporate free-riders in the environment area are those firms which undertake actions that get "bad" press for an industry. The chemical industry as a whole may clean up its act, but public perception of chemical dangers will be strongly influenced by the misbehaviour of the weakest firm in the industry. Leading business executives are also acutely aware that these corporate "bad" actors can promote public demand for greater breadth and specificity in laws and regulations and greater resources assigned to enforcement and public disclosure. Arranging for the government to enforce laws and regulations against the marginal firms is an acceptable way of reducing the potential for public and state engagement in environmental management.

It is less acknowledged in the business literature that environmental regulations can influence the structure of the market. Larger and well-established firms have a vested interest in having whatever environmental rules there are based on their current technology and management systems. These "state rules" can then serve to protect their engineering investments and act as barriers to entry for potential competitors.

What is most relevant for this chapter is that both individual business enterprises at the national level and the broader public in the long term share a common interest in a well-functioning state regulatory system. However, at any given historical period one can imagine having a "balancing rod", with a governmental environmental regulation system as the fulcrum, the public sector governance on one side, and private sector interest governance on the other side. During some periods of time the balance of forces favours the public sector. At other periods the balance beam has clearly tipped towards the private sector.

The strength of the public side is influenced by a good number of normal political pressures. Some of the environmental and health impacts of business activities have resulted in opposition by civil society. Public political pressure can prod states to take action to pressure the market to address the problem. On the health and safety front, organized coal workers and unions demanded safer work conditions and the state created an inspectorate to monitor mine safety. On air pollution, neighbourhoods near factories organized for cleaner air and less risk from industrial accidents, and governments were forced to create legal, regulatory, and administrative systems to address these concerns.

The private sector brings its weight to bear on the balance beam through providing political contributions to law-makers; lobbying law- and regulation-makers; using lawyers and the legal system to try to undercut specific rules and regulations; and advertising to affect public perception about environmental laws or regulations that business sees as a burden. However, there remains a structural limitation for the business community. In weakening the overall governmental regulatory framework, they still need to have justifiable and supported government standards to which the business community can refer as acceptable environmental practices.

Business leaders also want a government system that grants them as much flexibility as possible. The approach currently advocated by the private sector for maximum flexibility has been named by the business community as "self-regulation".[5] This term has been selected to capture the public support for "regulation" while transferring the leadership from the state regulatory system to the individual firm or industry association. For analytic clarity, this approach is probably more neutrally termed "voluntary environmental management" or VEM.[6]

The effort at corporate VEM in OECD countries seeks to shift the balance sharply towards greater corporate control while maintaining some of the necessary characteristics of a state environmental regulatory system. In doing so, VEM has created four parallel activities in the state regulatory system: internal voluntary standards, self-defined implementation standards, self-financed certification systems, and elective public reporting. These are reflected in Table 10.2.

There are of course significant differences between the state domestic environmental regulatory systems and the private sector "regulatory approach" in domestic markets. As indicated in Table 10.3, some of the differences are crucial to the shift in political balance towards commercial control of environmental matters while firms retain the vocabulary of a

Table 10.2 Parallel structures between components of state regulatory systems and voluntary environmental management systems

Components of a state regulatory system	Components of a corporate voluntary environmental management system
Laws	Voluntary codes and standards
Regulations	Self-defined implementation standards
Enforcement	Self-financed certification systems
Public disclosure	Elective public reporting

normal state regulatory approach. The effect, though, is to reduce broad public engagement in environmental matters, to reduce business "overhead" costs, and to build public support for private sector environmental management.

In the long term, however, VEM processes also weaken even that function of a state regulatory system that benefits the business sector. This can be seen by the dilemma faced by the business sector when civil society perceives a "new" environmental problem. Under voluntary environmental management, civil society is more likely to focus its attention directly on the private sector, rather than on public sector institutions.

The domestic experience of business executives, government officials, and civil society participants obviously spills over into the international arena. These actors bring with them the "successes" as well as the "failures" of their national history. In one type of OECD country, where negotiated understandings are worked out between the government and the business leaders, their representatives in international forums bring with them a sense of cooperative understanding. In other OECD countries, where it is the expectation that laws and regulations will be followed, their international delegations may well reflect their domestic history by heightened expectations about the precision of the drafting of any international agreement. This domestic understanding influences the initial perspective of corporate executives, government officials, and NGOs outside of their home country.

At the international level

On the international level, the dynamic between the business sector, state actors, and civil society is more complex than domestic practices in some ways and more straightforward in others.

On the governmental side, there is not really an equivalent body to the nation-state. The UN organizations, the WTO, and the existing col-

Table 10.3 Features that differentiate between VEM and a state regulatory system affecting business activities

Component of VEM system	Different features
Voluntary codes and standards	• Some industrial sectors have voluntary standards; other sectors are completely without industry standards • Industry standards vary widely in public policy implication • National standard-setting bodies are proposing an ever-expanding list of standards for broad use • Individual and trade associations' codes have limited acceptance in many social and environmental communities
Self-defined implementation standards	• Self-defined baseline of appropriate natural and human conditions • Self-defined thresholds for minimum performance standards • Self-defined level of public acceptance of specific implementation standards • Without a parliamentary forum or a public hearing, little way to engage stakeholders and determine the potentially conflicting views on a specific product or process level
Self-financed certification systems	• Almost no sanctions for a company even when its auditor discovers the violation of a VEM standard • Independence of auditing firm and auditor, and the legal status of the audit report, are not clear • Minimal supervision of environmental auditing bodies • Little agreement on auditor responsibilities beyond client firm • Few, if any, penalties for improper audit judgements
Elective public reporting	• Performance benchmarking nearly impossible • Evidence of "improvement" may or may not be relevant • Few performance standards for voluntary environmental reporting • Extensive information and images in corporate environmental reports and websites, but little that permits an inter-firm comparative assessment • Environmental management information is often completely independent from public environmental reporting

lection of multilateral environmental organizations all do have a role in governing the international market; but together they lack the political strength of any OECD national state. In this sense, the international system is quite simple: there are no parliamentary/congressional hearings, no courts with environmental jurisdiction, no international political parties or elections, and no civil transnational liability proceedings.

The relative weakness of the interstate regulatory system is also seen in the limited scope and number of environmental conventions, the weakness of convention rules, and the cumbersome enforcement arrangements though the conferences of parties (interesting in this connection is that the acronym happens to be COPs). It is also the case that, unlike domestic environmental law and regulations, international environmental agreements are often drafted in deference to the terms of international trade rules.

However, from the point of view of the enterprise, the multi-country character of the transnational corporation significantly increases the political options of a TNC as compared to a nationally based firm in managing its environmental relations to a "state". A given TNC can choose different geopolitical jurisdictions for its legal home, for its financial centre, for its tax obligations, for its production facilities, and for its managerial control. Of course, not all TNCs are internally structured in the same way. Some are managed as networks, some are more production-centred than customer-centred, and some are more source-centred than product-centred. But whatever the underlying management structure, a transnational corporation has more options in how it balances environmental protection, state oversight, and public perception.

On the international level, NGO actions have defined issues that have provided the basis for intergovernmental initiatives. Targeted campaigns on infant formula, tobacco, pesticides, banned products, and waste disposal have led the intergovernmental machinery to take on these specific problems. International civil society has also created the expectation that international action is necessary and has forced governments to confront issues that the international business community would rather not address. Public policy issues such as debt cancellations, reparations of illicit funds sent abroad, the Tobin tax, and corruption in international business transactions would not have appeared on the international agenda without a broad groundwork being laid by civil society bodies.

Proposals for a WEO, and other similar international proposals for strengthening international environmental governance, are intended in one way or another to change the balance of existing relations between the interstate system and the international firm. Seen in this fashion, it is not surprising that the international business community can be quite supportive of the current fragmented international system. While enhanced corporate global managerial control is of benefit to the international firm, the business community continues to prefer that the interstate system is without leadership and incoherent in environmental matters.

One of the current measures of the international business community's continued support for a weak interstate system is their insistence that the UN system is not a place to formulate even environmental guidance documents. If the United Nations was seen as a legitimate place to develop corporate environmental norms with interstate participation, international business leadership would be concerned that, over time, pressure might develop to change some of these corporate "norms" into more legally binding conventions. To the business community, these would be as unwanted as any new domestic laws and regulations. In the build-up to the WSSD, this effort to keep the UN system fragmented on corporate environmental matters is well reflected in the pre-conference issue on "what is a good Type 2 outcome".

Civil society organizations and some governments believe that the WSSD process should define a "sustainable public-private partnership", or at least specify the minimum conditions for recognizing that a particular public-private partnership is a sound sustainable development activity. The business community, along with many of the OECD governments, are strongly disinclined to have an interstate meeting express a formal standard for "sustainable corporate activity" as this might, over time, encourage more active interstate standards directly impacting on the corporate environmental activities of global firms.

However, as OECD domestic corporate environmental models vary widely, any new component of an international regulatory system for the environment is likely to be very experimental even on the governmental side. Given this reality, the proposals to strengthen interstate control of corporate environmental issues are likely to be an unusual combination of existing national practices or a wholly new structure at the international level. The latter new arrangements include some data-exchange arrangements, some "name-and-shame" approaches, and some multi-country scientific assessment panels.

At the interstate level there are also serious institutional obstacles that do not really operate at the domestic level. First there is the multi-jurisdictional character of global corporate law. How does one have states with different legal approaches and different environmental laws and regulations come to grips with a TNC that thrives on multi-state fragmentation? Second, governments in the international arena often provide "protection" for their "national" firms in their conflicts with other governments and their domestic firms. And third, there are the limitations on civil court decisions on environmental matters: firms can move assets easily to second or third states to avoid a civil liability pen-

Table 10.4 Special international aspects of voluntary environmental management

Component of VEM system	Special international aspect
Voluntary codes and standards	• International conventions bind states not firms • Very limited coverage of existing international environmental agreements • Most international environmental standards are now drafted by business-related bodies
Self-defined implementation standards	• Each conference of parties can make its own implementation standards • Some agreements use principally "market-based" implementations • Most agreements and systems currently seek to use incentives for "good behaviour" by creating profit opportunities for the private sector; no MEA can sanction firms for "bad behaviour"
Self-financed certification systems	• The WTO Technical Barriers to Trade Agreement gives favourable standing to ISO-type certification • Many certification systems are formulated in order to affect media campaigns and consumer opinion, not necessarily to check levels of corporate implementation of industrial association standards
Elective public reporting	• Current reporting requirements in MEAs bind states, not private actors • Current elective coverage of corporate environmental reports varies widely • The disclosure standards in ISO 14001 are entirely voluntary, except that ISO 14001 firms acknowledge that they are ISO certified • Major efforts are ongoing with the Global Reporting Initiative to formulate commonly accepted reporting standards

alty. These three additional weaknesses on the interstate side make it even easier for self-interested and short-term business concerns to thrive in a fragmented international environmental arena and to oppose a more balanced international environmental system.

Again there are special features in each of the four areas of an environmental corporate management system in current arrangements for an international corporate voluntary system of governance, as indicated in Table 10.4.

Consequently on the international level there is greater complexity in the private sector/state balance and a far higher concentration of environmental power in the private corporate sector in the international arena than in the domestic sector. As the international environmental governance system is so weak, it also fails to meet the long-term needs of the business sector. To meet the business need for legitimate market standards and references for good environmental performance, there is an increasing move internationally towards privatization of environmental rule-making.

Private environmental rule-making is the outgrowth of three developments: two at the international level and one at the domestic level. At the international level there has been the very successful work, over many years, in the development of technical product standards for the international business market under the aegis of the International Organization for Standardization (ISO). Second is the endorsement by the Marrakesh Agreement of a revision of the WTO Agreement on Technical Barriers to Trade that gives special trade status to ISO standards. Thirdly, private environmental rule-making on the international level is also a consequence of the withdrawal of governments from domestic regulatory activity: if states argue that they should not be making domestic environmental rules, they have little motivation or political support for making international environmental rules.

The ISO has for some 50 years been developing industrial product standards and maintains a highly diverse system of technical product and process standards-setting arrangements. The ISO estimates that, on any given day, some 30 ISO work groups are formulating or reviewing ISO product standards. These standards are for the most part drafted as engineering standards. However, since the build-up to the UNCED (Rio) conference, the ISO has moved increasingly into process standards and into areas where the ISO standard touches public policy concerns. The national teams developing ISO standards are largely corporate executives from firms affected by the standard who have been selected by their national standard-setting bodies to participate in the international working groups. While the best known of these newer public-policy-related standards is the ISO 14000 series, many other ISO series deal with various "engineering" aspects of noise, water discharge rates, air emissions, and waste management.

The 1994 GATT makes clear reference to international standards set by the ISO. When a country creates a national standard or guideline, then the international community acknowledges that this country is presumed to have avoided creating an unnecessary barrier to trade through the new regulations. Because of such text in the 1994 and in the current Technical Barriers to Trade (TBT) Agreement, standards developed by the ISO have acquired a very important status. At the same time, the new GATT created obstacles to using the recommendations of UN intergovernmental expert groups as global standards in the international trading system.[7]

Table 10.5 Possible tools to achieve a better balance between corporate interests and the interests represented by the interstate system

Public legal regime/ corporate voluntary codes and standards	• Complement state standards in MEAs with specific firm-level standards • Agree that existing MEAs have *de facto* obligations on private actors • Make legally binding existing industry codes of conduct in the absence of a relevant MEA • Establish an international court with jurisdiction on environmental matters
Public sector regulations/ corporate self-defined implementation standards	• Create corporate and civil society advisory bodies to the conferences of parties of MEAS • Enhance civil society participation in ISO decision-making • Establish other joint (industry, government, civil society) standard-setting bodies similar to the Forest Stewardship Council and the Marine Stewardship Council
Public sector enforcement systems/corporate self-financed certification systems	• Agree to joint investigation arrangements • Agree to joint enforcement arrangements • Create an international dispute settlement panel
Public reporting requirements/corporate elective public reporting	• Move towards a non-elective version of the Global Reporting Initiative (GRI)

International policy options

Over time, the interests of TNCs and needs of IGOs and global civil society need to be rebalanced, at least to incorporate the regulatory needs for surrogate representatives for "citizens", "nature", and "future generations".[8] Proposals for a WEO fall into this category. This chapter is intended to help define the functions of a WEO in terms of its potential role in the environmental activities of TNCs.

At the strategic level, both structural and interim changes can be explored. Structural changes would require a redefinition of the corporate charter of firms and the functions of nation-states, a reauthorization of international organizations, and a changed responsibility for NGOs. As long as TNCs and states exist as they now are, political imbalances in environmental protection will inevitably favour the short-term private sector interests. In the near term, and in a world with each of these institutions, there are nevertheless various approaches that could begin to recentre the balance beam. Some of these are included in Table 10.5.

The current balance between international corporate voluntary environmental management and public sector environmental management is, at least from the perspective of the environment, tilted too far in one direction. By recognizing the four components of environmental regulatory systems and the drivers at the national and international level, it is possible to construct a number of ways to recentre the political balance, to create a sustainable business climate, and to enhance global environmental protection.

Notes

1. This paper represents the author's own personal, professional views, not those of the United Nations.
2. UN Conference on Trade and Development Programme on Transnational Corporations. 1993. *Environmental Management in Transnational Corporations: Report on the Benchmark Corporate Environmental Survey*, Environment Series No. 4, ST/CTC/149. New York: United Nations; Gleckman, H. 1995. "Transnational corporations' strategic responses to sustainable development", in H. Bergensen and G. Parmann (eds) *Green Globe Yearbook*. Oxford: Oxford University Press, pp. 93–106; Baram, M. 1994. "Multinational corporations, private codes and technology transfer for sustainable development", *Environmental Law*, Vol. 24, No. 33, pp. 32–65; Roht-Arriaza, N. 1996. "Private voluntary standard-setting, the International Organization for Standardization, and international environmental law-making", in *Yearbook of International Environmental Law*. Oxford: Oxford University Press, pp. 105–161.
3. Financial incentives and disincentives in environmental management are not considered in this chapter, as they are relatively minor actors in national environmental management. This may be changing with the increase in interest from institutional and private investors in socially responsible investing (SRI), which screens for sound environmental management. The most optimistic accounts indicate that SRI investing accounts for one in eight dollars invested in the USA. See Social Investment Forum, SIF Industry Research Program. 2001. *2001 Report on Socially Responsible Investing Trends in the United States*. Viewed at www.socialinvest.org/areas/research/trends/SRI_Trends_Report_2001.pdf. On the other hand military actions and inactions affecting the environment were excluded because they are rather large and abrupt sources of environmental degradation and are not formally part of any OECD government environmental approach.
4. An example of this is when auto manufacturers cite government safety and fuel efficiency standards as performance benchmarks in their advertising and voluntary public environmental reports. On fuel efficiency, auto manufacturers cite Japanese Automobile Manufacturing Assocation and European Automobile Association (ACEA) standards, both of which apply in advance of government regulations, and EPA standards. Two examples are Ford Motor Company. 2000. *Building Relationships*. Viewed at www.ford.com/NR/rdonlyres/eriiydwcj54tyeuv4qcwf5zgiip3gyrk3iyrlhxhwyvpcdv7avwkvgwmht6uvx4rxurv2-hobmhdc66yvdvmp3k2bc6e/2000_ccreport4.pdf; and Toyota Motor Corporation reports globally and by region. In Japan, they report fuel efficiency against Japanese government standards. See www.toyota.co.jp/IRweb/corp_info/eco/index_frame.html?location=dev. For North America, Toyota reports against US EPA standards and also reports where each model performs relative to "best in class" on EPA benchmarks. See www.toyota.com/about/environment/news/enviroreport.html.

5. See Morelli, John. 1999. *Voluntary Environmental Management: The Inevitable Future.* Springer, UK.

6. The phrase "corporate environmental governance" might be another example of the private sector using governmental vocabulary to legitimize the private sector's encroachment on some of the functions of the state. In practice, the terms "corporate governance" and "corporate environmental governance" are used to describe the effectiveness of the process and the methods required for the board of directors and/or the management to control parts of their far-flung multinational firm. Corporate governance is not created or maintained in a public process, which would be normally accepted components of a "governance" system.

7. This argument is elaborated in Krut, Riva and Harris Gleckman. 1998. *ISO 14001: A Missed Opportunity for Sustainable Global Industrial Development.* London: Earthscan.

8. There are several leadership initiatives in this respect undertaken by business-NGO groups. States frequently do not play a role, so these are purely voluntary initiatives. A recent example is Earthwatch Europe, IUCN – The World Conservation Union, and World Business Council for Sustainable Development (WBCSD). 2002. *Business and Biodiversity: The Handbook for Corporate Action.*

11

The private business sector in global environmental diplomacy

Mikoto Usui

Introduction

This chapter deals with certain facets of the game change strategies being pursued by the "business and industry" sector[1] in global environmental diplomacy. This is a rather slippery and complex subject area that most NGO scholarships have tended to think light of. This introduction tries to provide an integrative perspective on this subject and a few important messages emanating from it, although the subsequent three sections address only selected dimensions of this perspective owing to space limitation.

"Diplomacy" implies the conduct of international relations by negotiation (rather than by force), propaganda, recourse to law, information exchange, or engendering goodwill and other peaceful means that are designed either directly or indirectly to facilitate negotiation.[2] In the context of this chapter the term is rather coterminous with "public diplomacy" that involves a myriad of non-state actors concerned with the management of interdependence on a more or less voluntary basis, exerting more or less tangible spillover effects on interstate policy-making arenas – a phenomenon that has assumed increased importance under the shadow of the Rio Summit and its subsequent globalized follow-up processes.

The preceding three chapters deal with non-governmental organizations (NGOs) as a genre of agency (i.e. creative actors attempting to bring about change) that promotes "public interests". In Chapter 8 Mori (in line with Article 71 of the UN Charter and ECOSOC Resolution 1296) tries to be lenient about the distinction between the two different categories of NGOs – not-for-profit civil society organizations (CSOs) and for-profit business organizations (FPOs) – but amply illustrates the difficulties of coordinating or reconciling the two camps for developing common NGO positions in conjunction with major global conference diplomacy on the sustainable development (SD) matter. Fisher (Chapter 9) explicitly differentiates the two categories, and sees CSOs as an analytically distinct institutional sector that is separate from both state and economy (industry and business). Chapter 10 (Gleckman) explicitly refers to the private business sector, but concentrates on the desiderata of business-state and business-IGO (intergovernmental organizations) relationships. In so doing, Gleckman adopts overtly a structuralist vantage point from which "self-interested and short-term business concerns" are seen to "thrive in a fragmented international environmental arena". He thus shares the same normative bias as embraced by many NGO scholarships in stressing need for stronger regulatory systems to rectify the political power balance. In contrast, the author of the present chapter tries to offer a rather diametrically different perspective in which business and civil society, as well as IGOs, are seen as creative agencies endeavouring to find space for interactive leadership for social change amidst the existing contradictory structures.

Business-society bifurcation

There are many provocative ways of caricaturing the FPO-CSO engagement, the latest version of which is "the Davos Man versus the Porto Alegre Protester". The Davos Man represents the community of large international corporations and believes in a liberal economy even though not totally negligent of the third pillar of the Johannesburg agenda: "poverty eradication". The Porto Alegre Protester condemns the "corporate power and government complicity in the rape of the planet", and is vociferous about the "foreign direct liability" accompanying foreign direct investment and the need for subjecting multinational corporations (MNCs) to some legally binding international codes of conduct.[3] Nevertheless, some more serious scholarship is required now to explore how to reap better whatever fragmented promises may be looming out of the emergent tri-sectoral interactions that are being shared by some, if not all, segments of the business sector.

A great deal of interest has been expressed in the notion of intersectoral "partnerships", although there is yet little clarity on what these do and do not entail in reality. Constructive arrangements for multi-stakeholder interaction are open-ended and still somewhat fuzzy in overall terms. As Keohane and Nye assert, the ever more pervasive rhetoric of partnership has not much altered the principle of global governance that continues to be characterized by *networked minimalism*.[4] "Networked" may be interpreted as signifying the predominance of flat or horizontal organizational forms that link individual independent actors without commitment to a common strategy or policy position. Being networked does not immediately lead to a negotiated order among the participants. Moreover, "minimalism" features the parallel, or poorly nested, connection among different networks, such that intrusion into the autonomy of each is kept minimal even when they share some broadly defined goals of cooperation. Thus NGO scholarships tend to locate the CSO in the political realm as an agency standing for the citizen's power and serving as a critical countervailing force against state and industry, while industry is an agency representing the economic power that has traditionally dominated state-society relationships. This perspective is embedded in a broader argument about the economy-society relationship in the so-called "reflexive" modernization process which has attracted much critical thinking. The critical reflection has engendered even an ideal type of CSO whose mission is "to serve undeserved or neglected populations, to expand the freedom of, or to empower, people to engage in advocacy for social change".[5] While NGO scholarships have tended to congeal with such a normative bias, they have left the FPO sector, particularly its relationship with environmental NGOs, as a grossly "under-researched" by the academic community.[6]

This chapter purports to span this gap with a reflection on the promises and problems of the FPO sector as another crucial genre of agency for change toward SD. It is about time that we should step away from the now classical stereotype of business-society relationship, a farcical description of which was given some 25 years ago by Dahl and Lindblom as something that "would appear peculiar to a man from Mars":

Business's superior power is derived from the fact corporations are charged by society to organize and manage its productive forces. The result of this responsibility is the "privileged participation of business" in government ... Societies operate by rules that require that businessmen be induced rather than commanded ... these societies must provide sufficient benefits or indulgencies to businessmen to constitute an inducement for them to perform their assigned tasks.[7]

A three-layered analytical perspective on corporate game change strategies

We then need to locate the FPO sector, too, in the "zone of plasticity" lying between *structure* and *agency*, just as NGO scholarships have done in order to assess the CSO role in social change. "Structure" implies existing institutionalized sets of statuses, roles, and prevalent rules of the game, and "agency" stands for those actors who voluntarily define their own goals and strategies for game change, i.e. reconstructing their relationships, norms, and rules.[8] It is in this zone of plasticity (alternatively called the state of "structuration") that the contradictory goals, roles, and values entrenched within extant structures give rise to space for creative agency.[9] Put differently (if not quite alternatively), Andrew Cooper, speaking of changing diplomacy in and around the UN system, conceptualizes a global model of *interactive leadership* to grasp the complex and open-ended processes in which more or less like-minded states and business and non-business NGOs "rub against and off each other in an uneven fashion".[10] So, our attention will centre on how relatively resourceful, innovative corporations endeavour to promote game change, individually or collectively, to cope with emergent social norms, external pressures, and constraints.

Within the FPO sector, such actors correspond to those whom Holliday and Pepper (co-chairs of the WBCSD) characterized as "innovators" and "market shapers" (as distinguished from "compliers" and "laggards/free-riders") when they tried to describe a "smart hierarchy" of environmental public policies.[11] In formal environmental policy arenas, the innovator/market shaper types of business actors are found in a relatively non-conspicuous, not very cohesive, but highly discretionary group of opportunists. Sprinz and Weiss refer to them as "Third party leaning toward Pusher", so distinguished from two other types of more vociferous interest groups, "Dragger/laggard" and "Pusher/leader".[12] One might ask such questions as how far are the "Third party" actors leaning to join the "Pusher/leader" group? What initiatives are they taking meanwhile to prepare themselves for enlarged future business opportunities? And what kinds of regulatory policy design would help them cross the threshold for rising up to coalesce with "Pushers"? These are among the major questions to be entertained in this chapter.

In order to capture the corporate game change strategies at multiple levels, a simplified analytical framework might be of help. Table 11.1 is one of the possible ways of describing it. It consists of three levels.

- *Global*: How to change international institutional setting.
- *Intermediate*: How to change individual business environments.
- *Local*: How to change products (or make intra-firm adaptations).

Various thematic dimensions or action areas are distinguished at each of these levels. Those listed in Table 11.1 are meant to be illustrative and not exhaustive. Individual actors may choose to act at more than one level simultaneously. Important from an analytical perspective is that moving from one level to the next can help trace the *local-global* nexus that flows across the multilayered processes of structuration.

Table 11.1 An integrative perspective on corporate game change strategies towards sustainability

Level	Thematic areas of action (major examples)	
Global Changing international institutional setting	I-A	Enhancing global advocacy networks for self-legitimization to cope with CSOs' confrontational diplomacy
	I-B	Partnership-building with IGOs and other stakeholders with problem-solving commitments (joining the UN Global Compact and the "Type 2" track of the WSSD process)
	I-C	Positive leadership-taking in the processes of interstate negotiation on global and regional conventions and protocols

Intermediate
Changing individual
  business
  environment
	II-A	Lobbying in national and local governmental policy-making processes

	II-B	Intra-industry alliance for developing voluntary standards and certification systems
	II-C	Partnership-building with CSOs for joint ventures and development of credible *de facto* standards (of more, or less, cross-border significance)
	II-D	Policy negotiation and voluntary environmental agreements with national governments (on climate change and other environmental and ethical issues)

Local
Changing own products
  and services (intra-
  firm adaptation)
	III-A	Changing products and processes through individual management systems (geared to such notions as eco-efficiency, zero emissions, natural steps, ecological marketing, etc.)

	III-B	Compliance-oriented environmental management policy (adopting broadly recognized standards such as ISO 14001, SA 8000, BiE, etc.)
	III-C	Stakeholder engagement to cope with zones of conflict at the grass-roots level (especially in the case of mining and minerals MNCs operating in developing countries)
	III-D	Self-motivated partnership-building with local community-developmental actors in developing countries

In fact, we will see the confrontational postures of the Davos Man and
the Porto Alegre Protester in global-level public diplomacy (action area
I-A) tend to subside quickly as we move down towards the lower levels
of the landscape. Actors from the two camps get enticed increasingly by
opportunities for engaging each other for mutual gain, e.g. by developing

jointly designed and administered credible standards and certification systems, if still mainly on a voluntary basis. Further down at the local level, problem-, issue-, and situation-specific multi-stakeholder dialogues are forced to assume boundary-spanning characteristics that would generate space for joint action and a negotiated order with responsibility allocation and joint problem-solving commitments. To discover the right pathways through this global-local nexus would be of utmost importance to improve regime design for further deepening and widening existing multilateral environmental agreements (MEAs).

It should be noted that the adoption of such a multilayered analytical framework would necessarily implicate a definition of *international institution* inclusive of both its soft/informal and hard/formal content. An effective regime must find the right mix of formal and informal rules of the game and the appropriate enforcement characteristics related to them. This neo-institutional perspective is highly relevant in speaking of institutional reforms in view of the evolving nature of SD regimes, most of which are at their early fledgling stages. As for the "organizational" dimension of institutional reform, there is an old saying of the classical functionalist that "form follows function".[13] Heeding the global-local nexus should make it desirable to add to it that "function follows shared problems". Within the state sector, IGOs have emerged as a separate agency on account of their functional role (in addition to their mandates originally given as interstate policy forums) as a coordinating and "synergizing" agent for concerted efforts by states, industry, and civil society for the supply of international public goods.[14] These IGOs' enhanced focus on implementation of existing agreements may or may not be a new "conceptual leap" enthusing the world community, but certainly demands improved participatory delivery mechanisms at multiple levels. For that matter, the "Type 2 outcomes" of the WSSD process would deserve continued attention as an avenue for reconsolidating and enriching the "vertical interlinkages" spanning through the global-local nexus of existing and new MEAs.

The structure of the rest of this chapter

Treating all the individual themes at full length for all the three levels shown in Table 11.1 would deserve more than a book project. Since the author of the present chapter has already given a fuller treatment of the three-level perspective on a level-by-level basis elsewhere,[15] the following three sections focus on selected dimensions remoulded so as to permit a return trip from global to local and then back to global. (The bracketed codes relate by and large to the corresponding themes/action areas shown in Table 11.1.)

- Public diplomacy grounded in networked minimalism [I-A]:
  - parallelism at the global level: the ICC environmental diplomacy
  - some theoretical reflections
  - adaptive developments from Rio to Johannesburg.
- Multi-stakeholder engagement with problem-solving commitments:
  - a bird's-eye view traversing through the local-intermediate-global nexus
  - evolving facets of stakeholder theory [II and III]
  - stakeholder engagement in zones of conflict [III-C]
  - voluntary standards and certification schemes [II-B and II-C]
  - self-motivated business-CSO partnerships [II-C]
  - self-motivated business-community partnerships in the bottom tier of the world market [III-D]
  - from the Global Compact to the "Type 2" track of the WSSD [I-B].
- Beyond the WSSD: regime design matters [I-B and I-C]:
  - horizontal and vertical interlinkages
  - how to coax industry to become "Pusher"
  - two parallel "Type 2" showcases and an agenda for future research.

Public diplomacy grounded in networked minimalism

While corporate legality continues to rest within a system of state law, world-renowned multinational corporations (MNCs) have begun to work harder at legitimizing themselves at the international level. Many CSO representatives, as well as NGO scholarships, are concerned about the private sector's own capability of generating *de facto* standards in cyberspace, financial markets, intellectual property rights, bond-rating institutions, etc. and effectively lobbying to their advantage in national and international policy-making processes. Cutler, Haufler, and Porter conceptualize this tendency as an act of claiming industry's own "private international authority", which complements, and sometimes even substitutes for, state authority.[16] It has power-game dimensions, such as controlling markets, reducing inter-firm transaction costs, capturing state regulations, and sometimes even using the state against other civil society actors. However, such power-political dimensions are no novelty. On the one hand, the "plural élitism" theory of state-society and business-society relationships has generated a number of studies on the advantages that the corporate sector has in terms of money and technology. And, on the other hand, the rules of the game have long allowed for an alliance in one form or another between IGOs and leading business actors to cope with problems of legitimacy and accountability posed by industry's "private authority".

Such reproachful remarks notwithstanding, there is still enough room left for us to tread back the historical course of international institutional adaptation and dynamics of structure-agency confluence in which industry's private authority has exhibited traces of both resilience and adaptive responsiveness to changing world requirements. Note that "adaptation" implies new activities being added without questioning underlying institutional values, some new means of action being altered, or some new objectives being added without worrying about their coherence with existing ones.[17] Let us first see how the ICC – the world's most powerful umbrella organization – has acted as the frontline spokesman for international business interests. Then, after some effort of theorizing about the pitfalls inherent in the ICC's public diplomacy at the global level, we will bring in on the scene more consciously SD-oriented actors such as the WBCSD and the UNED Forum. These actors have been particularly instrumental in creating space for institutional adaptation within the UN-orchestrated processes towards the Johannesburg Summit.

Parallelism at the global level: The ICC environmental diplomacy

The ICC, established in 1919, has been involved from the very outset in global politico-economic diplomacy at the highest levels. It was one of the earliest NGOs that enjoyed full voting rights and participated directly in League of Nations meetings. It outlived the League of Nations. Hocking and Kelly[18] give a fairly detailed account of the ICC involvement with the League of Nations as well as the UN system through the 1970s. In the early post-war years it was the ICC that stood firmly against the draft charter of the International Trade Organization and exerted pressure for creating the GATT instead. The ICC has been present at the UN Conference on Trade and Development (UNCTAD) from its first meeting in 1964. The UN-GATT Economic Consultative Committee, created under the ICC aegis in 1969, facilitated high-level discussions to guard the international business interest from the South's increasingly aggressive UN diplomacy, and proved instrumental for the later launch of the OECD *Guidelines for Multinational Enterprises* in 1976. Upon Maurice Strong's invitation, the ICC gave a 15-minute presentation at the first UN Conference on the Human Environment (UNCHE), Stockholm, in 1972.

The ICC Commission on the Environment was established as an outcome of its World Industry Conference on Environmental Management (WICEM), co-sponsored by the UN Environment Programme (UNEP) (the latter being the only immediate organizational innovation that Stockholm brought about). At that stage, the Commission began to spend most energy in arguing that environmental standards would hamper the market-place unless they were acceptable on an all-industry basis.

Harris Gleckman (then a staff member of the UN Center on Transnational Corporations (UNCTC)) gives an interesting insider's account of how the ICC lobbied against the UN initiatives during the preparatory process for the 1992 Rio Summit. While the ICC's *Business Charter of Sustainable Development* plagiarized from the UNCTC-authored *Criteria on Sustainable Management* without any acknowledgement, the ICC kept openly criticizing the UNCTC's work on environmental matters, contending that "the UN should reduce its attention to environmental matters affecting the international market".[19] Moreover, together with some OECD countries it "launched a frontal effort to avoid any reference to TNCs and their potential contributions to SD" and "resisted all attempts made by IGOs to table meaningful definitions of sustainable business and ignored offerings from citizens groups".[20]

In Rio, "the ICC three-day conference omitted any direct discussion of the future tasks expected from national industries or TNCs in Agenda 21".[21] Meanwhile, on the part of the CSO camps, a large coalition of international activists formed the International Non-governmental Forum (INGOF), which rallied in Rio at a distance from the ICC conference and was busy finalizing its own draft International NGO Treaty – a counter-proposal to Agenda 21.[22] At that time, no formally integrated rules of procedure existed for more than 1,400 participating NGOs. Ann Doherty's questionnaire study reveals the various complaints registered by CSO respondents about the presence of not-for-profit business associations (the ICC, the BCSD, the Association of Chemical Manufacturers, etc.) in the same capacity as other non-profit NGOs. They include statements such as "Business succeeded in escaping all regulations"; "Business reduced the scope of the conference"; and "Corporate interests ruled the agenda in favour of market-based approaches"; etc.[23]

During the preparatory process for the 2002 World Summit on Sustainable Development (WSSD), the ICC and the WBCSD jointly formed a new platform named Business Action for Sustainable Development (BASD). They jointly submitted a position paper to the multi-stakeholder dialogue segment of the WSSD/PrepCom IV. That paper was curt and in a reserved tone, but eloquently recapitulated their long-embraced strategic priority:[24] "Business solutions to sustainable development focus on *concrete actions and deliverable results rather than process and procedures*" (emphasis added). In contrast, the dialogue paper given by a group of NGOs on the same occasion reiterated at length the familiar CSO stance regarding how MNCs ought to be better tamed:[25] "The WSSD must endorse ... a *legally binding framework/ convention for corporate accountability and liability* under the UN, with independent mechanisms for monitoring progress and enforcement" (emphasis added).

In Johannesburg, the BASD organized a Business Day on 1 September 2002 – a high-profile open forum with panellists drawn from senior business leaders. It was accompanied by a new book entitled *Walking the Talk*.[26] The overarching themes of the Business Day were sustainable management of natural resources, making markets work for all (even for poor people's "sustainable livelihoods"), and accountability and transparency.[27] In parallel, however, on the very same day Friends of the Earth International organized "Art Action: Hear Our Voice" near the entrance to the Earth Summit hall. A six-metre-tall "Corporate Giant" (a super-fat inflatable businessman which had already toured in Europe), surrounded by 6,000 biodegradable statues representing the diverse voices of "peoples" victimized by MNCs, were meant to symbolize "corporate power and government complicity in the rape of the planet".[28]

The advocacy networks of CSOs and those of FPOs tend to be kept disparate. More often than not, each camp rallies by itself and for itself to mount campaigns for self-advocacy. This is the case even at forums for global conference diplomacy where they are officially given a consultative status. Mori notes that ECOSOC Resolution 1296 on NGOs with consultative status limits their role to consultation, and not negotiation (see Chapter 8). At the level of formal conference diplomacy, their activities consist mainly of submitting written statements for information in the hope of identifying differences and sharable values and objectives among different sectors and actors. The "multi-stakeholder dialogue" session of the UNCSD was inspired by the UNED Forum, which had been established in 1993 as an outgrowth of the Sustainable Development Unit of the UN Association of UK and Ireland, and later renamed the Stakeholder Forum for Our Common Future with its expanded international membership.[29] However, the dialogue at this high level of political aggregation has generated something even less than "positional bargaining", serving mostly just to highlight positional differences among different actors. Parallelism looms obstinately between the two camps when each attempts to present itself as though it were a single coalition. Mori (Chapter 8) speaks of the failure of the CSD Steering Committee for NGOs to develop common positions among the various caucuses of which the committee was comprised.

Some theoretical reflections

In terms of the structure-agency nexus, one can argue that the confrontation or parallelism between FPO and CSO issue networks stems from the leaders of each camp placing too much emphasis on the structural perspective at the expense of the agency perspective. CSOs' criticism is usually addressed at the "laggard/free-rider" segments of the business community, rather than its "innovator/market shaper" wings. The latter, as a lead agency for change, remain highly sensitive to critical social voices, but are often suspect of complicity with the former because they are all embedded in the same formal structure that the ICC represents.

A commonplace of organization theory is that "informal links among organizational participants congeal alongside formal structures" in the sense that such links "develop to confront issues defined in the formal structure".[30] Also, David Mitchell's model of "alliance security dilemma" in inter-institutional negotiation (which was adapted from the two-level game theory) may help explain, by analogy, the confrontational situation in which the two coalitions run into "the risk of being entrapped even when they are not really interested in it".[31] Other coalition-theoretic hypotheses, such as the one worked out by Lynn Wagner,[32] may be useful for predicting that negotiation tends to stop at a confrontational "we-they" differentiation when each coalition with low internal cohesion tries to project the appearance of a highly cohesive group by resorting to the lowest common denominator that is trenched on a highly simplified structuralist vision of social order. This is more likely to occur when the agenda is framed in terms of broad cross-sectoral issues, over which positional preferences tend to vary more greatly across different coalitions than within each coalition. If an attempt were made to fuse two such coalitions together, even the commonly shared SD agenda would easily result in positional parallelism of the "we-they" type.

Thus, some scholars (such as Jacques Fomerand[33]) question whether many of the UN global conferences are really serving the purpose of genuine public diplomacy, apart from the momentary media events which may not have lasting effects on state policies. One way of avoiding serious analytical enterprise in this matter might be to see their impact, as Paul Wapner[34] does, in the longer-term perspective of "dialectical" interaction through time among different contradictory forces. And, as Peter Haas says, while they may not have immediate direct effects on policies, they do in time provide indirect effects that may induce states to take more progressive steps toward SD.[35]

It is clear from the foregoing reflection that the author of this chapter would not think much of institutional reform proposals like the "World Environment Organization" (WEO) or "World Environment and Development Organization" (WEDO), although these are directly or indirectly heeded in many other chapters of this volume. An imagery of the "global corporatism" type of organizational arrangements[36] quickly stumbles on numerous thorny issues. Apart from the theoretical problem of conflating "institution" and "organization",[37] even the idea of "corporate and civil society advisory bodies" for MEA-COPs (suggested by Gleckman in this volume in his Table 10.5) would be unlikely to overcome the weaknesses of the CSO Multi-stakeholder Steering Group and the issue of democratic legitimacy of representatives from NGO sectors. It will be seen in the next section that the polarized nature of positional bargaining consciously grounded in contradictory structures tends to give in to exigencies of problem-solving requirements envisaged in stakeholder engagement at lower levels. Meanwhile, let us continue with our search for promises of institutional adaptation that have begun to loom in the post-Rio+5 phase of the Johannesburg process.

Adaptive developments from Rio to Johannesburg

Towards Rio+5, in the face of the ever-louder anti-globalization and anti-MNC voices from CSO circles, the ICC began to seek more sensible, politically neutralized, and intellectually credible ways of interfacing between its members' private interests and the increasingly wary public. One avenue was to build the WBCSD with a globalized sustainability-oriented professional mission by merging its Environment Commission's bureau for programme delivery[38] with the Business Council for Sustainable Development (BCSD) in 1995. The latter had been set up by Stephan Schmidheiny (then a corporate adviser to Maurice Strong, the UNCED Secretary-General) in association with 50 senior CEOs but independently of the ICC. The other was to find a major partnership role in the new agenda which was being contemplated by Kofí Annan for the United Nations.

The ICC charter continues to emphasize its role as a defender of business interests[39] and have its Paris-based international secretariat actively feed business views into the United Nations and other IGOs on any issues directly affecting business operations. In contrast, the WBCSD is mandated to concentrate on SD issues and environmentally desirable business practices[40] and take an independent professional stance. Unlike the ICC representatives, the WBCSD's members can speak, not on behalf of their corporations, but in their personal capacities. Now its membership includes CEOs from 160 of the world's largest and most influential companies, and its global network consists of more than 35 regional and national BCSDs, still growing to make inroads into more developing countries and countries in transition. Both the WBCSD and the ICC are equally actively involved with the United Nations, participating in the *ad hoc* inter-sessional working groups of the UNCSD and the conferences of the parties (COPs) of various major MEAs. The WBCSD's advocacy activities appear politically much lower profile than the ICC, but intellectually higher profile with active interaction with renowned international policy research institutions such as the World Resources Institute (WRI), the International Institute for Environment and

Development (IIED), and the Prince of Wales International Business Leaders Forum (IBLF), etc., as well as the World Bank and the UNDP.

The WBCSD adopts problem-solving approaches with its working groups specialized in specific issue areas of SD, such as climate and energy, sustainable development reporting, medicines and genes, biodiversity, and "sustainable livelihoods". This last issue area has been added (since 2001) to promote a view within the business community that "markets can be a major force for advancing sustainable development among the world's poor".[41]

With a view to finding a major role for the international business community to assume in Kofí Annan's Global Compact (GC) project, the ICC and the WBCSD began to have a number of meetings with Annan while endeavouring to cope with the unease and doubt being voiced by many member corporations. At the same time the ICC launched a series of seminars and press releases on public-private partnership, which culminated in the Geneva Business Dialogue (in September 1998).[42] Many CSOs were sceptical of this Global Compact process, and rallied to get it "hijacked" by their own proposal of a Citizens' Compact. The notion of the Citizens' Compact was dedicated to enhancing the CSO right of surveillance and the development of a legally binding framework to govern global corporations' behaviour. To counteract this, the ICC Environment Commission delivered an eloquent speech at the Rockefeller Foundation on the relevance of the "poverty eradication" dimension of the UN agenda for sustainability-conscious business actors. It even tried to reassure that "the time horizons of business are relatively long compared to democratic governments, seeking a renewal of their mandate every few years".[43] Apparently such a bold statement was made possible on the strength of the launch of the WBCSD working group on sustainable livelihoods mentioned above. The group's first report on the rationale of pro-poor business community engagement[44] was made available on the Business Day in Johannesburg, coupled with a more macro-oriented sister edition, *Investing for Sustainable Development*.[45] The latter was prepared jointly with the IUCN, the LEAD, Deutsche Bank, and the World Bank Institute, addressing the question of creating an enabling policy environment that should underpin business solutions to SD in terms of "concrete actions and deliverable results".

The UNED UK Committee, founded in the wake of the 1992 UNCED to promote national SD processes,[46] endeavoured increasingly to feed its experience in stakeholder dialogue as an input to international processes, and thus inspired the UNCSD to incorporate a dialogue segment into its regular sessions. The UNED Forum undertook a fairly serious research project (2000–2001) on multi-stakeholder partnerships (MSPs). This project was intended to review various examples of MSPs around intergovernmental bodies with a view to distilling an acceptable "template procedure" and methodological framework for the WSSD process.[47] The examples studied included the UNCSD multi-stakeholder dialogue (1997–), the UN Global Compact process (1999–), the Global Reporting Initiative (1999–), the World Commission on Dams (1998–2000), the WBCSD-IIED Global Mining Initiative (1999–2001), the Aarhus Convention Process, etc.

The result inspired the CSD again (acting then as the WSSD Prep-Com) towards official adoption of the "Type 2" track. The UNED Forum was then renamed as the Stakeholder Forum for Our Common Future and prepared to hold an implementation conference (IC) in Johannesburg (24–26 August 2002). The Stakeholder Forum was comprised of BP, Novartis, Unilever, and Ondeo Suez from the business community, along with the UN Foundation, UNEP, the World Bank, the IUCN, the International Confederation of Free Trade Unions (ICFTU), the Rockefeller Foundation, and other NGO groups. Twenty-five facilitators from its globalized membership worked out 14 draft Type 2 agreements in four issue areas (fresh water, energy, food security, and health). The Stakeholder Forum coordinator reporting on the IC outcome states:

The new partnerships are about action, not about lobbying governments. Impacting policy-making is not the primary concern of the participants who gathered at the IC. They [we] met to agree action to implement existing (and emerging) policy agreements. However, it is hoped that the stakeholders' actions and what we learn from them will indeed feed into policy-making in the future.[48]

Multi-stakeholder engagement with problem-solving commitments: A bird's-eye view traversing through the local-intermediate-global nexus

Multi-stakeholder processes come in many shapes at many levels. Their organizational forms and procedures need to be designed to suit specific situations, issues, or problems as well as the participants' abilities, needs, and other circumstances. In this overview, the focus is set on grasping how industry has come to heed a broader range of "stakeholders" than just shareholders to cope with emerging pressures and opportunities at grass-roots, as well as international, levels. In fact, upholding stakeholder thinking has been gaining greater currency with the advent of MNCs' increased global reach and the surging anti-globalization waves. Many corporate managers have begun to think about the need for "reintegrating business into society", as being urged by CSO activists and scholarships.

This section will first take a glance at key elements of the stakeholder theory which seem to be shared broadly by both social systems theorists and management scholarships concerned with issues of corporate social responsibility (CSR). Against such theoretical backgrounds it then discusses some of the important issues envisaged in practice, particularly the notion of "foreign direct liability" facing "asset-specific"[49] industries operating in developing countries; the proliferation of "bottom-up" standards in forestry and tourism industries; and self-motivated industry-community partnerships that would probably have positive implications for poverty eradication in poorer societies. These kinds of stakeholder engagement with problem-solving commitments will be seen to have led towards two noteworthy global-level institutional innovations: the Global Compact and the "Type 2 outcome" incorporated into the Johannesburg process.

Evolving facets of stakeholder theory

A broad consensus seems to be emerging regarding the practice and ethics of social systems design among social system theorists. Emphasis is put increasingly on the concept of stakeholder engagement and the methodologies for boundary-spanning dialogue. For instance, Ken Bausch[50] stresses the need for well-sustained and properly managed group processes in order that a "negotiated order" may be arrived at with an agreed allocation of rights and obligations among the stakeholders willing to engage in joint problem-solving. The thrust of such processes is to treat participants' differing perspectives on a given issue as resources for problem-solving rather than as antagonistic differences to be edited out or harmonized, and also to reconfigure power differences in terms of a balance of interests rather than a balance of forces or resources. Moreover, a sharable knowledge base is essential for *rationally* reconciling the participants' diverse *pre-rational* cognitive filters in order to engender space for joint action.

Such a visionary theory resonates well into recent CSR scholarship. CSR was originally (during the 1970s) conceived as "profitability + compliance + philanthropy", but has subsequently embraced additional thematic frameworks such as business ethics, corporate citizenship, and stakeholder engagement. The most recent version of stakeholder theory adopts, in addition to social "obligation" and "responsibility", an element of *social responsiveness*: i.e. attention to not just active interaction of business with a broad range of stakeholders but also anticipatory action committed to both social and economic goals. Much conceptual and empirical work has been undertaken to integrate relationship-building activities into stakeholder engagement.

Some interesting propositions can be found in the recent two-volume edition by Andriof *et al.* entitled *Unfolding Stakeholder Thinking.*[51] One of them is that the ethical facet of CSR may be a consequence of, rather than an exogenous causal factor for, multi-stakeholder learning dialogue. While participants in the dialogue process are usually faced with "messy systemic problems" characterized by a dissensus-generating dichotomy between "self" and "other", a more "sense-making" process can ensue when a shared vision of relational responsibilities starts emerging, leading to "co-construction" of multilateral negotiated orders.[52] In order to explain the positive role of big corporations in this process, Duane Windsor[53] draws upon the logic of "consequentialism": namely, through sustained stakeholder dialogues it would become easier to trace and specify responsibility for consequences (including distant repercussions), which may lead to negotiated outcomes pertaining to distributive equity, and a change from the *status quo* directed towards the least advantaged in any given situation. Corporate managers amid the zone of conflict in developing countries are faced with a perceived imbalance in the public's conceptualization of business responsibilities. Thus they learn sooner or later more stringent lessons than other stakeholders, to the effect that they become increasingly inclined to lead the way towards a collective action effort to solve a shared problem. These are certainly among the promising theoretical possibilities, but need to be buttressed by further empirical studies.

Stakeholder engagement in zones of conflict

Field studies available on the realities of CSR practices of mining and minerals MNCs operating in developing countries confirm that CSR and good ethical behaviour are means of improving relationships with local stakeholders. But the yet-unresolved question is: what are the best means of promoting CSR among those MNCs – voluntary codes of conduct, international regulations, or host government intervention? MNCs' self-regulatory initiatives alone would not guarantee good CSR practice unless host governments are equipped with a sophisticated legal system and effective mechanisms for their enforcement. And such preconditions vary greatly from country to country.[54]

As for international regulations, the negotiations of the UN Commission on Transnational Corporations for an MNC code of conduct started in 1974, dragged on throughout the decade, and then subsided without a definitive outcome with the advent of more urgent negotiations for debt relief and "adjustment with a human face" early in the 1980s. The OECD revised twice its 1976 MNC guidelines. In the 1990s the Multilateral Agreement on Investment (MAI) faltered in the face of the fierce protest of environmental and anti-MNC CSOs arguing that it protected the rights of corporations without paying equivalent attention to their responsibilities.[55] The 2000 revision of the OECD guidelines for MNCs[56] provides for monitoring by designated national contact points, but it is yet to be seen if it will result in a really effective international regulatory instrument.

The Mining, Minerals, and Sustainable Development (MMSD) Project would deserve particular mention in this conjunction. This two-year research and consultation project was contracted to the International Institute for Environment and Development (IIED) through the WBCSD by nine of the world's largest mining companies, for the purpose of creating a sustainable future vision of the minerals sector. Its final report, entitled *Breaking New Ground*,[57] disseminated on the IUCN Business Day in Johannesburg (31 August 2002), was an outcome of the "MMSD process" involving a broad range of stakeholders – four regional partnerships (Southern Africa, North America, South America, and Australia), some 20 national projects, and 23 international workshops and seminars. Its policy prescription includes establishing a sort of "sectoral global compact" that embraces a framework agreement on norms and principles, a global declaration and protocol, and national and regional industry codes of conduct, as well as capacity-building action plans at community, national, and global levels. The MMSD Project's office is now closed (with at least part of it being taken over by the ongoing WBCSD Global Mining Initiative). But the process can be regarded as a valuable experimentation of industry-specific multi-stakeholder engagement with explicit heed to global-local interlinkages.

Voluntary standards and certification schemes

Industry's self-regulatory initiatives include more, or less, internationally accredited voluntary standards and certification schemes. In fact there exists a plethora of such initiatives. Some represent merely the self-promotional gimmicks of intra-industry mini-lateral alliances (Level II-B); some involve partnering between reputable MNCs and CSOs that bear particularly upon the development of voluntary standards and certification schemes of cross-border significance (Level II-C). There is also multi-stakeholder engagement in the form of business-community partnerships geared to development of locally adapted "bottom-up" standards (Level III-D).

For example, the number of certification initiatives on forestry and forestry products has more than doubled since 1996, and over 40 new schemes are under development in more than 30 countries. Many of them assume characteristics of oligopolistic competition rather than voluntary self-regulation. Critics jeer at them as a "classical example of the fox guarding the henhouse".[58] This tendency corroborates with the fact that forestry is a domain where only a very weak, fragmentary regime exists. The International Tropical Timber Agreement (ITTA: 1983) and the Tropical Forestry Action Program (TFAP: 1985) were the results of interstate negotiations including forestry-related MNCs and tropical timber-producing and timber-importing countries among major stakeholders. Both initiatives came under fierce criticism by environmental NGOs in that they were donor-driven rather than country-driven, lacking clear priorities in their decision processes, and had centralized administration "disenfranchising" a broader spectrum of stakeholders.[59] The 1992 UNCED could only agree on a "Non-Legally Binding Authoritative Statement of Principles" (Forestry Principles), which offered only a starting point for protracted negotiations by the Intergovernmental Panel on Forests (IPF), subsequently renamed as the Intergovernmental Forum on Forests (IFF). Earlier conferences of the parties of the Convention on Biological Diversity (CBD: 1992) could not launch a work programme on forestry owing to the strong blocking coalitions involving timber-producing and timber-exporting developing countries and major forest-exploiting MNCs. Of the world's forests, 140 million hectares are exploited by fewer than 50 MNCs under short-term exploitation permits.[60] Such short-term contracts leave little incentive for the multi-million-dollar timber industry to plan and manage for longer-term exploitation. Industry competition for acquiring renewed and new exploitation permits is accompanied by self-promotion and legitimization, resulting in a proliferation of would-be SD-oriented timber certification schemes both within industry and created by third parties. This implies creating differentiated thresholds for "good practices" that are used to claim comparative social advantage for insiders over potential new entrants.

The Forest Stewardship Council (FSC) is one of the major *de facto* standards engineered by MNC-CSO partnerships which are often likened to soft conventions of global significance. It originated from a defensive partnership of B&Q (a company specializing in "do-it-yourself" wood products) with the WWF-UK in response to the repeated anti-DIY demonstrations mounted jointly by the Rainforest Action Group, FoE UK, and timber industry labour unions in 1991. Although the FSC is nearly globally accredited, critics point out that its structure and operational practice lack equity in that the competitive interests of "excellent producers just above the FSC threshold of acceptable forest management" are favoured, often at the expense of the almost equally good producers just below it.[61] So the FSC has not successfully contained the plethora of locally inspired standards and certification initiatives on forestry and forestry products. Generally speaking, globalized standards tend to be process-based, as most ISO management standards (such as the ISO 9000 and 14000 series) are. This makes difficult their across-the-board application to asset-specific industries operating in different countries.

However, differentiated thresholds for good practice are not always a bad thing. If they are based on business-community partnerships at locality-specific levels and well administered, they can stimulate locally better-adapted innovation and competition. Especially where SD-conscious CSOs are actively involved in local conservation activities, the multi-stakeholder process can serve as a sort of real-time policy forum and help raise societal expectations for better-than-legal practice and accountability. Locality-specific visions and standards can possibly get linked to some "bottom-up" pathways connecting between the local and the global. Thus, Bass, Font, and Danielson argue that "exploring locality-specific visions and standards is a necessary precursor to certification schemes in order to avoid inequity from top-down standards".[62]

The norms well shared among local producers would in time permeate into consumer preference, which would in turn induce buyers' groups to shift their sourcing strategy in favour of more broadly credible certification systems, stimulating development of national or regional certification and labelling schemes. Examples of this kind include the emergence of the Pan-European Certification Initiative in 1999, and the effort of the African Timber Organization to develop a regional scheme based on the ITTO (International Tropical Timber Association) criteria and indicators. Mexico, Malaysia, and Tanzania, with the support of the IUCN, the WWF, and the UK Forestry Commission, have just launched (in March 2003) a region-specific sub-regime, the Global Partnership on Forest Landscape Restoration.

In the domain of tourism, the picture is somewhat different. Actions for tourism certification took off no earlier than around 1998 but have already resulted in over 100 different voluntary labels and schemes. This industry, too, has an asset-specific characteristic, since key tourism infrastructures (such as beaches, national parks, and historical sites) are often publicly owned, except related hotel businesses, and most voluntary local standards and certification schemes are administered jointly with local governments. They are seldom run for profit but the majority are heavily government-subsidized. Besides, cooperative ventures between private business actors and local communities in this domain are increasingly promoted by biodiversity conservation NGOs, rural developmental programmes, and ODA donors as a means of making the tourism industry beneficial to all parties, not only by providing access to capital and international tourists for local communities but also by facilitating the industry's access to natural and cultural resources in host developing countries. However, because of the international nature of tourism, tourists would rather wish to see internationally consistent and well-accredited standards established. Thus, proposals are emerging to develop something comparable to the FSC, such as a global "Sustainable Tourism Stewardship Council". In fact, the World Tourism Organization's (WTO) rather "top-down" initiative has launched (as of 2000) the Tour Operator Initiative for Sustainable Development (TOISD) jointly with UNESCO and UNEP.

Privatization of utilities in urban-peripheral areas has expanded scope for privately financed infrastructure (PFI) businesses. These typically involve business-government partnerships, and sometimes tripartite business-government-community partnering arrangements. In developing countries both bilateral and multilateral donor agencies, mandated increasingly to alleviate poverty, get involved particularly in the phase of such partnering arrangements requiring substantial capacity-building for the community citizens concerned. Suez/Ondeo's Water for All programme for drinking water in needy rural provinces in South Africa, its Aguas Argentinas Consortium with the municipality and community CSOs in Buenos Aires, and other water system initiatives targeted for below-the-poverty-line people in Bolivia, the Philippines, Morocco, etc. are among the often-cited examples in UN policy documents, as well as in WBCSD documents.[63]

Self-motivated business-CSO partnerships

Not a few cases of business-CSO partnerships have arisen out of self-motivated collaborative arrangements without formal involvement of IGO facilitators. Examples of industry-specific *de facto* voluntary standards of global significance that are based on MNC-CSO partnerships include, in addition to the FSC mentioned above, the Unilever-led Marine Stewardship Council (MSC: since 1995) and the Tea Sourcing Partnership (TSP: since 1997). Jem Bendell's *Terms of Endearment*[64] offers many more of such examples, and points to the emerging tendency that major environmental NGOs like the WWF and Greenpeace, which used to pay little attention to market-based mechanisms, have come to enter strategic partnering agreements with major industrial MNCs. These are to serve the objectives of these NGOs' mainstream advocacy activities, as well as to help improve the environmental/ethical performance of their partner companies.

Negotiations between the two different institutional (and also professional) cultures would take time. But, after such differences have been mutually recognized through sustained negotiation, the outcome may be

Table 11.2 Rational motivations for mutual engagement of multinational corporations and environmental NGOs

Motivations for MNCs to engage with environmental NGOs	Motivations for environmental NGOs to engage with MNCs
• Creating new markets	• Disenchantment with government policies
• NGOs' credibility with the public on social issues and priorities	• Gaining greater leverage through business links with government
• Avoiding negative public confrontations	• Access to more funds and technical and managerial resources
• Cross-fertilization of thinking for the future	• Cross-fertilization of thinking for the future
• Cooptation of new stakeholders	• Access to supply chains

hinged on rationally calculated merits of collaboration, as illustrated in Table 11.2 in general terms.

One might feel that such motivational compatibility could augur a possibility for *civil regulation* to tame MNC behaviours. But Bendell points out that notion would soon crumble in the face of serious limitations on the part of CSO power, particularly with respect to the social reach of consumer politics of today. While CSO power is practically linked to consumers' spending power, citizens in Southern countries have far less of such power than their counterparts in the North.[65]

A few more warnings may well be in order. Firstly, corporate partners would sooner or later face great difficulties in accommodating the increasingly demanding sustainability agenda of their CSO partners that would threaten the corporate short-term financial time horizon. Secondly, the CSO partners would face conflicts with their memberships and their own fundraising base. And thirdly, resourceful CSOs may not exist so ubiquitously as one would wish to think. Elkington and Fennel[66] even predict that the reserve army of well-resourced independent CSO partners is likely quickly to run short of the now rising demand from corporate players. They thus suspect that "the corporations leading off in forging strategic alliances with key CSOs may be doing so just to enjoy a 'first-mover' benefit".

Nevertheless one may venture to argue that there should be an ontologically tenable reason for believing that both FPOs and CSOs seek opportunities for mutual direct engagement in one form or another for the purpose of their individual organizational survival and growth. This is because any organization, be it private or public, for-profit or not-for-profit, is necessarily "Janus-faced" in the sense that it consists of a mixture of two programmatic ideal types: *action* and *politics*. For a business corporation, if its mainstream business activities stand for its "action" programme, then its political programme consists, like corporate public relations activities, of "reflecting" as faithfully as possible the diverse, inconsistent demands and ideologies of its external stakeholders. The two types of programme normally abide side by side within the same organization, and need to be managed separately with radically different organizational ideologies and professional cultures. There always remain some imbalances or inconsistencies between the two programmes, and yet to maintain a right mixture of the two is a necessary condition for organizational survival and growth. Thus a CSO, too, would need to buttress its mainstream advocacy activities (action) with occasional contractual engagement with appropriate business corporations, if focused only on selected niches of the larger issue areas with which it is concerned.[67] By the same token, one can argue that such CSO-FPO partnerships need not, and ought not, be sustained on such a longer-term basis as to precipitate them into the danger of mutual cooptation.

Self-motivated business-community partnerships in the bottom tier of the world market

Now, reverting to the stakeholder engagement scenes in developing societies, the "Pyramid Laboratory" and its contribution to the WBCSD activities deserve particular attention. The WRI-organized Sustainable Enterprise Summit in October 1999 had before it a provocative research paper entitled "Strategies for the bottom of the pyramid".[68] It drew attention to the bottom tier of the world market that was worth about $2 trillion (some 4 billion people living mostly in rural villages, shanty towns, and urban slums, with less than $1,500 annual income per capita) – a market not insignificant, although smaller than $10–15 trillion of the mid-tier of the pyramid. The paper made a strong case for the relevance of businesslike approaches for international corporations to engage themselves with local CSOs and public authorities to assist in community developmental activities in developing societies.

The examples cited then were limited to only a few countries (especially India) involving only a few MNCs, but showed a reasonable range of variations, including local infrastructural development projects (such as Grameen phones in Bangladesh and rural telephones in India); microcredit facilities with the collateral requirement replaced by local peer group evaluation (and often with a focus on women); corporate sourcing direct from indigenous local firms and smallholder farms for globally marketable products; product development and distribution systems engaging a local supply chain involving micro-firms in villages and towns; and renewable energy servicing systems for off-grid rural areas. Table

Table 11.3 Key dimensions of pro-poor business-community partnerships for addressing the bottom tier of the world market

Key dimensions/business models	Illustrative examples
Local infrastructural development involving private sector technical and managerial resources	• Rural telephones (India); Grameen phones (Bangladesh) • Suez/Ondeo's Water For All programme for drinking water in two needy rural provinces of South Africa • Aguas Argentinas Consortium (between Suez/Ondeo, the municipality, and community NGOs) for the water and wastewater system in Buenos Aires; Ondeo's water system initiatives targeted for below-the-poverty-line people in Bolivia, Chile, Indonesia, the Philippines, and Morocco
Micro-credit with local peer group evaluation instead of collateral	• Deutsche Bank's Microcredit Development Fund cooperating with local financial agents and CSOs to create community-owned for-profit micro-credit companies • Citibank's micro-lending services in Bangalore, India • International SRI funds catering for small-scale investments, such as Pax World Funds and Calvert New Africa Fund • HSBC (international financial service) contributing its employees' time to Investing In Nature, a joint project with Earthwatch, the WWF, and Botanic Gardens Conservation International
Sourcing direct from indigenous firms and smallholder farms in developing countries	• Indigenous Designs, a Californian clothing producer, sourcing high-quality garments from indigenous firms in Ecuador and Peru for sale in the USA • Starbucks' "shade-grown coffee" and M&M Mars' "sustainably grown cocoa" sourced from small farmers in developing countries • Sappi-Monds partnership with smallholder tree growers in South Africa
Product development and distribution systems engaging a network of micro-firms in villages and towns	• Unilever in India adopting the practice of a prosperous local detergent producer, Nirma • Ruf and Tuf Jeans (ready-to-make jeans components) created by Arvind Mills, India, with a network of 4,000 tailors located in small rural towns and villages • Aventis' partnership with the WHO, MSF, and Bristol-Myers Squib

Table 11.3 (cont.)

Key dimensions/business models	Illustrative examples
Renewable energy servicing systems for off-grid rural areas in developing countries	• Waterhealth International's solar-powered Ultra Violet Waterworks technology for developing societies • Partnership between SUDERETA (Tanzanian NGO) and North-South Initiative e.V (Germany) for setting up "Enterprises of Trust" for production and sale of renewable energy systems in rural regions • Environmental Enterprises Assistance Funds (with IFC, Calvert Social Investment Foundation, Energy House Capital Corp, USAID, etc.), including a Solar Development Group that supports 26 PV companies servicing off-grid rural areas in 14 developing countries • Eskom's electrification programme in South Africa • BP Solar rural development projects • G8 Renewable Energy Task Force (co-chaired by Sir Mark Moody Stuart of Shell) to identify the barriers and solutions to increased use of renewable energies in developing countries

11.3[69] lists key dimensions of pro-poor business-community partnerships with several illustrative examples for each dimension.

Prahalad and Hart[70] tried to appeal to the international business community by offering a plausible framework of management economics underlining these pro-poor business models. In a nutshell, as in the case of electronic commerce, the argument rests on the merits of recouping return on investment via "capital efficiency" (rather than labour efficiency to be achieved with capital-using technology); achieving it by intensive use of local labour and other resources, including local small businesses; reducing transaction and organization costs through partnership agreements with local community authorities and CSO groups; and achieving high-volume sales with low margin unit return.

The Pyramid Laboratory vision and theory may have appeared just a pie in the sky at that time. But the idea has since quickly made an inroad into the WBCSD work programme in the form of its "Sustainable Livelihoods" project (already mentioned in the preceding section). The WBCSD initiative in this direction may have been in part politically prompted in the course of its negotiation with Kofí Annan for the Global

Compact and its subsequent engagement in the preparatory process for the WSSD. The first report on this project[71] still devotes much energy to persuading the business community about the business-friendly project rationale by emphasizing "deregulation and privatization", "market opportunities", and "licence to operate". The project is meant to be an "honest broker" facility to help bring together like-minded companies, NGOs, and governments, local, national, and international. The report indicates that the project has already collected over 60 case studies on pro-poor business ventures which are to be published in a fuller report in a few years' time.

Certainly, truly developmental business-community partnerships do not occur in a vacuum. Where daunting power asymmetry exists between international corporations and local communities, negotiations would require some third-party brokers or facilitators, and even an extra programme for pre-training community partners for improved negotiation capability and power. International development agencies are often called on for assistance in such situations. In fact, the WBCSD has offered a sister publication on this matter[72] which heeds, among other factors, the need for "entrepreneurial capacity incubators" – a practical multi-partner approach for deepening and expanding local supply chains and facilitating entrepreneurial development in developing societies. Such incubator projects are supported by IGOs such as the GEF, UNEP, and UNIDO, as well as the WBCSD, the IUCN, the LEAD and the WRI. Thus, "business-IGO" partnership has become correlative with the win-win strategy for pro-poor business ventures. And it has become an important dimension of institutional adaptation on the part of the UN system.

From the Global Compact to the "Type 2" track of the WSSD

A number of global partnership models have emerged whereby the UN Development Programme (UNDP), the World Bank, the International Finance Corporation (IFC), UNCTAD, and other UN agencies have taken substantial "brokering" initiatives for multi-stakeholder engagement at the concrete problem-solving level in the context of development cooperation. Relatively well-known examples include the Consultative Group on International Agricultural Research (CGIAR), the Global Water Partnership (GWP), the Global Alliance for Vaccines and Immunization (GAVI), the UN Fund for International Partnership (UNFIP), the UNDP MicroStart programme, the GEF-supported IFC funds for supporting environmental enterprises, the UNDP-World Bank Advisory Facility for Public-Private Infrastructure, etc.[73]

There are several other examples of multi-sectoral partnership in which major FPO actors assumed a lead role. Particularly noteworthy in the context of business-community partnership is the Business Partners for Development (BPD) – a three-year study project initiated in 1999 by the World Bank together with multi-sectoral partners including BP, Shell, Kellogg's, Rio Tinto, Care International, Vivendi, the IBLF, etc. Its objective was to investigate empirically how private businesses, civil society, and public administrations could work together in the field to deliver benefits to both business and communities in developing countries. The research was completed by December 2001 and its report[74] consists of an analytical compilation of the lessons learned from the 30 "focus projects" that involved more than 120 different organizations in 20 different countries. The ICC-UNCTAD partnership for promoting foreign investment, initiated in 1998, was to assist the world's poorest countries in upgrading the managerial and technological capacity of their small and medium-sized firms by facilitating their supply and distribution linkages with MNCs. Its Bio-Trade Initiative is to increase market access for biodiversity products from developing countries.

Still another noteworthy example is the UNEP-orchestrated Cleaner Production (CP) network. It has been in existence since 1989, involving many national CP centres and allied CP centres (now more than 100) operating across some 40 countries. It has a pragmatic and proactive banner of "pollution prevention", with gradually increased emphasis on achieving greater "eco-efficiency" through reduced resource (and energy) inputs, reduced wastes, and reduced environmental risks. Although not linked to any formal MEAs, its International Declaration on Cleaner Production (IDCP), launched in 1998, has served a sort of framework accord whereby signatory countries, business firms and associations, local autonomies, and productivity centres show their voluntary commitment to the CP banner. With the advent of the WSSD process, a new 10-year work programme is being proposed with a broader-scoped agenda of "sustainable consumption and production".[75]

As well-documented information on those proactive initiatives reached the UN General Assembly and the CSD forums, two institutional innovations came into being to complement the conventional interstate mechanisms for international policy-making. One was the Global Compact (GC), initiated by the UN Secretary-General's "good office" (i.e. not based on General Assembly resolutions) with an intention to advance "global corporate social responsibility". The other is the "Type 2" avenue introduced by the UNCSD (acting as the WSSD/PrepCom) by way of an open assembly hall for voluntary multi-party partnerships/initiatives with problem-solving commitments of cross-border significance. Such partnerships/initiatives are defined as "action-oriented coalitions focused on deliverables" that will "contribute to translating political commitments into action"[76] and involve CSOs, FPOs, IGOs, bi-lateral aid donors, and local autonomies as appropriate.

In retrospect, those two innovations were interdependent in the sense that the GC paved the way toward the Type 2 outcome for the WSSD process. And the ICC, the WBCSD, and their allied think-tanks had much to do with this development. The GC office, once established (in June 2000), proved instrumental in having the UN Secretary-General present his report to the UN General Assembly on UN cooperation with the private sector.[77] The report minimized the element of policy advocacy by simply presenting the results from a comprehensive factual survey on UN organizations' ongoing partnership activities with the private sector (the GC being treated as one of them). The survey was prepared by the IBLF, and its findings were shaped in consultation with a large number of member governments and UN agencies.

Meanwhile, the GC triggered various complementary initiatives at regional and national levels with the support of major international business associations and their member companies. By the time the Type 2 track to the WSSD was proposed, the GC's outreach and network-building activities had exposed many countries and institutions in Africa, Asia, and Latin America to the promises of issue-specific proactive private-public partnerships on the field. The GC "policy dialogues" included annual conferences on the theme of business and SD, and several working groups specialized in issues such as multi-stakeholder partnerships, sustainable investment, and sustainable entrepreneurship.[78]

When the Type 2 track was proposed by the WSSD PrepCom chairman, many developing countries, as well as CSO caucuses, voiced suspicion that both the GC and this proposal would result in "privatization of sustainable development",[79] and argued for a restrictive definitional clause stressing more or less immediate positive spillovers to the Type 1 (i.e. intergovernmental) negotiations at the WSSD. But after some negotiations, the chairman removed such initial restrictions to open the track for voluntary action-oriented partnerships and initiatives, both new and ongoing, as long as they could "demonstrate added value in the WSSD context". However, critics still continue to challenge the definitional ambiguity of Type 2 outcomes and raise issues such as commitments to project funding and procedures for monitoring, evaluation, and compliance.

Beyond the WSSD: Regime design matters

We now return to the global level, this time paying particular attention to the formal policy- and rule-making dimension of regime formation and maintenance. Firstly, the notion of "vertical interlinkages" will be elaborated with emphasis on the local-global nexus. This is followed by a discussion on the "Stiglerian threshold" – a critical condition for pulling in the "Third party leaning towards Pusher" on formal rule-making initiatives at the interstate level. The section then addresses some issues concerning regime design, hinting at certain policy research strategies of relevance in the post-WSSD context.

Horizontal and vertical interlinkages

Much attention is being paid to scope for "interlinkages" among the UNCED instruments on climate change, biodiversity, anti-desertification, forest sustainability, hazardous chemicals, etc., and also between these and major economic instruments like the WTO and the OECD MAI. The objectives of such interlinkages are by and large twofold: a greater administrative efficiency in intergovernmental negotiations and policy management at national and international levels; and an enhanced cognitive base needed for international agreement-making. The logic of synergistic merits is quite clear. Less clear, however, are the processes through which the synergies would help dissolve recurring political deadlocks in multilateral treaty-making.

A multi-party forum necessarily involves multiple issues even when it deals with an agenda focused on a single issue area at a time. Ernst Haas' typology of international agreement suggests that an agreement based only on politically sponsored tactical issue linkage in the absence of a consensual knowledge base would be short-lived.[80] Even when the expert knowledge for ambitious problem-solving exists and is accepted by politicians, issue linkage may remain at best fragmented if the shared political goal is static or fragmented. Then the resulting agreement may be of only pragmatic value and subjected to further amendments in line with increased knowledge. However, Haas simply juxtaposes four ideal types of international agreement without postulating any a priori correlation between knowledge consensualization and political goal-sharing.[81] Sharing an improved cognitive basis alone may or may not promote the sharing of an expanded and interconnected political goal. So, interlinking different MEAs at the cognitive level is one thing, while reconciling among the different, more or less short-sighted, political goals embraced by different participants is another.

In fact, international regimes have been traditionally constructed as "decomposable" hierarchies, each being based on more or less fragmented issue linkages. Multilateral conference diplomacy allows for behind-the-door trading between different issues of interest to different parties. So, in reality, we are accustomed to the subtle mechanism of negotiation whereby multiple issues provide the "means" rather than the subject of agreement. The outcome tends to be at best of pragmatic value, and we know it would be hubris to dream of a grand package of fully nested MEAs that would cover the immensely complex whole of problems and causalities simultaneously. For example, after reviewing the theory and practice of linkage, Lawrence Susskind suggests that negotiators should be able not only to add issues and parties but also to subtract issues and parties to help hold winning coalitions together.[82] And he recommended in conjunction with the pre-UNCED Salzburg Initiative (1990–1991) adopting a bottom-up approach which would build decentralized coalitions that cut across typical North-South lines on a (bio)regional basis and then aggregate increasingly larger clusters of states and NGO interests into coalitions of like-minded stakeholders.[83]

So, the best pragmatic way out may be to work simultaneously on both *horizontal* interlinkages among relevant MEAs (to broaden the cognitive base on which they stand) and *vertical* interlinkages, or strategic "issue divisions", that can connect individual MEAs with relevant issue-specific sub-agreements and multi-stakeholder action programmes. "Cognitive evolution encompasses the ability to compose and then decompose a nested problem set",[84] because decomposition is required for the purpose of making organized action possible. Vertical interlinkages become particularly important for facilitating clearer responsibility allocation among all the relevant stakeholders so as to ensure clear-cut and effective compliance mechanisms for individual MEAs.

How to coax industry to become "Pusher"

This leads us back to the question posed earlier in the introduction: under what conditions or situations will the "Third-party leaning towards Pusher" be likely to step forward and begin to coalesce with "Pusher" (hard-nosed environmentalists and green parties) to support a new legislative proposal on the table? One possible answer is an appropriate issue division that would make a Stiglerian situation perceptible sooner than otherwise. The Stiglerian situation refers to one in which leading firms (of the innovator/market-shaper type) begin to perceive a newly envisaged regulation as an opportune leverage for them to earn quasi-monopoly rents on their new products and technologies. This theory, named after George Stigler's decades-old article,[85] draws straightforwardly on standard business economics without invoking a normative notion like CSR. It points to the situation in which regulatory *benefits* concentrate on a relatively few leading business actors, while *costs* are thinly distributed over many. Important for introducing a new regulation is not only the way the regulatory proposal is designed, but also precisely when it is tabled officially. The timing should match the relevant industrial actors' perception of a ripening Stiglerian situation that can prompt them to move for game change. That timing may well be called the "Stiglerian threshold" for brevity's sake.

Relevant examples at the domestic level abound. Among those policies which saw quick international assimilation after the first adoption in one country, one can recall, for example, the ban on use of leaded gasoline (which promised higher profits for producers of unleaded gasoline); the banning of the domestic sale of DDT in OECD countries (which gave a competitive edge to producers of more sophisticated pesticides); the regulatory initiative in Germany for recycling packaging materials and automotive parts (which other countries feared would imply a new technological trade barrier); and the Japanese automobile industry's adoption (as early as in 1978) of the then world's most stringent NO_x emission regulation – the so-called Japanese resurrection of the American Muskie law (which the Japanese auto industry began to think would help enhance its international competitiveness). More generally, one can look back in time to identify the Stiglerian thresholds which triggered successful adoption of a variety of individual regulatory measures of the command-and-control type, introduced by governments covering specifically designated products and processes at a time.

One of the salient cases at the level of multilateral environmental negotiations is the unexpectedly swift adoption of the Montreal Ozone Protocol in 1987 – only two years after the adoption of the equivocal framework convention at Vienna. It can be attributed to the changed perception of leading chlorofluorocarbon producers, particularly DuPont, followed by Imperial Chemical Industries, about the commercialization prospect of substitution products in the pipeline.[86] Besides, in regard to regulatory design it should be noted that the ozone regime was, unlike the climate change regime, focused on a very narrow range of specific products. One can also recall the 1962 OILPOL amendment which introduced provisions requiring tankers to install specific technology (the load-on-top procedure), and the 1978 Protocol to MARPOL which introduced further a new vessel-building technology (the segregated ballast tanker). In these cases, the major improvement in enforcement of the convention was triggered by switching from performance standards to equipment standards, which made it easier to detect violations during regular port inspections. And the ease of detecting and prosecuting equipment violators eliminated the tanker owners' fear that complying with the more costly technology would put them at comparative disadvantage. Thus, Ronald Mitchell contrived his thesis on "regime design matters".[87] The thrust of his argument is that "specific" regimes of the classical type, each specialized in a single well-specified issue area, could more effectively induce compliance, and that it was more clearly the case when the regimes relied on technology-based standards than on performance-based standards (i.e. specifying only discharge limits).

Here, some warnings are in order. Public policy is not usually supposed to favour resourceful, privileged economic actors at the expense of a larger number of weaker, less innovative actors. Technologically advanced firms that can readily reap upon the Stiglerian threshold are hardly in need of public subsidy or governmental promotion policy. And, once a Stiglerian strategy succeeds, the public authority must then work hard to look after stragglers.[88] Besides, the more narrowly specified are the target actors for regulation, the fewer will be the laggards suffering from it and the lesser the sense of shame on the part of the government. In fact, this explains why *both* government and industry favour the step-by-step piecemeal adoption of product- and equipment-specific command-and-control policies which cumulate in an altogether not very coherent arsenal of public policy instruments in many countries.

The DuPont-supported Montreal Ozone Protocol did in fact put many minor, technologically less prepared, producers at a disadvantage, and required its London revision (1990) for compensating developing countries in the form of a special multilateral fund to support their phase-out efforts.[89] Also, the DDT ban within OECD countries (in the mid-1970s) has had a lasting awkward aftereffect, in that many laggard small producers continued to seek an outlet for their traditional, potentially hazardous, pesticides.[90] We ought to learn hard lessons from these instances. It is not enough just to say that "public shaming" through information disclosure is a very effective tactic for large, reputation-sensitive corporations, because the same tactic would not make sense when dealing with small firms which have no reputation to protect. Moreover, the sustainability issues are too pressing to stay calm just on the grounds that no policy would be better than a bad policy.

After acknowledging all those warnings, the author would like to contend that an industry-government collusion, coopting hard-nosed environmentalist groups on a Stiglerian threshold, can drive a wedge into powerful anti-regulatory coalitions that would otherwise continue to insist on the *status quo*. For that matter, regulatory design matters. Great care should be exercised to design issue-specific sub-regimes that would be effective enough to coax potential leaders, to deepen or widen existing regimes, and to get the tide turned for steadier advancement toward SD.

Potential win-sets perceived at the international level may not always prove domestically feasible. But, in some cases, even the same industry that has opposed a domestic legislation may come forth to promote a similar one at the international level. Elizabeth DeSombre provides a number of examples of industry-environmentalist coalitions which came to support forward-looking regulatory proposals in the areas of endangered species, air pollution, and fisheries.[91] She says that industry's interest in these cases is mainly in seeking "a new level playing field for international competition". This is a typical argument put forward by the winning coalition emerging on a Stiglerian threshold, even though she is speaking in the context of domestic catching-up legislation in technologically less-advanced developing countries.

Fortunately, loftier principles and norms tend to prevail in multilateral policy arenas than in domestic policy processes, the latter being exposed more readily to stragglers' backlash tactics. Multilateral diplomacy does not only help bridge over the discrepancy between problem space and political action space, but can often function as a change agent that stimulates the diffusion of policy innovations across national borders. Indeed, such a reverse tide of influence[92] may generally prove more effective for smaller countries whose internal capacity for policy development and administration is severely limited. But the picture may well be quite different for cross-border coalition-building within the like-minded leading business actors. The "responsible care" activism offers a case in point. It has steadily made inroads into many industrial countries and proved highly instrumental for the launch of the OECD *Guidelines for Pollutant Release and Transfer Registers* (PRTRs),[93] as well as for the recent conclusion (in 2001) of the Convention on Persistent Organic Pollutants (POPs). Certainly, more empirical research is desirable to look into such reverse paths whereby the outcomes of multilateral policy discourse exert positive influence upon domestic policy processes, and to examine the role being played by leading industry agents in manoeuvring such pathways.

Two parallel Type 2 showcases and an agenda for future research

The Johannesburg plan of implementation has designated the CSD as the focal point for Type 2 partnerships/initiatives. As of January 2004, the CSD Secretariat posts 266 partnerships (and some activities in the process of initiating partnerships) on its website.[94] The CSD-11 (May 2003) agreed to a set of criteria and guidelines for scrutinizing and following up on the registered projects. The CSD-12 (April 2004) will have a "Partnerships Fair" such that both existing and potential new partners can create synergies between partnerships, launch new partnerships, and present ideas on the CSD follow-up process.

One-third of the projects approved for the CSD registry were submitted by national governments as leading partners, nearly 40 per cent led by UN agencies/funds and programmes and other IGOs (UNEP, the UNDP, the World Bank, UNIDO, and UNESCO being particularly active), and about a quarter led by the so-called (non-governmental) major groups. However, the CSD registry scarcely includes projects with business-oriented approaches. Ninety-odd industry-led partnerships/initiatives adopting business-oriented approaches used to be posted on the BASD website until late 2002. The site has recently been taken over by a newly established portal called "Partnerships Central" and is now administered by the Center for Advancement of Sustainable Development Partnerships (CASDP) – a newly created, independent, non-profit organization governed by a board of directors chaired by Lord Holm of Cheltenham (former vice-chairman of the BASD).[95] Thus we are currently left with a pair of parallel showcases of Type 2 projects and programmes, as shown in Table 11.4.

Many of the projects in the CSD showcase are focused on training, policy research, and information-sharing. The WBCSD/BASD Partnerships Central showcases offer a number of schemes of business-NGO and business-NGO-IGO partnering in which ICC/WBCSD member companies and associations play some leading roles. Many of them are already fairly large-scale international programmes of the "sectoral global compact" type. Major examples include the Global Reporting Initiative (GRI), the Global Alliance for Vaccine and Immunization (GAVI), the Global Mining Initiative, the Sustainable Asset Management (SAM), the Marine Stewardship Council (MSC), the Responsible Care programme, etc. This compendium is complemented by the WBCSD publication *Walking the Talk*,[96] which offers as many as 64 case studies (or success stories) on SD-oriented corporate activities and programmes.

One might question here again: "Why such a parallelism between the two showcases?" Part of the possible answer may be associated with the tramline nature of public diplomacy of CSOs and FPOs (as discussed earlier). Another possible answer may be that, given the scepticism about the Type 2 approach being voiced by some CSOs and Southern delegations, the international business community may have chosen not to spoil the success it has had in promoting its long-embraced approach to SD. Its emphasis on "concrete actions and deliverable results rather than process and procedures" has resonated well into the proactive Type 2 outcome of the WSSD process.

Both showcases are at best illustrative of ongoing and newly evolving initiatives. Many of the CSD-registered projects may be suspect of fundraising artifice on the part of advocacy NGOs (even though quite a few seem to have succeeded in attracting donors' attention). Besides, it is most disappointing that only three partnership projects are classifiable primarily into the "poverty eradication" category, in spite of the high weight given to it in the WSSD trilogy. The number would increase to a dozen or so, but not much more than that, if one included rural en-

Table 11.4 Type 2 outcomes: Two parallel showcases of multi-party partnerships/
initiatives

The UNCSD Type 2 registry	The BASD partnership initiatives
Over 260 projects, mostly oriented to training, information-sharing, and policy research, clustered by major thematic areas: – production and consumption patterns (9) – energy (23) – natural resource base (70) – education (14) – other means of implementation (39) – local authorities and urbanization (14) – other new partnerships being initiated (33) • Geographical coverage: – global (60%) – regional (40%) • Financial commitments: two-thirds being funded (total some $1.2 billion) • Leading partners: – governments (65%) – IGOs (33%) – NGOs, including private sector, local authorities, and research institutes	Showcase A Over 50 projects posted on the BASD website, including: – Business Partners for Development – Environmental Enterprises – Global Reporting Initiative – Global Mining Initiative – Energy Wisdom Program – Global Alliance for Vaccines and Immunization – Marine Stewardship Council – Sustainable Forestry Program – Rio Tinto-Earthwatch Initiative Showcase B: Partnerships Central About 130 projects (as of March 2004) clustered in the WEHAB themes: – water and sanitation (12) – energy (36) – health (14) – agriculture (29) – biodiversity (38)

ergy and community water projects. The "self-motivated" business-community partnerships being considered by the WBCSD's Sustainable Livelihoods project do not seem to have made inroads into the CSD registry.

As Uli Piest points out, there is a need for clearer mechanisms for ensuring accountability and monitoring of these Type 2 projects in their implementation phases in order to strengthen their links to decision-makers at national, regional, and global levels.[97] At the present stage the CSD registry may be, on the whole, not much more than a fuzzy and disorderly showcase of self-proclaimed promises. Before attempting to impose any hasty bureaucratic standards on these bottom-up initiatives, careful research would be needed for objectively calibrating their individual credibility and feasibilities in politico-institutional, technical, and financial terms.

A similar qualification would apply to the BASD Partnerships Central showcase. As for *Walking the Talk*,[98] the 27 cases shown in the chapters on "corporate social responsibility", "from dialogue to partnership", and "making markets work for all" are particularly appealing, while many others are focused on intra-firm or intra-industry SD initiatives. Many of the success stories may be suspect of public-relational bias. Objective scholarly research would be desirable here too. Although the corporate wall of self-advocacy is likely to be tough to crack, action research on these sustainability business models may be focused on the ongoing voluntary programmes of the "sectoral global compact" type with a view to developing an appropriate IGO-mediated mechanism for enhancing their accountability and third-party monitoring. Also, it might be particularly rewarding to conduct a series of closed-door interviews or talk-shops with the like-minded corporate executives who seem increasingly leaned to become "Pusher" towards whatever new international regulatory initiatives may fit their individual speciality niches. Such an enterprise might help find out whether, and in what ways, leading-edge industrial actors communicate among themselves, if only very privately, to assess the ripeness of relevant Stiglerian thresholds for them to lead forward in international environmental rule-making.

Follow-up research on the Type 2 showcase projects and programmes may generate important stepping-stones by way of a "bottom-up" approach to the deepening and widening of existing MEAs. It may well be complemented by some "top-down" approaches to issue division.

In discussing examples of the Stiglerian threshold, the author attempted to shed light on the possible merits of product- and equipment-specific regime designs, but at the same time warned about the built-in bias of governmental regulations in favour of command and control. This does not mean that all good regimes must be of that kind. Some critics, particularly economists, argue that most of the low-hanging fruits for command and control have been picked or that such an approach is no longer suited to meet the enormous global challenges of SD. But the author would rather argue to the contrary. SD is yet a highly contested concept, and even a value consensus about its nature is fragile. So there must be scope for further pragmatic "issue division" for deepening of extant MEAs.

For example, Ronald Mitchell, who cared much about regime design in conjunction with the OILPOL and the MARPOL, invites attention now to the pending issues of the Kyoto Protocol. In an article co-authored with Edward Parson, he suggests possibilities for improving the overall procedural system for the Clean Development Mechanism (CDM), again with particular attention to its monitoring and compliance dimension.[99] He points to a need for the practice of honest self-reporting to appropriately designed project criteria, and a balanced approach for responding to project performance including the credits to be awarded to successful project completion and to be withheld for under-performing projects, etc. As for the Kyoto Protocol, David Victor[100] predicts that its future COPs will have to revive sooner or later the "policies and measures" (PAMs) approach (an *à la carte* menu from which countries are free to choose), coupled with "pledge and review" (PAR) rounds. The PAMs-PAR approach was once proposed by the EU (tacitly supported by Japan) in the early phase of the protocol negotiations but sidelined in favour of the USA's (would-be) business-friendly idea of emissions trading. This approach might require a separate protocol because of the complexity of international policy coordination that would demand GATT/WTO-like successive negotiation rounds.

The Climate Change Convention alone can envisage many other niches for multilateral sub-agreements in which green competition appears to be precipitating towards Stiglerian thresholds, among others within the energy and transport sectors. In addition to the schemes already mentioned in Tables 11.3 and 11.4, the potential of a tradable renewable energy certificate (TREC) system has gathered increasing attention, especially in the OECD countries. With some due adaptations, the TREC may find legitimate links to the CDM of the Kyoto Protocol.[101] The Biodiversity Convention, too, is such an expansive platform that many more protocols are to come into the pipeline in addition to the recently concluded (somewhat evasive) protocol on living modified organisms (LMOs). A detailed discussion on these specific possibilities is beyond the scope of this chapter. It is hoped that the international policy research community will explore more systematically the potentialities of these and other plausible angles for improved environmental regime design.

Concluding remarks

This chapter attempts to locate "business and industry" in the agency structure perspective, and highlight the various strategic options envisaged by the relatively creative industrial actors endeavouring to find space for game change and interactive leadership towards sustainable development, in parallel to, as well as in cooperation with, other non-state actors. An effort is made to "de-mythologize" the confrontational public diplomacy of the "Davos Man versus the Porto Alegre Protester" all too often observed at the global level, with the help of some coalition-theoretic reflections and also by presenting a multi-layered perspective on multi-stakeholder engagement with problem-solving commitments.

Industry's emphasis on "concrete actions and deliverable results" can be seen to have resonated well with IGOs' growing inclination towards the implementation of existing global commitments at local and cross-border levels. Heed is given to both promises and problems of corporate social responsibility, business-NGO partnerships (facilitating development of locally adapted and/or internationally credible standards), and business-community partnerships (with pro-poor community developmental implications).

This multi-layered perspective suggests that the international institution, construed inclusive of both its formal and informal content, is not at all thin, but has grown ever denser during the decade from Rio to Johannesburg. But it is on the whole yet too fuzzy and fragmented, especially with respect to (not just intellectually obvious but) politically effective pathways between the local and the global. In seeking ways of improving regime design, timely perception of the "Stiglerian threshold", coupled with an appropriate degree of issue division, is considered crucial for coaxing SD-oriented industrial actors to become "Pusher" for international rule-making.

The author of this chapter would shy away from making any wishful propositions regarding the "organizational" aspect of the global environmental institution, but would rather say "form follows an agreed function, which in turn follows a well-nested set of shared problems". Some lines of policy-oriented research are suggested with a view to developing improved "vertical interlinkages" that would serve for further deepening and widening of existing and newly evolving multilateral environmental accords in the post-WSSD context. They include, among others, bottom-up action research, preferably large-scale and participatory, for monitoring and consolidating the "Type 2" initiatives for effective interlinkages with regional and global conventions; a skilfully managed consultation process with SD-oriented industrial leaders with a view to making informed prediction of specific regulatory niches auguring Stiglerian thresholds of interest to them; and a series of case studies exploring the role of "Third party leaning towards Pusher" in promoting policy innovations at the international level and then manoeuvring the flow of their impact back on to national policy processes.

Notes

1. "Business and industry" is one of the nine "major groups" of society as identified in Section III of Agenda 21. It is synonymous with the "private business sector" in the chapter's title, and is variously referred to as "industry", "business", "for-profit organizations" (FPOs), etc. for brevity's sake. This sector includes not-for-profit business associations, business-sponsored think-tanks, and umbrella organizations such as

the International Chamber of Commerce (ICC) and the World Business Council for Sustainable Development (WBCSD).
2. Berridge, G. R. 1995. *Diplomacy: Theory and Practice*. Hertfordshire: Prentice Hall/ Harvester Wheatsheaf.
3. Desai, N. 2002. "Notes on a Statement by Nitin Desai, UN Under-Secretary-General", WSSD Round Table, Copenhagen, 21 February, available at www.iied.org/wssd/. Friends of the Earth International (FoEI) organized an anti-MNC campaign, "Art Action: Hear Our Voice", on the same day that a "Business Day" was held by Business Action for Sustainable Development (BASD) during the Johannesburg Summit, 1 September 2002. They also organized the World Social Forum (WSF) in Porto Alegre, Brazil, and then the "Public Eye on Davos" in Davos, Switzerland in January 2003. These were meant to be world CSO summits in competition with the World Economic Forum (WEF).
4. Keohane, R. O. and J. S. Nye Jr. 2000. "Introduction", in J. S. Nye and J. D. Donahue (eds) *Governance in a Globalizing World*. Washington, DC: Brookings Institution, pp. 1–41, at p. 14.
5. McCarthy, K. D., V. Hodgkinson, and R. Smariwalla. 1992. *The Non-profit Sector in the United States*. San Francisco: Jossey-Bass, p. 3.
6. Rittberger, V. 2000. "(I)NGOs and global environmental governance: Introduction", in Pamela S. Chasek (ed.) *The Global Environment in the Twenty-first Century: Prospects for International Cooperation*. Tokyo: United Nations University Press, p. 86; Breitmeier, H. and V. Rittberger. 2000. "Environmental NGOs in an emerging global civil society", in Pamela S. Chasek (ed.) *The Global Environment in the Twenty-first Century: Prospects for International Cooperation*. Tokyo: United Nations University Press, p. 156.
7. Dahl, R. A. and C. E. Lindblom. 1976. *Politics, Economics and Welfare*. New Haven: Yale University Press, Preface. It should be noted that "businessmen" in this description ought not be taken as individual persons, but representing just the economic sector as such in the modern world of functional differentiation.
8. This terminology is drawn from the structuration theory in the realm of sociology which conceptualizes collective social action (formal or informal groups or organizations) as being neither purely structural nor purely agential but resulting from the interplay of structure and agency, or the confluence of operating structure and purposely acting agents. See Harper, C. L. 1996. *Environment and Society*. Upper Saddle River, NJ: Prentice Hall, p. 281.
9. Broadbent, J. 1998. *Environmental Politics in Japan: Networks of Power and Protest*. Cambridge: Cambridge University Press, Annex I. For example, Paul Wapner says that "Openings in the system arise from contradictions; NGOs work the contradictions" – see Wapner, P. 2000. "The transnational politics of environmental NGOs: Governmental, economic, and social activism", in Pamela S. Chasek (ed.) *The Global Environment in the Twenty-first Century: Prospects for International Cooperation*. Tokyo: United Nations University Press, p. 104. The CSO and FPO sectors are not self-subsisting entities with circumscribed properties but have numerous contradictory tendencies within them. Dana Fisher (Chapter 9 in this volume) notes that the state, economy, and civil society are analytically distinct institutions enjoying relative independence from one another in modern society, even though they are empirically interpenetrating. But Wapner pays heed to the dialectical character of tri-sectoral interpenetration and includes the economy within the civil society – see Wapner, P. 1997. "Governance in global civil society", in O. R. Young (ed.) *Global Governance: Drawing Insight from the Environmental Experience*. Cambridge, MA and London: MIT Press, p. 305, note 6.

10. Cooper, A. F. 2002. "Like-minded nations, NGOs and the changing pattern of diplomacy within the UN system: An introductory perspective", in A. F. Cooper, J. English, and R. Thakur (eds) *Enhancing Global Governance: Towards a New Diplomacy?*. Tokyo: United Nations University Press, p. 7.

11. Holliday, C. O. and J. Pepper. 2000. "Sustainability through the market: Seven keys to success", paper contributed on behalf of the WBCSD at the WRI Sustainable Enterprise Summit, Washington, DC, 19–20 September, p. 33. These four categories of actors in terms of the degree of innovativeness are correlated with four different types of public policies: voluntary initiatives, negotiated policy or agreement (such as the Dutch covenants), economic incentives, and command-and-control regulations.

12. Sprinz, D. F. and M. Weiss. 2001. "Domestic politics and global climate policy", in U. Luterbacher and D. F. Sprinz (eds) *International Relations and Global Climate Change*. Cambridge, MA and London: MIT Press, Table 4.2. "Third party leaning towards Pusher" consists, most typically, of providers of renewable energy, leading innovators on substitution technologies, and sustainability consulting businesses providing services on environmental monitoring and eco-investment portfolios; "Draggers/laggards" are typically polluting industries or pollution-inducing consumers; and "Pushers/leaders" are typically victims of environmental impacts, environmental NGOs, and "green" parties.

13. Mitrany, David. 1946. *A Working Peace System*, 4th edn. London: National Peace Council; Mitrany, David. 1975. "The prospect of integration: Federal or function", in P. Taylor and A. J. R. Groom (eds) *Functionalism: Theory and Practice in International Relations*. New York: Crane, Rusak. For a more recent review of functionalism in international relations, see for example Burley, Anne-Marie. 1993. "Regulating the world': Multilateralism, international law, and the project of the new deal regulatory state", in J. G. Ruggie (ed.) *Multilateralism Matters: The Theory and Praxis of an International Form*. New York: Columbia University Press, pp. 125–156.

14. Kaul, I., I. Grundberg, and M. Stern (eds). 1999. *Global Public Goods: International Cooperation in the 21st Century*. Oxford: Oxford University Press.

15. Usui, M. 2003. "Sustainable development diplomacy of the private business sector: An integrative perspective on game change strategies at multiple levels", *International Negotiation*, Vol. 8, No. 2, pp. 267–310.

16. Cutler, A. C., V. Haufler, and T. Porter. 1999. *Private Authority and International Affairs*. New York: SUNY Press, p. 339.

17. Haas, Ernst B. 1990. *When Knowledge Is Power: Three Models of Change in International Organizations*. Berkeley, CA and Oxford: University of California Press, p. 3.

18. Hocking, B. and D. Kelly. 2002. "Doing the business? The International Chamber of Commerce, the United Nations, and the Global Compact", in A. F. Cooper, J. English, and R. Thakur (eds) *Enhancing Global Governance: Towards a New Diplomacy?*. Tokyo: United Nations University Press.

19. Gleckman, H. 1995. "Transnational corporations' strategic responses to sustainable development", in Fridtjof Nansen Institute (ed.) *Green Globe Yearbook of International Cooperation on Environment and Development*. New York and Oxford: Oxford University Press, pp. 93–106.

20. *Ibid.*, p. 100.

21. *Ibid.*, p. 106, note 18.

22. See for example Finger, M. 1994. "Environmental NGOs in the UNCED process", in T. Princen and M. Finger (eds) *Environmental NGOs in World Politics: Linking the Local and the Global*. London and New York: Routledge, pp. 186–213; Mori, S. 1999. *NGOs and Environmental Governance*. Tokyo: Tsukiji-shokan (in Japanese).

23. Doherty, A. 1994. "The role of non-governmental organizations in UNCED", in B. I.

Spector, G. Sjostedt, and I. W. Zartman (eds) *Negotiating International Regimes: Lessons Learned from the United Nations Conference on Environment and Development.* London, Dordrecht, and Boston: Graham and Trotman/Martinus Nijhoff.

24. UN General Assembly. 2002. *Dialogue Paper by Business and Industry.* A/CONF/..../ Add. 7. Note by the Secretary-General for PrepCom IV, 27 May–7 June 2002.

25. UN General Assembly. 2002. *Dialogue Paper by Non-governmental Organizations.* A/CONF/..../Add. 4. Note by the Secretary General for PrepCom IV, 27 May–7 June 2002.

26. Holliday, C. O., S. Schmidheiny, and P. Watts. 2002. *Walking the Talk.* Sheffield: Greenleaf Publishing.

27. *Ibid.* This book was authored by Charles Holliday Jr (former WBCSD chairman), Sir Philip Watts KCMG (of the Royal Dutch/Shell Group), and Stephan Schmidheiny (now WBCSD's honorary chairman). Schmidheiny was the principal author of *Changing the Course* and a founder of the Business Council for Sustainable Development (predecessor of the WBCSD) 10 years ago.

28. See note 3 above, and also www.foei.org/.

29. See www.earthsummit2002.org/msp/.

30. Gordenker, L. and T. G. Weiss. 1996. "Pluralizing global governance: Analytic approaches and dimensions", in T. G. Weiss and L. Gordenker (eds) *NGOs, the UN and Global Governance.* Boulder, CO and London: Lynne Rienner, esp. pp. 34–35.

31. Mitchell, D. 2001. "International institutions and Janus faces: The influence of international institutions on central negotiators within two-level games", *International Negotiation*, Vol. 6, No. 1, pp. 31–37.

32. Such arguments are related to Lynn Wagner's study on coalitional types and expected outcomes. Wagner, L. M. 1999. "Negotiations in the UN Commission on Sustainable Development: Coalitions, processes and outcomes", *International Journal*, Vol. 4, No. 2, pp. 107–131. See also Usui, note 15 above.

33. Fomerand, Jacques. 1996. "UN conferences: Media events or genuine diplomacy?", *Global Governance*, Vol. 2, No. 3, pp. 361–375.

34. Wapner 2000, note 9 above.

35. Haas, P. M. 2002. "UN conferences and constructivist governance of the environment", *Global Governance*, Vol. 8, No. 1, p. 73.

36. About "global corporatism", see Ottaway, M. 2001. "Corporatism goes global: International organizations, nongovernmental organization networks and transnational business", *Global Governance*, Vol. 7, No. 3, pp. 265–292.

37. Young, O. R. 1989. *International Cooperation: Building Regimes for Natural Resources and the Environment.* Ithaca and London: Cornell University Press, Chapter 2.

38. That bureau was reformed after Rio into a more proactive and larger-scale World Industry Council of the Environment (WICE). The ICC meant to see this in competition with the BCSD for a while.

39. The ICC homepage is clear and loud about its preferred rule of the game based on self-regulation: "Self-regulation is a common thread running through the work of the Commissions. The conviction that business operates most effectively with a minimum of government intervention inspired ICC's voluntary codes." See www.iccwbo.org/.

40. The WBCSD is mandated to be "the leading advocate for sustainable development in the world business community", and to "work on various areas of policy research" to investigate "how industry can become more sustainable" and/or "where business's involvement can make a difference" for SD (quoted phrases from www.wbcsd.ch/). Major financial support, as well as personnel and research data, come from the member corporations, more than half of which are major European-based environment-conscious MNCs. See Broadhurst, A. I. and G. Ledgerwood. 1998. "Environmental

diplomacy of states, corporations and non-governmental organizations: The worldwide web of influence", *International Relations*, Vol. XIV, No. 2, pp. 1–19, at p. 9.

41. See www.wbcsd.ch/.
42. At the Geneva Business Dialogue, Helmut Maucher, the ICC chair, retorted to the NGO activism, stating that "emergence of activist pressure groups risks weakening the effectiveness of public rules, legitimate institutions and democratic processes. These organizations should place emphasis on legitimizing themselves, improving their internal democracy, transparency and accountability." See Geneva Business Declaration 1998, available at www.iccwho.org/home/icc_and_united_nations/.
43. "From the relief of the poverty to the creation of sustainable livelihoods – The business contribution", speech given by Lord Holm of Cheltenham, chair of the ICC Commission on the Environment, to the Rockefeller Foundation, 23 September 1999. See www.iccwbo.org/home/environment_and_energy/sustainable_livelihoods.asp.
44. World Business Council for Sustainable Development (WBCSD). 2002. *Sustainable Livelihoods: The Business Connection*. Johannesburg: WBCSD, downloadable from www.wbcsd.ch/.
45. World Business Council for Sustainable Development (WBCSD). 2002. *Investing for Sustainable Development – Getting the Conditions Right*. Johannesburg: WBCSD, IUCN, World Bank Institute, Deutsche Bank, and Leadership for Environment and Development (LEAD), downloadable from www.wbcsd.ch/.
46. The UNED UK Committee served as a multi-stakeholder forum on domestic and international policy matters related to the environment and development. Its members comprised individuals/experts selected from all the nine "major groups" of NGOs as defined by Agenda 21 (including the ICC and the WBCSD as well). See www.unedforum.org/.
47. See www.earthsummit2002.org/msp/. The project was undertaken in collaboration with Novartis (Switzerland), BP Amoco plc, and the Ford Foundation. Minu Hemmati, who worked as MSP project coordinator, has produced a large volume of practical guide on MSP processes: Hemmati, M. 2002. *Multi-Stakeholder Processes for Governance and Sustainability – Beyond Deadlock and Conflict*. London: Earthscan.
48. Quoted from www.earthsummit2002.org/ic/.
49. Asset specificity means that a company is tied to locality-specific natural resources, community people, and infrastructural facilities so that it can not easily become footloose.
50. Bausch, K. 2001. *The Emerging Consensus in Social Systems Theory*. New York: Kluwer Academic/Plenum Publishers.
51. Andriof, J., S. Waddock, B. Husted, and S. S. Rahman. 2002. *Unfolding Stakeholder Thinking: Theory, Responsibility and Engagement*. Sheffield: Greenleaf Publishing.
52. Payne, S. L. and J. M. Calton. 2002. "Towards a managerial practice of stakeholder engagement: Developing multi-stakeholder learning dialogue", *Journal of Corporate Citizenship*, Vol. 6, June, pp. 37–52.
53. Windsor, D. 2002. "Stakeholder responsibility: Lessons for managers", *Journal of Corporate Citizenship*, Vol. 6, June, pp. 19–35.
54. Eweje, G. 2001. "Corporate social responsibility and developing countries: Natural resource exploitation in Nigeria, South Africa, and Zambia", unpublished PhD thesis, University of London, Royal Holloway and Bedford New College, esp. Chapter 8.
55. Haufler, V. 2002. "Industry regulation and self-regulation: The case of labour standards", in A. F. Cooper, J. English, and R. Thakur (eds) *Enhancing Global Governance: Towards a New Diplomacy?*. Tokyo: United Nations University Press, pp. 162–186.

56. OECD. 2002. Text of the OECD Guidelines for Multinational Enterprises, adopted 27 June, available at www.oecd.org/.
57. MMSD (Mining, Minerals, and Sustainable Development) Project. 2002. *Breaking New Ground: The Report of the MMSD Project*. London and Sterling, VA: Earthscan, for the IIED and the WBCSD.
58. For example, Food and Agriculture Organization (FAO). 1999. *Sustainable Forest Management*. Issue paper commissioned by the World Bank, available from www. worldbank.org/; Rugge, I. 2000. *Progress in Timber Certification Schemes Worldwide*. London: Forests Forever.
59. Kolk, A. 1996. *Forests in International Environmental Politics: International Organizations, NGOs and the Brazilian Amazon*. Utrecht: International Books.
60. Mayers, J. and S. Bass. 1999. *Policy That Works for Forests and People*, Policy That Works Series No. 7. London: International Institute for Environment and Development; Sears, R. R., L. M. Davalos, and G. Ferraz. 2001. "Missing the forest for the profits: The role of multinational corporations in the international forest regime", *Journal of Environment and Development*, Vol. 10, No. 4, pp. 345–364.
61. Bass, S., X. Font, and L. Danielson. 2001. "Standards and certification: A leap forward or a step back for sustainable development?", *The Future Is Now*, Vol. 2, November, pp. 21–31, available from www.iied.org/.
62. *Ibid.*, esp. p. 30.
63. See for example UN General Assembly. 2001. "Cooperation between the United Nations and all relevant partners, in particular the private sector", Report of the Secretary-General to its 56th Session, Item 39 of the Provisional Agenda (Towards Global Partnerships), A/56/323; Holliday and Pepper, note 11 above; Holliday, Schmidheiny, and Watts, note 26 above.
64. Bendell, Jem. 2000. "Civil regulation: A new form of democratic governance for the global economy?", in Jem Bendell (ed.) *Terms of Endearment: Business, NGOs and Sustainable Development*. Sheffield: Greenleaf Publishing in association with New Academy of Business, pp. 239–254.
65. *Ibid.*, pp. 252–253. The International Organization of Consumer Unions (IOCU), founded in 1960 and now renamed CI (Consumers International), has a membership of more than 273 organizations in as many as 121 countries. The ISO's Consumer Policy Council (COPOLCO) has been given new terms of reference (since 2000) to study means of assisting consumers in developing countries to benefit from standardization, and to develop means of improving their participation in international standardization. The CI has long led the campaign for NGOs to be accorded the right to participate in ISO Technical Committees, and the right has been granted as of October 2001.
66. Elkington, J. and S. Fennell. 2000. "Partners for sustainability", in Jem Bendell (ed.) *Terms of Endearment: Business, NGOs and Sustainable Development*. Sheffield: Greenleaf Publishing in association with New Academy of Business, pp. 152–153.
67. Usui, note 15 above. This argument is inspired by Nils Brunsson's theory of "organization of hypocrisy" – see Brunsson, N. 1989. *The Organization of Hypocrisy: Talk, Decisions and Actions in Organizations*. Chichester, New York, Brisbane, Toronto, and Singapore: John Wiley & Sons. A similar argument is developed in characterizing the relationship between the WBCSD and the ICC by Usui, *ibid*.
68. Prahalad, C. K. and S. L. Hart. 1999. "Strategies for the bottom of the pyramid: Creating sustainable development", draft dated August 1999, accessible through the website of the WRI Management Institute for Environment and Business, www. wri.org/meb/.

69. The table is drawn from *ibid.*; WBCSD, note 44 above; G8 Renewable Task Force. 2001. *Final Report.* www.renewabletaskforce.org/; WSSD/PrepComIV list of partnerships/initiatives.

70. Prahalad and Hart, note 67 above.

71. WBCSD, note 44 above.

72. WBCSD, note 45 above.

73. See UN General Assembly, note 63 above.

74. Business Partnership for Development (BPD). 2002. *Putting Partners to Work – Report on BPD.* www.bpdweb.org/.

75. See www.uneptie.org/pc/cp7/; UNEP. 2002. *Cleaner Production: Global Status Report.* Draft as of May 2002 available from the Environmental Management Center, Mumbai, India, www.emcenter.com/cpglblstatus/. The UNEP Seventh High-level Seminar on Cleaner Production (April 2002) also recommended that this CP network should develop a synergy with various existing MEAs and that UNEP should play an expanded role in establishing such linkages.

76. The quoted phrases are from the PrepCom IV chairman's explanation. Initially, Type 2 partnerships/initiatives were confined to ones that were new and developed specifically in the context of the WSSD, although such restrictions were subsequently softened considerably. See www.johannesburgsummit.org/htm/documents/prepcom4docs/bali_documents/.

77. See UN General Assembly, note 63 above.

78. See UN Global Compact Office. 2002. *The Global Compact: Report on Progress and Activities.* www.unglobalcompact.org/un/gc/unweb.nsf/.

79. For example, "WSSD tuned into partnership market" – a criticism voiced at www.cseindia.org/.

80. Haas, note 17 above, esp. pp. 78–80.

81. *Ibid.*

82. Susskind, L. E. 1994. *Environmental Diplomacy: Negotiating More Effective Global Agreements.* New York and Oxford: Oxford University Press, Chapter 5.

83. *Ibid.*, pp. 124–125.

84. Haas, note 17 above, p. 192.

85. Stigler, George. 1971. "The economic theory of regulation", *Bell Journal of Economics*, Vol. 2, pp. 3–21.

86. Oye, K. A. and J. H. Maxwell. 1995. "Self-interest and environmental management", in R. O. Keohane and E. Ostrom (eds) *Local Commons and Global Interdependence.* London and New Delhi: Sage Publication, pp. 191–221.

87. French, H. F. 1997. "Learning from the ozone experience", in L. R. Brown *et al.* (eds) *State of the World 1997.* New York: W. W. Norton for the Worldwatch Institute. Mitchell, R. B. 1993. "Intentional oil pollution of the oceans", in P. M. Haas, R. O. Keohane, and M. A. Levy (eds) *Institutions for the Earth: Sources of Effective International Environmental Protection.* Cambridge, MA and London: MIT Press; Mitchell, R. B. 1994. "Regime design matters: International oil pollution and treaty compliance", *International Organization*, Vol. 48, No. 3, pp. 425–458.

88. Usui, M. 1999. "Multilateral environmental diplomacy: Science-politics and industry-politics interface and issue linkages in the emerging system of multilateral negotiations", *Cross-cultural Business and Cultural Studies*, Vol. 3, No. 1, pp. 179–196.

89. Oye and Maxwell, note 86 above.

90. The multilateral negotiation to build the prior informed consent (PIC) regime for pesticides export to developing countries was protracted until the mid-1980s, with the leading coalition of UNEP, the WHO, and PAN (Pesticides Action Network) struggling against the blocking coalition of the FAO and GIFAP (a Brussels-based agro-

chemical industry association). Paarlberg, R. L. 1993. "Managing pesticide use in developing countries", in P. M. Haas, R. O. Keohane, and M. A. Levy (eds) *Institutions for the Earth: Sources of Effective International Environmental Protection*. Cambridge, MA and London: MIT Press.

91. DeSombre, E. 2000. *Domestic Sources of International Environmental Policy: Industry, Environmentalists and the US Power*. Cambridge, MA: MIT Press.

92. Kanie (Chapter 5 in this volume) refers to this as the "second image reversed" mode of domestic-international interaction.

93. OECD. 1996. *Pollutant Release and Transfer Registers (TRPRs): A Tool for Environmental Policy and Sustainable Development: Guidance Manual for Governments*, available at www.oecd.org/.

94. The portal used to be freely accessible to the public at www.johanesburgsummit.org. It is now available on www.un.org/esa/sustdev/partnerships.

95. Lord Holm of Cheltenham serves also as co-chair of the WBCSD Working Party on Corporate Social Responsibility, co-chair of the ICC Environment and Energy Commission, and is also director of the LEAD. UN organizations, other IGOs, UN-defined major non-governmental groups, and some governments participate in the Advisory Committee of the CASDP (www.casdp.org). The CASDP-administered Partnerships Central Portal (www.partnershipscentral.org) is still under construction, but already carries some 130 projects as of March 2004.

96. Holliday, Schmidheiny, and Watts, note 26 above.

97. Piest, Uli. 2003. "A preliminary analysis of the interlinkages within WSSD 'Type 2' partnerships", *Works in Progress*, Vol. 17, No. 1. Tokyo: United Nations University.

98. Holliday, Schmidheiny, and Watts, note 26 above.

99. Mitchell, R. B. and E. A. Parson. 2001. "Implementing the climate change regime's Clean Development Mechanism", *Journal of Environment and Development*, Vol. 10, No. 2, pp. 125–146.

100. Victor, D. G. 2001. *The Collapse of the Kyoto Protocol and the Struggle to Slow Global Warming*. Princeton and Oxford: Princeton University Press.

101. Different TRECs are evolving in the UK, Europe, Australia, several US states, Japan, and some developing countries. TRECS received much attention at the First Asia-Pacific Green Power Conference, Tokyo, March 2003. For the worldwide network for information exchange on TRECs, see www.treckin.com. There have also been intergovernmental initiatives such as the G8 Renewable Energy Task Force, which was established upon the recommendation of the Twenty-sixth G8 Summit Meeting in Okinawa (July 2000), with a view to increased use of renewable energy sources, particularly in developing countries. This task force, co-chaired by Sir Mark Moody Stuart (Royal Dutch Shell), has issued its final report (July 2001) suggesting further consideration of "tradable renewable certificates" (TRCs) at both national and global levels. See www.renewabletaskforce.org/.

Conclusion

12

Conclusion: Institutional design and institutional reform for sustainable development

Peter M. Haas, Norichika Kanie, and Craig N. Murphy

Introduction: The WSSD and sustainable development

The WSSD marked a step in an ongoing effort to reform international environmental governance to promote sustainable development, and maintained momentum towards sustainable development by averting an erosion of the Rio goals. Since environmental governance – or at least what is now called environmental governance, and was called environmental cooperation at the time – entered the international agenda in 1972 at the UNCHE, the UN system has developed a wide array of institutions and regimes to address many aspects of environmental threats. Unlike the post-war financial and commercial regimes, which were organized around a small number of formal institutions with fairly clearly demarcated norms and rules, environmental governance has evolved incrementally over the last 30 years, and now encompasses a wide array of international institutions, laws, and regimes. In addition it now includes many actors who were not represented in earlier periods of governance.

The debates over sustainable development and institutional reforms to improve the prospects for sustainable development are sure to continue for the foreseeable future. It is now widely recognized and appreciated that the principal characteristic of international issues is their complexity. Yet traditionally international institutions have been designed according to an organizational logic that addresses problems individually. Sustainable development requires a reorientation of collective understanding and of formal institutions to focus on the key intersecting and interacting elements of complex problems. This volume hopes to contribute to that ongoing dialogue. This chapter looks at how well this system has performed, and potentials for its reform.

From environmental protection to sustainable development

International environmental governance was the buzzword for 20 years, but has now been supplanted by sustainable development, with a new array of governance techniques designed to advance it. Initially environmental protection operated in a delicate balance with the goal of economic development. In the preparations for the 1972 United Nations Conference on the Human Environment (UNCHE) environmental protection was wedded to economic development under the substantive linkage of environment and development.[1] Development economists from the North and South concurred that environmental protection required financing from economic development, and that economic growth would not spawn development unless it took heed of the environment as well. While there was a substantive core amongst academic and élite economists who agreed to the compromise, its fuller acceptance at the UNCHE rested on a tactical linkage to satisfy the developing world's demands for financial assistance. Since the UNCHE there has been the expectation – seldom fulfilled – that additional development costs in the developing world for environmental protection would be paid by Northern ODA and multilateral development finance, if not the private sector itself.

In 1987 the World Commission on Environment and Development released the seminal report, *Our Common Future*.[2] The report served as the justificatory document for the 1992 UN Conference on Environment and Development, and put forward a new doctrinal approach to economic development that "meets the needs of the present without compromising the ability of future generations to meet their own needs". Sustainable development urges a simultaneous assault on pollution, economic development, unequal distribution of economic resources, and poverty reduction. It argues that most social ills are non-decomposable, and that environmental degradation cannot be addressed without confronting the human activities that give rise to it. Thus sustainable development dramatically expanded the international agenda by arguing that these issues needed to be simultaneously addressed, and that policies should seek to focus on the interactive effects between them.

The core of the new sustainable development agenda reflected new thinking among economists and the development community about the linkages between issues on the international agenda.[3] Yet critics wondered how the agenda was to be defined (namely what *does not* count as an element of sustainable development?) and by what policies these aspirations were to be achieved. After all, the justification for these elements was not always clear, and it seemed that many of the items on the sustainable development agenda had been added capriciously or to bolster political support without substantive warrants.[4] Critics also contended that the new agenda threatened to divert attention from the fundamental goals of fighting poverty, reducing military expenditure, increasing respect for human rights, and promoting democracy. Conversely, though, the broad agenda helped to offer the prospect of tactical linkages between small policy networks in the international development community which lacked sufficient autonomous influence to be able to shape agendas or policies.

Sustainable development has two core components. The first is substantive, as discussed above, that stresses the need for an integrative approach to economic development which includes environmental protection along with other goals of growth, social equity, and, according to some advocates, democratization. The second is procedural. Sustainable development and Agenda 21 call for radically broader participation in decision-making. Sustainable development is no longer the pure domain of national sovereignty. Agenda 21 called for multiple stakeholder participation ("major groups") at multiple levels of international discussions, including NGOs, scientists, business/industry, farmers, workers/trade unions, and local authorities, as well as indigenous people, women, and youth and children.

Collective governance is necessary in order for governments individually to pursue sustainable development. Paula Dobriansky, US Under-Secretary of State for Global Affairs, announced in September 2001 that:

governance is a foundation for sustainable development ... effective multilateral treatment of transboundary and global environmental threats rests on capacity building, effective institutions, public access to information, informed and science-based decision-making, public participation and access to justice and enforcement.[5]

Governance and sustainable development

Governance is now performed by a multitude of actors operating at different levels of the international system.[6] This book presents two major findings consistent with current consensus from studies of globalization.[7] First, many new actors are involved in international and global governance.[8] Second, there is a distinct set of governance functions which must be performed in order for countries to be able to develop sustainably. An important research challenge is to develop a fuller taxonomy of which actors perform which functions, and who is best at performing which. The WSSD stressed the value of partnerships between states and multiple other actors in conducting sustainable development projects as represented in the so-called "Type 2" (non-negotiated) partnership outcome.[9] The partnerships would not be able to be effective unless actors fill in the functions that are appropriate for each of them.

Multiple actors interact at different levels of the international system.[10] Since the 1992 Earth Summit NGOs have proliferated in number, and in the extent and intensity of their political involvement in environmental governance. NGOs are active in agenda-setting, sounding alarms about new problems, public education and mobilization, and verification and informal enforcement of international environmental regimes.[11] NGOs may also provide expertise. Many NGOs are also subcontracted by foreign aid agencies and international financial institutions to conduct training and administer conservation projects in developing countries. International institutions, at the global and regional levels, play an important role in providing a venue for states to coordinate policies and transfer resources to other actors.[12] Infrequently, but often enough to be significant, international institutions contribute to social learning by other members of the international community.[13] Scientists, particularly transnational networks of scientists, have been active in agenda-setting, environmental monitoring and issuing early warnings, interest formation, and policy-making.[14] Private sector firms are increasingly recognized as vital partners in sustainable development, as they are responsible for foreign investment and own and develop the technology that will ultimately enable more sustainable development.[15] International law, as well, can exercise an influence over the choices of states.[16]

Effective governance rests on the performance of multiple governance functions. Some functions are formally performed: that is, by the direct commitment of some body to a clear actor to perform the designated function or functions. Others may be performed indirectly: that is, the functions may be observed but are not the consequence of intended action by those contracting some set of activities to be performed by the relevant actors.

This volume has been seeking to identify the elements of global environmental governance and improve their effectiveness.[17] Its findings received a positive hearing at side events at WSSD preparatory meetings and at the WSSD.[18] The authors have found the actors and functions shown in Table 12.1 to be core elements of the current global environmental governance apparatus.

Table 12.1 Matrix of functions

Function	Formal/direct	Informal/indirect
Issue linkage	• Intergovernmental negotiations • New information provided by epistemic communities • Through financial mechanisms (GEF) • IOs (GEO/WEO)	• Scientists • Business/industry
Agenda-setting	• IOs and member states	• NGOs • Media • Scientists
Developing usable knowledge	• Scientists	• Scientists • NGOs
Monitoring	• IOs • Committees nominated by MEA secretariat • MEA signatory governments	• NGOs (particularly in developing countries) • Scientists
Rule-making	• Negotiations by national governments	• Business/industry (*de facto* standards) • NGOs (principled standards)
Norm development	• Epistemic communities	• NGOs (equity and environmental preservation) • Business/industry (efficiency)
Policy verification	• Governments	• NGOs • IOs
Enforcement	• Hard law • WTO and MEA rules	• NGO campaigns
Capacity-building (technology transfer)	• Official technical assistance (national and local governments) • Business/industry • Science community (education/training)	• Business/industry (joint venture)
Capacity-building (organizational skills)	• IOs • NGOs • Science community (education/training)	• Business/industry
Promote vertical linkage	• IOs • National and local governments	• NGO • Scientific community
Financing	• Governments (ODA) • Regional development banks • Multilateral bodies	• By business/industry

The following points elaborate some of the most salient aspects of governance as performed by this wide array of new actors.

- *Issue linkage*, such as linking different activities contributing to environmental degradation, or linking environmental issues to the full sustainable development agenda. This function has been provided by negotiations on comprehensive sustainable development issues (such as the WSSD), by new scientific information, by international organizations and coordination between functional organizations related to sustainable development (including MEA secretariats), and by financial mechanisms such as the GEF. In this regard the decision in the WSSD to include the Convention on Desertification in the GEF project is expected to promote a closer linkage with other regimes.
- *Environmental monitoring* and early warning of new threats. International organizations, MEA-related committees, and signatory governments to MEAs have provided monitoring. Informally, this is a role for scientists and grass-roots NGOs.
- *Rule-making*, including sponsoring negotiations, and providing policy advice. Officially national delegates to negotiations do this. NGOs can also share formal rule-making by providing principled standards (such as the precautionary principle). Business and industry make rules by providing *de facto* standards.
- *Norm development*, such as the ability to establish higher-order systemic norms that cut across all areas of multilateralism, trump other principles of governance, and can be defended as aspirations in other settings (i.e. sovereignty, respect for market principles, sustainable development). Providing such a function is a role for epistemic communities. Informally NGOs develop norms on equity and environmental preservation, and business and industry develop norms on efficiency.
- *Policy verification*, which is a function for governments, although NGOs and international organizations (IOs) may collect information on government compliance and circulate it as part of a strategy of naming and shaming.
- *Enforcement*, such as through direct/legal application of sanctions, liability, and indirect shaming, or NGO campaigns.
- *Capacity-building* (public education, technical training, technology transfer, and improving the national administrative influence of national environmental authorities). Technology transfer can include the establishment of information clearing-houses about best available technologies and best environmental practices. This function has been provided by national and local governments through official technical assistance, business and industry, and the science community. Business and industry can also provide the function informally through joint-venture projects. The capacity-building function also rests on international organizations and NGOs when it comes to organizational skills.

- *Developing vertical linkages.* Establishing principles and norms for sustainable development is a function of NGOs and IOs. Once such broad shared aspirations are established, discussions of issues will take account of such higher-order ideas, both in terms of presumptive policies and in terms of which IOs will be regarded as appropriate venues for addressing sustainable development issues. Developing environmental advocacy at or against the WTO is one example of developing new principles under which specific approaches can be nested.
- *Linking international and domestic arenas* and narrowing the gap between the two is the function that international organizations and national and local governments can provide. NGOs and scientists may narrow the remaining gap.
- *Financing.* National and multilateral official financing institutions as well as the private sector provide financing for governance.

Some activities may have multiple indirect effects. For instance, by publicizing issues norms and standard-setting may be achieved. By verifying and providing resources one may achieve compliance. By mobilizing civil society governance efforts may promote agenda-setting and framing, and thus define new national preferences which narrow the range of feasible negotiated outcomes. Educating élites and governments may have similar effects.

Institutional reform

The present international environmental governance system is organized around a core consisting of UNEP, established in 1973. But over the years many other organizations have acquired environmental responsibilities, including the World Bank, the IPCC, the UNCSD, and the GEF, as well as numerous non-state actors; and widespread frustration is often expressed at the Byzantine operation of the current environmental governance system. Those who are poorly informed about it tend to dismiss the ability of this patchwork quilt of governance arrangements to govern effectively, because of the failings of some of its more visible elements, but, as argued in this volume, the governance system is best understood and evaluated as part of a governance system of many interconnected and interactive elements.[19] Thus far, comprehensive agenda-setting and regime development have been far more successful than has compliance.

UNEP began in 1973 as the "conscience" of the UN system. It was responsible for developing environmental norms and rules for the UN system. UNEP tried to induce other international institutions to recognize environmental externalities, to urge the creation of national authorities, and to build the profile and influence of top national environmental authorities. Convening the UNCHE had the effect of triggering institutional reform, as most governments were forced to create new domestic authorities to prepare for the conference. Annual (and later biannual) UNEP meetings served to create transgovernmental linkages between environmental bureaucrats, many of whom found they had more in common with counterparts in other countries than with those at home. They could commiserate about their relatively weak and marginalized positions *vis-à-vis* other ministries/bodies within their own governments, and exchange information about how to improve domestic influence to promote their functional responsibilities in their own governments.

UNEP has also performed a number of concrete governance functions. It coordinated projects with other UN agencies, and mobilized funding from the UNDP to finance environmental projects throughout the UN system. UNEP helped to train national officials in new environmental protection and sustainable development techniques, as well as providing scientific equipment for monitoring environmental quality. UNEP helped conduct research in new ecological management policies. It helped generate mass environmental consciousness by sponsoring educational campaigns. One of its most important tasks has been global environmental monitoring. UNEP helped sponsor and administer over 70 international treaties for a variety of transboundary and global environmental problems.

One of UNEP's first major projects was the Earth Watch programme, which in fact took over a decade to become fully operational.[20] UNEP is now capable of collecting and disseminating environmental monitoring data on the quality of many major global ecosystems, and publishes the *Global Environmental Outlook*.

After the UNCHE, UNEP was the only international institution responsible for environmental protection. Since then, however, most international institutions have assumed some environmental responsibilities. The international environmental governance system has not been significantly overhauled in three decades, and many critiques have been raised about UNEP and the overall environmental governance system. To some extent, UNEP's success has led to its own obsolescence, because it is no longer equipped to conduct its activities or to serve as the UN system's conscience on environmental issues now that the system has become so robust and decentralized.

Critics suggest that UNEP is now too small, too poor, and too remote to coordinate and promote sustainable development effectively.[21] Its secretariat only has between 250 and 300 professionals, and many of the best officials have been lured away to jobs in other international institutions since those bodies have come to assume environmental and sustainable development responsibilities; its headquarters in Nairobi is remote and expensive for delegates to attend meetings (or for UNEP officials to attend meetings elsewhere); and the budget is inadequate to cover the ambitious array of programmes assigned to it by member governments. In addition, most of the UNEP budget is based on voluntary contributions to programme-based trust funds, so the organization lacks discretion in the use of its money. Such a lack of discretion is often particularly troublesome when member states are late or irregular in their payments.

Recent evaluations of environmental governance more broadly suggest that there are administrative overlaps in the international system, as institutions have assumed new responsibilities for the environment, and inefficiencies in the system. Financial support comes now from the World Bank, the GEF, and the UNDP. UNEP has little influence over these large international financial institutions.

At the national level institutional barriers inhibit comprehensive policy-making and sustainable development. The functional narrowness of most decision-making units at the national level and the separation of funding authorities from those with operational responsibilities prevent national administrations from formulating and pursuing comprehensive sustainable development efforts.

UNEP was created to perform many environmental governance functions, and had more assigned to it as it grew. UNEP is now widely criticized, often justly, for its inability to perform adequately all aspects of such an ambitious mission. It is somewhat remarkable that it has accomplished so much.

Over the years many reform proposals have been offered.[22] UNEP pursued internal efforts at streamlining its activities and achieving synergies amongst its various projects in its 1990 System-wide Medium-term Environmental Plan (SWMTEP). The 1997 Task Force on Environment and Human Settlements, instigated by UN Secretary-General Kofi Annan, suggested strengthening UNEP by elevating it to a specialized agency (and thus making it entitled to a fixed and regular budget) and by improving its ability to coordinate activities with other specialized agencies, although with no clear guidelines about how such coordination was to be achieved in the absence of strong political will by member governments or the heads of the agencies. This prompted the task force to make the recommendation that an "issue management" approach be set up under the United Nations. This approach would be used to address issues that cut across the mandates of specific institutions concerned with environment and sustainable development, such as UNEP and the UNDP. Under this proposed reform the High-level Advisory Board on Sustainable Development would be discontinued and supplanted by the establishment of an environmental management group to be chaired by

272 HAAS, KANIE, AND MURPHY

the executive director of UNEP. The group would assist in the coordination of activities between UNEP, the UNDP, and other UN agencies, and "adopt a problem-solving, results oriented approach that would enable United Nations bodies and their partners to share information, consult on proposed new initiatives and contribute to a planning framework and develop agreed priorities and their respective roles in the implementation of those priorities in order to achieve a more rational and cost-effective use of their resources".[23] A revitalized UNEP has also been supported by UNEP's 1997 Nairobi Declaration on the Role and Mandate of the United Nations Environment Programme.[24]

More dramatic proposals have called for the creation of a new world environmental organization (WEO) or global environmental organization (GEO) which would possibly replace UNEP, and would certainly have stronger and more centralized resources and influence.[25] Proponents have called for creating a centralized WEO/GEO assigned many of the responsibilities currently distributed throughout the UN system.[26] It would be responsible for articulating environmental policy and sustainable development policy for the international community, have resources to verify compliance, and enforce sanctions on those in non-compliance. Such a GEO might even have the legal authority and staff to be able to advocate for the environment in WTO trade and the environment arbitration panels, or even claim authority to adjudicate such disputes on its own. In addition it would consolidate the vast array of environmental regimes (or multilateral environmental agreements – MEAs) in one place, easing the administrative burden on governments trying to keep up with the vast array of international environmental obligations, as well as bolstering the political influence of environmental officials within their own governments because they would be collectively housed in a centralized environmental embassy. The GEO initially received a favourable reception from Germany and three other countries. Yet the proposal has met with institutional resistance from institutions that would lose responsibilities, and with disinterest by much of the UN community.

A hybrid version of a GEO combined with a more streamlined UNEP has also received recent attention to encourage "a new governance approach" based on partially decoupled links amongst formal institutional bodies.[27] Some redistribution of authority would occur, as a GEO would be established to develop policy, to coordinate the MEAs, and to counterbalance the WTO. The GEO would work loosely with other international institutions and promote non-state participation. UNEP would continue to coordinate international environmental science management. The United Nations University sponsored an interlinkages initiative in 1999 which stressed possible synergies between environmental agreements.[28]

Various visionary schemes have also been proposed. The Club of Rome and others have suggested transforming the Trusteeship Council into an environmental or sustainable development body. In 1992 Gus Speth raised the prospect of a massive North-South bargain for sustainable development.[29] Mahbub Ul Haq's proposed focus on human security offers a similar grand systemic focus that would reorganize all institutional efforts.[30]

The preparatory process for the WSSD clearly demonstrated the extent to which many governments were willing to undertake extensive institutional reforms. The February 2002 Cartagena meeting issued a declaration on international environmental governance which made it clear that governments wished to retain UNEP as the centre of the governance system, around which other efforts would revolve.[31] This meeting concluded a series of six often wishy-washy preparatory meetings held at the ministerial level by the Intergovernmental Group of Ministers.[32] The Cartagena Declaration suggested that "the process [of institutional reform] should be evolutionary in nature ... A prudent approach to institutional change is required, with preference given to making better use of existing structures." Moreover, the ministers proposed:

- sustainable development requires better coordination between ministries at the national level
- the increasing complexity and impact of trends in environmental degradation require an enhanced capacity for scientific assessment and monitoring and for provision of early warnings to governments
- environmental policy at all levels should be tied to sustainable development policies
- NGOs, civil society, and the private sector should be involved more extensively with all areas of decision-making within and between governments
- LDCs should be treated "on the basis of common but differentiated responsibility"[33]
- capacity-building and technology transfer are vital elements of governance
- retain UNEP/Nairobi as a meeting centre
- strengthen UNEP with regular financing – elevate it to a UN specialized agency with "predictable" funding
- the clustering approach to MEAs should be considered.

The ministers also proposed that a new global ministerial environment forum (GMEF) should be the cornerstone of the international institutional structure of international governance for the environment and sustainable development. The GMEF idea remains vague and the specific architecture of the GMEF remains to be seen, as well as how an institution which would rotate between governments would interact with formal institutions with fixed secretariats. At the very least it needs to clarify its primary mission, its relationships with the COPS of the MEAs, whether the GMEF gets a permanent secretariat, and the locations for its meetings.

The WSSD also asserted the importance of the MEAs, and the need to keep them intact from WTO challenges. Many governments are narrowly organized so that responsible ministries are incapable of recognizing the consequences of their actions for other ministries, or of coordinating effectively to prevent them. Many foreign ministries are still structured along the lines of pursuing traditional notions of national interest, and lack trained personnel or stable channels of information flow to be able to engage effectively in international discussions about environmental protection or sustainable development. For instance, it was not until the late 1990s that the USA established environmental positions in all foreign embassies and an office of global affairs was created within the State Department. Even so, the funding for these new institutions to fulfil their functions adequately has not been forthcoming. There is a further need for introducing environmentally trained personnel into the traditional lines of activity of most governments in order to enssure that environmental consequences of policies are anticipated and averted. The World Bank provides a useful model of how a handful of environmental experts in line positions can encourage more sustainable development projects.

Political analysis of climate and potential for reform

While ongoing pressures for institutional reform are likely to come from NGOs and an internationally organized academic network,[34] the inconclusive preparatory conferences leading up to the WSSD should give us pause about the political prospects of state support for multilateral institutional reform for sustainable development. The negotiation on Chapter 10 of the Johannesburg Summit Plan of Implementation shows that there exists a will in the international community to discuss sustainable development institutions, but little political momentum exists to move it forward. In fact, around 10 undecided paragraphs in Chapter 10 had to be deleted at the end of the negotiation in Johannesburg. To create a new international governance system supporting sustainable development would, at minimum, require the agreement of the major industrialized countries whose economic activities do the most to harm the global environment and whose financial resources would be needed to overcome the development losses that might otherwise be suffered by new manufacturing giants and the states waiting to follow them into the industrial world.

The USA, in particular, has recently tended to impede efforts to strengthen or deepen multilateral governance in almost all realms. The recent Bush administration has clearly signalled a retreat from multilateralism, as well as a profound disinterest in multilateral environmental governance and sustainable development. While domestic groups of academics and NGOs may support sustainable development reforms, the overall administration is uninterested.

The EU seems supportive of the idea of sustainable development, although it has not been able to pass a carbon tax or adopt measures which entail significant economic costs for its members. G7 and G8 summits have adopted declarations endorsing sustainable development, although such proclamations are vague and lack details. The collective purpose of the industrialized countries is currently mobilized behind combating terrorism rather than promoting sustainable development, and there is some degree of institutional exhaustion in the wake of the WSSD. The Netherlands and Scandinavia continue to support reforms. Domestic progressive elements within Canada and Italy may support multilateral institutional reform and sustainable development, but they are too small a coalition to sway the industrialized bloc. Germany and France are strong advocates of institutional reform and the establishment of a world environmental organization. Japan remains supportive in principle, but is blocked by bureaucratic decision-making processes and current financial exigencies.

The developing world remains suspicious of some of the policy goals pursued by the industrialized world, and is adamantly opposed to any reforms that would entail the movement of the headquarters of the principal international institution away from a developing country. The G77+ China has had difficulty in mobilizing collective pressure in the United Nations, and remains loath to exercise any confrontational tactics.

Finance and the limits to effective sustainable development

An enduring problem is finance.[35] Estimates of the costs of accomplishing the full list of Agenda 21 initiatives for sustainable development were in the order of $625 billion per year, or twice the annual level of ODA. Since then ODA has declined, leaving the gap even larger. Groups are increasingly looking to private sources of DFI to make up the difference. Private capital flows have replaced ODA as the principal source of external financing for most developing countries. Current patterns of DFI, though, reveal that flows go largely to a small number of mid-level industrializing countries, leaving most of the developing world starved for capital for sustainable development. Moreover, there remain few political pressures on firms to invest in sustainable sectors' activities, or to ensure that their firms and affiliates apply the cleanest technologies or best available practices. Some rays of hope are evident, though. MNCs tend to apply common practices worldwide which reflect the regulatory expectations in their home countries, so that local regulations and oversight may in fact make little difference for actual corporate practices.[36] Secondly, successful firms are becoming increasingly concerned about their environmental reputations, at least in countries with mobilized environmental populations and with a concerned consumer movement in their home markets. Examples of this latter case include NGO boycotts against forest products from countries that pursue non-sustainable timber practices.

Conclusion: Lessons and policy guidance

Much progress has been made in international environmental policy since Stockholm. The system remains fragile, however, and requires continual support and new recruitment to bolster its many policy networks and maintain the pressure on governments for continued environmental protection. The current political climate does not bode well for massive reform efforts. Indeed, the enemy of the good is the great. Given an assessment of limited political will within the next five years or so, the authors suggest that some streamlining of the international governance system may be the most politically tractable option for encouraging sustainable development. These proposals seek to reform international governance structures that satisfy the major functions of international governance while providing for participation by the principal actors involved in international governance. Financing remains problematical, and further research is necessary on the international division of labour in terms of who performs which functions most effectively.

According to current organizational thinking, decentralized information-rich systems are the best design for addressing highly complex and tightly coupled problems.[37] Thus, international governance for sustainable development may be best served through a decentralized architecture coordinated by an electronically sophisticated hub that is capable of quickly accessing usable information and transmitting it to the appropriate institutional nodes in the network. Concerns about redundancy and efficiency are red herrings for such design principles. Redundancy amplifies the political influence of policy networks involved in governance, and also assures that the governance system persists even if one of the nodes suffers political setbacks. Redundancy in funding sources may also compensate for episodic shortfalls in financing from principal funding sources. Similarly, efficiency is a principle that obscures the symbiotic influences between the elements of the network. Such decentralized systems do not cede full autonomy to states or markets: rather they seek to engage states and markets with actors and policy networks which are sensitive to possible abuses of unfettered free markets.

UNEP's initial responsibility was overloaded. It is now recognized that UNEP cannot perform all its tasks, and the authors feel that it should concentrate on the science function and coordinate scientific activities throughout the UN system. UNEP would oversee environmental monitoring, and provide the information to the international community through a variety of channels. If monitoring activities were clustered across environmental media it would be possible to gain economic efficiency and also to accelerate the flow of timely early-warning information. Because most environmental monitoring done in the context of multilateral environmental agreements has taken place on the regional level, and given the assessment of the current political environment and limited political will, accumulating experience at a smaller scale may facilitate bigger changes when the political environment changes. In this sense, regional institutions such as UNEP's regional offices may serve as a starting point for reform. Some knowledge is organized regionally and not globally, such as for regional seas.

At present, UNEP lacks the resources to perform all its functions effectively and to pressure states to pursue environmentally sustainable policies. UNEP has a comparative advantage in the UN system for its scientific expertise, and should be preserved as a monitoring and environmental assessment body. UNEP should also help develop rosters of experts for use by governments, international organizations, NGOs, and the private sector for assessing new environmental risks as they are identified. UNEP also has long-standing experience with coordinating loose, decentralized networks around the world. Thus it may still be capable of serving a coordinating function to ensure that the multiple elements of MEAs are coordinated, to anticipate any gaps, and to keep members of international policy networks in touch with one another. It would serve as an air-traffic controller for issues on the international environmental agenda, as well as for the multitude of associated ongoing studies and negotiations.

A GEO should be established to fulfil the policy and technology-based functions that provide institutional support for multilateral environmental governance. A GEO would consolidate environmental policy research, technology databases, and clearing-houses; conduct training; and centralize the secretariats that administer current environmental regimes.

Centralizing these secretariats would facilitate the creation of a broader global policy network across specific environmental issues, and justify the creation of national environmental embassies to represent states and participate in future negotiations. A GEO could also serve as a legal advocate for environmental protection and regulations to counterbalance the WTO by collecting a roster of international environmental lawyers to participate in WTO panels. The GEO should have high-profile annual ministerial meetings to address all environmental issues to ensure widespread involvement in environmental policy networks and galvanize rapid responses to new alerts. Ongoing efforts would continue to be addressed through the existing secretariats and conferences of parties. The GEO could even have a panel of environmental inspectors available to verify compliance by states and firms with multilateral environmental agreements.

The GEO location would probably be in Bonn or Geneva. Creative organizational structures are possible for such an organization so that it can enjoy legitimacy and also maximize its contact with civil society. Several institutional examples exist from which lessons may be borrowed. The IUCN and the ILO provide for tripartite representation and voting on delegations. A bicameral structure would greatly enhance the legitimacy of the institution and advance the mission of engaging civil society. States could vote in one chamber and non-state actors could vote in the other; although the legal meaning of decisions taken in each chamber might not be equivalent. The division between the EU and EP is similar. The now defunct UN Commission on Transnational Corporations had standing observers from business, labour, and academia.

The authors also recommend a few detailed reforms to accompany this grander institutional design.

- Greater involvement from the scientific community, NGOs, industry, and civil society more generally should be encouraged at all levels of governance.
- Scientists should be encouraged to develop consensus in the absence of political oversight. Science advice should be decentralized, but monitored.
- Create a High Commissioner for the Environment, such as already exists for human rights and refugees. This should be a high-profile individual capable of commanding normative respect by virtue of his or her own individual reputation.
- Create an NGO capable of verifying state and industry compliance with environmental MEAs, akin to Amnesty International. Promote tripartite boundary-spanning engagement with problem-solving commitments and synergize them towards further deepening and widening of existing environmental regimes.

Governance occurs through complex synergies between networks of actors across all levels of international politics. Current governance arrangements remain a crazy quilt of overlapping activities, about which many environmental analysts in governments and NGOs express misgivings. It is probably too complex to grasp easily, yet should not be dismissed because a cursory view treats such arrangements as incoherent – fragmented institutions are not necessarily incoherent. Gus Speth embraces this decentralized arrangement, stressing its potential for innovation.[38] The authors suggest that more attention be paid to clarifying the key actors and the governance functions they perform for addressing particular environmental threats. Only then can the environmental, social, and economic aspects of sustainable development be integrated in a concrete manner.

Notes

1. UNEP. 1981. *Development and Environment: The Founex Report: In Defence of the Earth*, Basic Texts on Environment, UNEP Executive Series 1. Nairobi: UNEP.
2. World Commission on Environment and Development. 1987. *Our Common Future*. New York: Oxford University Press, p. 8.
3. Pronk, Jan and Mahbub Ul Haq. 1992. *Sustainable Development: From Concept to Action*. The Hague: Ministry of Development Cooperation, New York: UNDP, and Conches, Switzerland: UNCED; Holmberg, Johan (ed.). 1992. *Making Development Sustainable*. Washington, DC: Island Press; Nelson, Joan and Stephanie J. Eglinton. 1995. *Global Goals, Contentious Means*, Policy Essay No. 10. Washington, DC: Overseas Development Council.
4. Lele, Sharachchandra M. 1991. "Sustainable development: A critical review", *World Development*, Vol. 19, No. 6, pp. 607–621; Tisdell, Clem. 1988. "Sustainable development: Differing perspectives of ecologists and economists, and relevance", *World Development*, Vol. 16, No. 3, pp. 373–384; Bernstein, Steven. 2001. *The Compromise of Liberal Environmentalism*. New York: Columbia University Press; Timberlake, Lloyd. 1989. "The role of scientific knowledge in drawing up the Brundtland Report", in Steinar Andresen and Willy Ostreng (eds) *International Resource Management*. London: Belhaven Press.
5. www.state.gove/g/rls/rm/2001/5083.htm. See also Dowdeswell, Elizabeth. 2001. "Design for the real world: Ideas for achieving sustainable development", text of a speech delivered at Harvard University, 12 December, mimeo.
6. According to the Commission on Global Governance, governance is the sum of the many ways in which individuals and institutions, public and private, manage their common affairs. See Commission on Global Governance. 1995. *Our Global Neighbourhood: The Report of the Commission on Global Governance*. Oxford: Oxford University Press, p. 2; O'Brien, Robert, Anne Marie Goetz, Jan Aart Scholte, and Marc Williams. 2000. *Contesting Global Governance: Multilateral Economic Institutions and Global Social Movements*. Cambridge: Cambridge University Press.
7. For instance see Slaughter, Anne-Marie. 1997. "The real new world order", *Foreign Affairs*, September/October, pp. 183–197; Keohane, Robert O. and Joseph S. Nye. 2000.

"Globalization", *Foreign Policy*, Spring, No. 118, pp. 104–119; Schaeffer, Robert K. 1997. *Understanding Globalization*. Lanham, MD: Rowman and Littlefield; Held, David, Anthony McGrew, David Goldblatt, and Jonathan Perraton. 1999. *Global Transformations*. Stanford: Stanford University Press; Hoffmann, Stanley. 2002. "The clash of globalizations", *Foreign Affairs*, Vol. 81, No. 4, pp. 104–115; Slaughter, Anne-Marie, Andrew Tulumello, and Stepan Wood. 1998. "International law and international relations theory", *American Journal of International Law*, Vol. 92, No. 3, pp. 367–397.

8. Keck, Margaret E. and Kathryn Sikkink. 1998. *Activists Beyond Borders*. Ithaca: Cornell University Press; Reinecke, Wolfgang H. and Francis M. Deng. 2000. *Critical Choices*. Toronto: IDRC; Florini, Ann M. (ed.). 2000. *The Third Force*. Washington, DC: Carnegie Endowment for International Peace; Wapner, Paul. 1996. *Environmental Activism and World Civic Politics*. Albany: SUNY Press.

9. See www.un.org/esa/sustdev/partnerships/partnerships.htm for the full list of registered partnership projects.

10. See Chapters 4 and 5 in this volume.

11. See Chapters 8 and 9 in this volume.

12. See Chapters 1, 2, 3, and 4 in this volume.

13. Haas, Peter M. and Ernst B. Haas. 1995. "Learning to learn", *Global Governance*, Vol. 1, No. 3, pp. 255–284; Social Learning Group. 2001. *Social Learning and the Management of Global Environmental Threats*, 2 vols. Cambridge, MA: MIT Press.

14. See Chapters 6 and 7 in this volume.

15. See Chapters 10 and 11 in this volume.

16. See Chapters 1, 4, and 5 in this volume.

17. See www.ias.unu.edu/research/multilateralism.cfm. See also UNU Inter-Linkages website at www.geic.or.jp/interlinkages/index.html. The result of the ongoing project is going to appear as two UNU volumes in 2004.

18. See UNU/IAS report "International Sustainable Development Governance: The Question of Reform: Key Issues and Proposals Final Report", August 2002. Tokyo: UNU/IAS.

19. For a similar analysis of compliance, see Victor, David G., Kal Raustialla, and Eugene Skolnikoff (eds). 1998. *The Implementation and Effectiveness of International Environmental Commitments*. Cambridge, MA: MIT Press.

20. Gosovic, Branislav. 1992. *The Quest for World Environmental Cooperation*. London: Routledge; Fritz, Jan Stefan. 1998. "Earthwatch twenty-five years on", *International Environmental Affairs*, Vol. 10, No. 3, pp. 173–196.

21. For summaries of these critiques see Downie, David L. and Marc A. Levy. 2000. "The United Nations Environment Programme at a turning point", in Pamela Chasek (ed.) *The Global Environment in the Twenty-first Century*. Tokyo: United Nations University Press, pp. 355–375; Gehring, Thomas and Matthias Buck. 2002. "International and transatlantic environmental governance", in Matthias Buck, Alexander Carius, and Kelly Kollmann (eds) *International Enviromental Policymaking*. Munich: Okom Verlag, pp. 21–43.

22. Dodds, Felix. 2000. "Reforming the international institutions", in Felix Dodds (ed.) *Earth Summit 2002*. London: Earthscan; Charnovitz, Steve. 2002. "A world environment organization", *Columbia Journal of Environmental Law*, Vol. 27, No. 2, pp. 323–362.

23. General Assembly Document A/53/463, para. 11. Although proposed in 1998, these reforms remain largely unimplemented.

24. Dodds, note 22 above; Charnovitz, note 22 above.

25. The second volume from this project, edited by W. Bradnee Chambers, investigates

closely the proposals for a WEO or GEO. The discussion shown here regarding a WEO/GEO is a kind of summary, and for more detailed account see the second volume.

26. Esty, Daniel. 1994. "The case for a global environmental organization", in Peter B. Kenen (ed.) *Managing the World Economy*. Washington, DC: Institute for International Economics, pp. 287–310; Biermann, Frank. 2001. "The emerging debate on the need for a world environment organization", *Global Environmental Politics*, February, pp. 45–55; Biermann, Frank. 2000. "The case for a world environment organization", *Environment*, Vol. 42, No. 9, pp. 22–31; German Advisory Council on Global Change (WBGU). 2001. *World in Transition 2*. London: Earthscan.

27. Esty, Daniel C. and Maria H. Ivanova (eds). 2002. *Global Environmental Governance*. New Haven: Yale School of Forestry and Environmental Studies; Haas, Peter M. 2001. "Pollution", in P. J. Simmons and Chantal de Jonge Oudraat (eds) *Managing Global Issues*. Washington, DC: Carnegie Endowment for International Peace.

28. See www.geic.or.jp/interlinkages/.

29. Speth, Gus. 1992. "A post-Rio compact", *Foreign Policy*, No. 88, Fall, pp. 145–161.

30. Haq, Mahbub Ul. 1995. *Reflections on Human Development*. New York: Oxford University Press.

31. Governing Council of the United Nations Environment Programme "Global Ministerial Environment Forum". S.S. VII/I. International Environmental Governance. UNEP/GC/21.

32. UNEP/IGM/5/2 and *Earth Negotiations Bulletin*, Vol. 16, No. 20. IGM-NYC Final Summary, www.iisd.ca/linkages/unepgc/iegnyc/.

33. "Common but differentiated responsibility" was agreed as Principle 7 of the Rio Declaration on Environment and Development (A/CONF.151/26) in 1992.

34. Biermann 2000, note 26 above; Biermann 2001, note 26 above; Esty, note 26 above; Biermann, Frank and Udo Simonis. 1998. *A World Environment and Development Organization*, SEF Policy Paper No. 9. Berlin: SEF; Ulfstein, G. 1999. "The proposed GEO and its relationship to existing MEAs", paper presented at the International Conference on Synergies and Coordination between Multilateral Environmental Agreements, United Nations University, Tokyo, 14–16 July; UNU/IAS Report, note 18 above.

35. Gwin, Catherine. 2001. "Development assistance", in P. J. Simmons and Chantal de Jonge Oudraat (eds) *Managing Global Issues*. Washington, DC: Carnegie Endowment for International Peace, pp. 154 and 158.

36. Hoffman, Andrew J. 2001. *From Heresy to Dogma: An Institutional History of Corporate Environmentalism*. Stanford: Stanford University Press; Leonard, H. Jeffrey. 1988. *Pollution and the Struggle for the World Product*. Cambridge: Cambridge University Press; Gladwin, Thomas and Ingo Walter. 1980. *Multinationals Under Fire*. New York: John Wiley; Wheeler, David. 2001. "Racing to the bottom? Foreign investment and air pollution in developing countries", *Journal of Environment and Development*, Vol. 10, No. 3, pp. 225–245.

37. Aggarwal, Vinod (ed.). 1998. *Institutional Designs for a Complex World*. Ithaca: Cornell University Press; Ansell, Christopher K. and Steven Weber. 1999. "Organizing international politics", *International Political Science Review*, Vol. 20, No. 1, pp. 73–93; Ostrom, Elinor. 2001. "Decentralization and development: The new panacea", in Keith Dowding, James Hughes, and Helen Margetts (eds) *Challenges to Democracy: Ideas, Involvement and Institutions*. New York: Palgrave Publishers, pp. 237–256.

38. Speth, Gus. 2002. "A new green regime", *Environment*, Vol. 44, No. 7, pp. 16–25.

Acronyms

AAG	Association of American Geographers
ACC	UN Administrative Committee on Coordination
ACEA	European Automobile Association
AGBM	Ad Hoc Group on the Berlin Mandate
AGGG	Advisory Group on Greenhouse Gases
AIC	advanced industrialized country
ANPED	Northern Alliance for Sustainability
AOSIS	Alliance of Small Island States
APEC	Asia-Pacific Economic Cooperation
AWIP	Another World Is Possible
BASD	Business Action for Sustainable Development
BCSD	Business Council for Sustainable Development
BIRPI	UN International Bureau for the Protection of Intellectual Property Rights
BPD	Business Partners for Development
CAN	Climate Action Network
CASDP	Center for Advancement of Sustainable Development Partnerships
CBD	Convention on Biological Diversity
CCAMLR	Committee for the Conservation of Antarctic Marine Living Resources
CDM	Clean Development Mechanism
CEO	chief executive officer
CFC	cholorofluorocarbon
CGIAR	Consultative Group on International Agricultural Research
CGP	Japan Foundation Center for Global Partnership

CI	Consumers International
CIDIE	Committee on International Development Institutions on the Environment
CIESIN	Center for International Earth Science Information Network
CITES	Convention on International Trade in Endangered Species of Wild Flora and Fauna
CMS	Convention on Conservation of Migratory Species of Wild Animals
COP/MOP	conference/meeting of the parties
CP	cleaner production
CSD	Commission on Sustainable Development
CSO	civil society organization
CSR	corporate social responsibility
CTE	WTO Committee on Trade and Environment
DAC	OECD Development Assistance Committee
DFI	direct foreign investment
DOEM	Designated Officials for Environmental Matters
DSB	WTO Dispute Settlement Body
EAEC	East Asian Economic Caucus
ECOSOC	UN Economic and Social Council
EIT	economy-in-transition country
ELCI	Environment Liaison Center International
EMEP	European Monitoring and Evaluation Programme
EMG	Environmental Management Group
EP	European Parliament
EPA	Environment Protection Agency (USA)
ESC	Economic Security Council
EU	European Union
FAO	Food and Agricultural Organization
FAR	IPCC first assessment report
FCCC	UN Framework Convention on Climate Change
FIELD	Foundation for International Environmental Law and Development
FoE	Friends of the Earth
FoEI	Friends of the Earth International
FPO	for-profit organization
FSC	Forest Stewardship Council
GATS	General Agreement on Trade in Services
GATT	General Agreement on Tariffs and Trade
GAVI	Global Alliance for Vaccines and Immunization
GC	Global Compact
GCLP	AAG Global Change and Local Places Research Group
GDP	gross domestic product
GEF	Global Environment Facility
GEO	global environmental organization
GESAMP	Group of Experts on Scientific Aspects of Marine Pollution
GHG	greenhouse gas

GMEF	global ministerial environmental forum
GO	governmental organization
GRI	Global Reporting Initiative
GWP	Global Water Partnership
IA	implementing agency
IACSD	Inter-Agency Committee on Sustainable Development
IAEA	International Atomic Energy Agency
IAECG	Inter-Agency Environmental Coordination Group
IBLF	Prince of Wales International Business Leaders Forum
IBRD	International Bank for Reconstruction and Development
IC	implementation conference
ICAO	International Civil Aviation Organization
ICC	International Chamber of Commerce
ICES	International Council for the Exploration of the Sea
ICFTU	International Confederation of Free Trade Unions
ICJ	International Court of Justice
ICLEI	International Council for Local Environmental Initiatives
ICSU	International Council of Scientific Unions
IDA	International Development Association
IDCP	International Declaration on Cleaner Production
IEO	International Environmental Organization
IFAD	International Fund for Agricultural Development
IFC	International Finance Corporation
IFF	Intergovernmental Forum on Forests
IGBP	International Geographic-Biological Programme
IGO	intergovernmental organization
IIASA	International Institite for Applied Systems Analysis
IIED	International Institute for Environment and Development
ILO	International Labour Organization
IMCO	Intergovernmental Maritime Consultative Organization
IMF	International Monetary Fund
IMO	International Maritime Organization
IMO	International Monetary Organization
INGO	international non-governmental organization
INGOF	International Non-governmental Forum
IO	international organization
IOC	Intergovernmental Oceanographic Commission
IOCU	International Organization of Consumer Unions
IPCC	Intergovernmental Panel on Climate Change
IPF	Intergovernmental Panel on Forests
IPR	intellectual property rights
IR	international relations
ISO	International Organization for Standardization
ITTA	International Tropical Timber Agreement
ITTO	International Tropical Timber Organization
ITU	International Telecommunication Union

IUCN	International Union for Conservation of Nature and Natural Resources (World Conservation Union)
IWC	International Whaling Commission
LDC	less developed country
LEAD	Leadership for Environment and Development
LMO	living modified organism
LRTAP	Convention on Long Range Transport of Atmospheric Pollution
MAI	Multilateral Agreement on Investment
MARPOL	International Convention for the Prevention of Pollution from Ships
MEA	multilateral environmental agreement
MEDPOL	Mediterranean Pollution Research and Monitoring Programme
MMSD	Mining, Minerals, and Sustainable Development Project
MNC	multinational corporation
MOU	memorandum of understanding
MSC	Marine Stewardship Council
MSD	multi-stakeholder dialogue
MSP	multi-stakeholder partnership
NAFTA	North American Free Trade Area
NASA	National Aeronautics and Space Administration
NEPP	national environmental policy plan
NGO	non-governmental organization
NGOWG	NGO Working Group on the World Bank
NSSD	national strategy on sustainable development
ODA	official development assistance
OECD	Organization for Economic Cooperation and Development
PAMs	policies and measures
PAN	Pesticides Action Network
PAR	pledge and review
PFI	privately financed infrastructure
PIC	prior informed consent
POP	persistent organic pollutant
PRTR	Pollutant Release and Transfer Register
REO	regional environmental organization
SAM	Sustainable Asset Management
SAR	IPCC second assessment report
SBSTA	subsidiary body for scientific and technical advice
SBSTTA	subsidiary body on scientific, technological, and technical advice
SCOPE	Scientific Committee on Problems of the Environment
SD	sustainable development
SDIN	Sustainable Development Issues Network
SEPAC	South-East Pacific
SMO	social movement organization
SPM	IPCC summary for policy-makers
SPS	Sanitary and Phytosanitary Agreement
SR	IPCC special report

SRI	socially responsible investing
SWMTEP	UNEP System-wide Medium-term Environmental Plan
TAR	IPCC third assessment report
TBT	Technical Barriers to Trade Agreement
TFAP	Tropical Forestry Action Program
TNC	transnational corporation
TOISD	Tour Operator Initiative for Sustainable Development
TR	IPCC technical report
TRC	tradable renewable certificate
TREC	tradable renewable energy certificate
TRIMs	Trade-Related Investment Measures Agreement
TRIPs	Agreement on Trade-Related Intellectual Property Rights
TSP	Tea Sourcing Partnership
TWN	Third World Network
UNCED	UN Conference on Environment and Development
UNCHE	UN Conference on the Human Environment
UNCSD	UN Commission on Sustainable Development
UNCTAD	UN Conference on Trade and Development
UNCTC	UN Center on Transnational Corporations
UNDP	UN Development Programme
UNECE	UN Economic Commission for Europe
UNED	UN Environment and Development
UNEP	UN Environment Programme
UNEPO	UN Environment Protection Organization
UNESCO	UN Educational, Scientific, and Cultural Organization
UNFCCC	UN Framework Convention on Climate Change
UNFIP	UN Fund for International Partnership
UNGASS	UN General Assembly Special Session
UNHCR	UN High Commissioner for Refugees
UNICEF	UN Children's Fund
UNIDO	UN Industrial Development Organization
UNU	United Nations University
UNU/IAS	United Nations University Institute of Advanced Studies
UNITAR	UN Institute for Training and Research
UPU	Universal Postal Union
VEM	voluntary environmental management
WBCSD	World Business Council for Sustainable Development
WEDO	world environment and development organization
WEF	World Economic Forum
WEHAB	WSSD Water, Energy, Health, Agriculture, and Biodiversity
WEO	world environmental organization
WG	working group
WHO	World Health Organization
WICE	World Industry Council of the Environment
WICEM	World Industry Conference on Environmental Management
WIPO	World Intellectual Property Organization

WMO	World Meteorological Organization
WRI	World Resources Institute
WSF	World Social Forum
WSSD	World Summit on Sustainable Development
WTO	World Tourism Organization
WTO	World Trade Organization
WWF	Worldwide Fund for Nature

List of contributors

Norichika Kanie
Associate Professor, Department
of Value and Decision Science,
Graduate School of Decision
Science and Technology, Tokyo
Institute of Technology, 2-12-1
Ookayama, Meguro-ku, Tokyo
152-8552, Japan

Norichika Kanie is an associate
professor at the Tokyo Institute of
Technology (TITech), Japan. He is
also a visiting researcher at the
Institute for Global Environmental
Strategies. Before joining TITech he
was an associate professor at the
Faculty of Law and Policy Studies,
University of Kitakyushu. He
received his PhD in media and
governance from Keio University,
after studying in the UK and the
Netherlands. His research interests
include global environmental
governance and multilateral
diplomacy. He has published
extensively on environmental
governance issues in both Japanese
and English, with particular focus on
climate change.

Peter M. Haas
Professor, Department of Political
Science, Thompson Hall, University
of Massachusetts, Amherst,
MA 01003, USA

Peter M. Haas is a professor of
political science at the University of
Massachusetts at Amherst. He
received a PhD in political science
from the Massachusetts Institute
of Technology. He has published
extensively on international
environmental subjects, including
pollution control in the
Mediterranean, pollution control in
the Baltic and North Seas, UNEP's
regional seas programmes,
stratospheric ozone protection, and
international environmental
institutions. He has also published
works on international relations

theory, focusing on the interplay between knowledge and power in international policy coordination.

Laura B. Campbell
Director, Environmental Law International, 740 West End Avenue, Suite 112A, New York, NY 10025, USA

Dana R. Fisher
Assistant Professor, Department of Sociology and Columbia Earth Institute, Columbia University, 813 IAB; Mail Code 3355, 420 West 118th Street, New York, NY 10027, USA

Harris Gleckman
Programme Officer, Financing for Development (FFD) Coordinating Secretariat, United Nations Department of Economic and Social Affairs (DESA), FFD Coordinating Secretariat Room DC2-2162, United Nations, New York, NY 10017, USA

Toru Iwama
Professor, Department of Law, Seinan-Gakuin University, 6-2-92 Nishijin, Sawara-ku, Fukuoka-city, Fukuoka 814-8511, Japan

Yasuko Kameyama
Senior Reseacher, National Institute for Environmental Studies, 16-2 Onogawa, Tsukuba, Ibaraki 305-0053, Japan

Satoko Mori
Associate Professor, Meisei University, 2-1-1 Hodokubo, Hino-city, Tokyo 191-8506, Japan

Craig N. Murphy
Professor of Political Science, Wellesley College, Wellesley, MA 02481-8203, USA

Jonathan R. Strand
Assistant Professor, Department of Political Science, University of Nevada Las Vegas, 4505 Maryland Parkway, Box 455029, Las Vegas, Nevada 89154-5029, USA

Mikoto Usui
Professor Emeritus, Tsukuba University, 1-10-5 Shintomi-cho, Kashiwa-city, Chiba 277-0856, Japan

Jacob Werksman
Environmental Institutions and Governance Adviser, United Nations Development Programme, ESDG/BDP, 304 East 45th Street, New York, NY 10017, USA

Index

Administrative Committee on Coordination
(ACC) 23, 29
Agenda 21
  attempts to implement 86
  barriers to implementation 99
  major groups 161
  NGO involvement 161
  resource limitations 105
Annan, Kofi 228
Another World Is Possible protest 187–194

Bush, George W. 71
Business Action for Sustainable
Development 224–225, 250
business *see* transnational corporations

Chambers, Bradnee 6–7
Chang, Ilse 186
Chirac, Jacques 6
civil society
  Another World Is Possible protest
  187–194
  business-civil society partnerships
  235–237
  business-society bifurcation 217–218
  corporate public diplomacy 222–229
  corporate social responsibility 230–231
  disassociation index 164–185

dynamics 177–182
engagement in environmental
  governance 176–196
Human Dike protest 186–194
international NGOs 178–182
protest movements 178–182
protesters 188–192
protests at international meetings
  182–185
Pyramid Laboratory 237–240
role of transnational corporations
  203–214
social movement organizations 185–192
stakeholder engagement 231–232
stakeholder theory 230–231
transnational social movements
  178–182
Climate Action Network 165–166, 182
Clinton, Bill 71, 78
Commission on Sustainable Development
(CSD)
  NGO involvement 160–164
  proposals for reform 28–29
  role in environmental governance 20
  strengths and weaknesses 163–164
Cooper, Andrew 93

DeSombre, Elizabeth 247

Dobriansky, Paula 265
Doherty, Ann 224

ECOSOC
  access for NGOs 158–160
  role in environmental governance 17, 26
environmental governance
  achievements in 3
  Administrative Committee on
    Coordination 23, 29
  basic science 124–126
  business-civil society partnerships
    235–237
  business-government interface 10–11
  centralized policy-making 76
  civil society engagement 176–196
  coordinating institutions 22–24
  coordinating treaty organs 29–30
  corporate game change strategies
    218–221
  differences in national regimes 204
  domestic-international linkage 87–90
  financial constraints 275–276
  financing science 132
  forces through NGOs 90–92, 9899
  forestry management 233–234
  horizontal linkages 243–244
  horizontal restructuring 26–30
  ICC environmental diplomacy 223–225
  idealized bargaining model 81
  implications of civil society protests
    194–196
  industry sector 216–252
  institutional linkages 93–98, 100–104
  institutional reform 263–279
  institutionalization of NGO
    involvement 157–173
  inter-institutional coordination 23–24
  inter-treaty organs 23–24
  International Environment
    Organization 25–26
  international organizations with
    environmental functions 74–75
  international relations 88–90
  intra-institutional coordination 22
  lack of information network 104
  language barriers 104–105
  links between policies and funding 30
  matrix of functions 11, 267
  mobilizing networks of scientific
    expertise 131–132

moves towards sustainable development
    264–269
  multi-stakeholder processes 98, 101–102,
    106, 229–243
  multilateral institutions 7–8, 15–22
  policy advice 129–131
  policy integration 96–97
  policy linkages 93–98, 100–104
  political interaction 88–90
  political potential for reform 274–275
  power of knowledge 92–93, 99–100
  private business sector 216–252
  proposals for a WEO 30–31
  proposals for world environmental
    organization 73–77
  provisions for science in MEAs 120–123
  Pyramid Laboratory 237–240
  regime design 243–251
  regional environmental organizations
    71–82
  resource limitations 105
  restructuring multilateral institutions
    24–30
  role of CSD 20, 28–29
  role of ECOSOC 17
  role of GEF 8, 21, 35–49
  role of ICJ 17–18
  role of IPCC 137–152
  role of NGOs 9–10, 266
  role of regional organizations 79–81
  role of transnational corporations
    203–214
  role of treaty organs 21–22
  role of UN General Assembly 16–17
  role of UN Secretariat 18
  role of UN Security Council 17
  role of UN specialized agencies 18–19
  role of UNDP 28
  role of UNEP 19–20, 27–28
  role of WTO 21
  science policy 115–133
  science-politics interface 4–5, 9
  scientific functions 118–124
  scientific monitoring 126–129
  scientific uncertainty 115
  second image reversed mode 88
  stakeholder engagement 231–231
  stakeholder theory 230–231
  target group approach 95–96, 101
  tourism 234–235
  transnational social movements 178–182

environmental governance (cont.)
  Trusteeship Council 25
  two-level games mode 88–89
  UN organs 16–21
  usable knowledge 116
  vertical linkages 8–9, 86–109, 243–244
  vertical restructuring 25–26
  voluntary environmental management
      206–208, 211
  World Bank institutional coordination 22
  WSSD Type 2 outcomes 240–243,
      248–251

Framework Convention on Climate Change
      (FCCC) 137, 138, 142, 144
  accreditation process 164–165
  Human Dike protest 186–194
  NGO involvement 164–166
  participation modalities 164–165
  strengths and weaknesses 166
forestry management 233–234

Gleckman, Harris 224
Global Environment Facility (GEF)
  background history 35–37
  financial resources 48
  GEF Council 41–45
  GEF Instrument 38–40
  managing conflicts 38–45
  operational methods 37–38
  operational problems 39–40
  primary responsibilities 37–38
  project-level operations 45–46, 48–49
  promoting synergies 38–45
  relationship with COPs 41–44, 47–48
  relationship with implementing
      agencies 44–45, 49
  role in environmental governance 8, 21,
      35–49
  strengthening capacity 76
  structural reform 46–47
Gunningham, Neil 247

Haas, Ernest 53
Human Dike protest 186–194

industry see transnational corporations
Inter-Agency Committee on Sustainable
      Development 23
Intergovernmental Panel on Climate
      Change (IPCC)

additional roles 138
channel for epistemic community
    146–148
forum for political agreements 145–146
forum for scientific agreement 148
historical background 138–140
legitimacy 138–139, 143–145
limitations to authority 130
official mandate 141
provider of scientific knowledge 142–143
public information role 150
publications 140
roles 140–150
scientific uncertainty 147
stakeholder expectations 140–150
structure 139–140
tool for negotiators 149–150
tool for obtaining research funding
    149
use of social scientists 4–5
working groups 144
International Atomic Energy Agency
    (IAEA) 21
International Chamber of Commerce
    (ICC) 223–225, 227–228
International Council for Local
    Environmental Initiatives 103
International Court of Justice (ICJ)
  role in environmental governance 17–18
  role in intellectual property rights 63
International Organization for
    Standardization (ISO) 212
international relations
  conceptualizing interactive diplomacy 90
  forces through NGOs 90–92
  hegemonic power 94–95
  idealized bargaining model 81
  institutional linkages 93–98
  policy linkages 93–98
  second image reversed mode 88
  target group approach 95–96, 101
  two-level games mode 88–89

Joint Group of Experts on Scientific
    Aspects of Marine Pollution
    (GESAMP) 130
Juniper, Tony 186, 187

Keohane, Robert 53
Kyoto Protocol 71, 100, 101, 137, 144, 148,
    251

Mining, Minerals, and Sustainable
    Development Project 232
Mitchell, David 226
Mitchell, Ronald 246, 251
Montreal Protocol 100, 146, 245, 246

Netherlands
    greenhouse gas negotiations 92–93
    Human Dike protest 186–194
    national environmental policy plan 101
    policy integration 96–97
    target group approach 95–96, 101
non-governmental organizations (NGOs)
    access to UN system 158–160
    action against transnational
        corporations 209
    Another World Is Possible protest
        187–194
    business-civil society partnerships
        235–237
    Climate Action Network 165–166, 182
    coordination of activities 161–162, 168
    extent of involvement in environmental
        governance 172–173
    funding for protesters 191–192
    Human Dike protest 186–194
    implications of civil society protests
        194–196
    institutionalization in policy
        functions 157–173
    institutionalization of public policy
        dialogue 171–172
    involvement in FCCC 164–166
    involvement in the CSD 160–164
    involvement with World Bank 167–171
    multi-stakeholder dialogue 162–163
    observers at international meetings 184
    participation in international
        meetings 193
    role in environmental governance 266
    scientific monitoring 128
    transnational networks 165–166
    transnational social movements 178–182
    vertical linkages 90–92, 98–99

Palmer, Sir Geoffrey 25–26
Piest, Uli 249
Pronk, Jan 193
Pyramid Laboratory 237–240

Ruggiero, Renato 5, 74

Salim, Elim 1
science policy
    basic science 124–126
    financing science 132
    IPCC as provider of scientific
        knowledge 142–143
    mobilizing networks of expertise 131–132
    monitoring 126–129
    national capabilities 124
    policy advice 129–131
    political legitimacy 117
    provisions for science in MEAs 120–
    scientific functions 118–124
    scientific uncertainty 115
    usable knowledge 116
    WEO scientific organization 150–152
Sinclair, Darren 247
Speth, Gus 273
Stigler, George 245
Strong, Maurice 99
sustainable development see environmental
    governance

transnational corporations
    adaptive developments 227–229
    balancing corporate interests and
        interstate system 213
    Business Action for Sustainable
        Development 224–225
    business-civil society partnerships
        235–237
    business-society bifurcation 217–218
    certification schemes 232–235
    corporate game change strategies
        218–221
    corporate social responsibility 230–231
    domestic markets 204–207
    features of VEM systems 208
    ICC environmental diplomacy 223–225
    incentives for environment-friendly
        policies 244–248
    International Organization for
        Standardization 212
    international markets 207–213
    international policy options 213–214
    multi-stakeholder processes 229–243
    networked minimalism 222–229
    NGO activities 209
    organizational theory 225–227
    pro-poor initiatives 238–239
    proposal for WEO 209–210

transnational corporations (cont.)
  public diplomacy 222–229
  Pyramid Laboratory 237–240
  stakeholder engagement 231–232
  stakeholder theory 230–231
  Stiglerian thresholds 244–247
  UN system 210
  voluntary environmental
    management 206–208, 211
  voluntary standards 232–235
  WSSD Type 2 outcomes 240–243,
    248–251

Ul Haq, Mahbub 273
UN Conference on the Human
  Environment 15
UN Development Programme (UNDP)
  relationship with GEF 44–45, 49
  role in environmental governance 28
UN Environment Programme (UNEP)
  Cleaner Production network 241
  centralizing role 133
  institutional reform 269–272
  inter-institutional coordination 23
  Mediterranean Action Plan 129
  proposals for strengthening 27–28
  proposed future role 277
  relationship with GEF 44–45, 49
  role in environmental governance 19–20
  scientific monitoring 126, 128
  structural problems 157
United Nations
  Global Compact 241–242
  International Environment
    Organization 25–26
  NGO access to UN system 158–160
  role of Secretariat in environmental
    governance 18, 27
  role of UN General Assembly in
    environmental governance 16–17
  role of UN Security Council in
    environmental governance 17, 27
  transnational corporations 210
UNU/IAS research project 6–7
USA
  formation of NAFTA 78
  hegemonic power 94–95
  lack of interest in sustainable
    development 275
  regional environmental organization 79
  scientific uncertainty 147

usable knowledge 117
withdrawing from Kyoto Protocol 71, 137

Victor, David 251
voluntary environmental management
  206–208, 211

Waltz, Kenneth 88
World Bank
  50 Years is Enough campaign 181–182
  institutional coordination 22
  NGO involvement 167–171
  non-institutionalized pressures 169–170
  participation modalities 167–168
  relationship with GEF 44–45, 49
  strengths and weaknesses 170–171
World Economic Forum 187–193
world environmental organization (WEO)
  arguments against 76–77
  capacity-building function 76
  centralized policy-making 76
  implications of civil society protests
    194–196
  inadequacies of present system 71–74
  international organizations with
    environmental functions 74–75
  international policy options 213–214
  lessons from other global
    organizations 51–52
  need for scientific organization 150–152
  organizational problems 226–227
  proposals for 272, 277–278
  questions regarding form and function 72
  recommendations for 5–7, 30–31
  regional stepping-stones 77–79
  transnational corporations 209
World Intellectual Property Organization
  (WIPO)
  acceptance by stakeholders 65
  classification treaties 59–60
  compliance over intellectual property
    rights 63
  dispute resolution 63–64
  effectiveness 61–65
  functions 61
  government participation in treaties 62
  historical background 56–57
  intellectual property rights protection
    57–59
  knowledge management 64–65
  mandate 61

measuring effectiveness 52–53
overview of effectiveness 51–52
registration treaties 59
societal values 60–61
World Summit on Sustainable Development
    (WSSD) 1, 6, 178, 224
  Cartagena Declaration 273
  moves towards sustainable development
    263–264
  Type 2 outcomes 240–243, 248–251, 266
World Trade Organization (WTO)
  acceptance by NGOs 56

dispute among member states 55–56
future policy regime 56
governance participation 54
historical background 53–54
managing social issues 56
mandate 54
measuring effectiveness 52–53
overview of effectiveness 51–52
problem-solving capability 55
role in environmental governance
    21
Seattle protests 179, 182, 187